THE REBEL
ROMANOV

Also by Helen Rappaport

In Search of Mary Seacole
After the Romanovs
The Race to Save the Romanovs
Caught in the Revolution
The Victoria Letters
Four Sisters
Magnificent Obsession
Beautiful for Ever
Conspirator: Lenin in Exile
Ekaterinburg
No Place for Ladies
Queen Victoria
Encyclopedia of Women Social Reformers
Joseph Stalin

With William Horwood
Dark Hearts of Chicago

With Roger Watson
Capturing the Light

THE REBEL
ROMANOV

Julie of Saxe-Coburg,
the Empress Russia Never Had

HELEN RAPPAPORT

SIMON &
SCHUSTER

London · New York · Amsterdam/Antwerp · Sydney · Toronto · New Delhi

First published in Great Britain by Simon & Schuster UK Ltd, 2025

Copyright © Helen Rappaport, 2025

The right of Helen Rappaport to be identified as the author of this work has been
asserted in accordance with the Copyright, Designs and Patents Act, 1988.

1 3 5 7 9 10 8 6 4 2

Simon & Schuster UK Ltd
1st Floor
222 Gray's Inn Road
London WC1X 8HB

www.simonandschuster.co.uk
www.simonandschuster.com.au
www.simonandschuster.co.in

Simon & Schuster Australia, Sydney
Simon & Schuster India, New Delhi

The author and publishers have made all reasonable efforts to contact
copyright-holders for permission, and apologise for any omissions or errors in the form
of credits given. Corrections may be made to future printings.

A CIP catalogue record for this book is available from the British Library

Maps and family trees by Martin Lubikowski

Hardback ISBN: 978-1-3985-2596-2
eBook ISBN: 978-1-3985-2597-9

Typeset in Sabon by M Rules
Printed and bound in the UK using 100% Renewable Electricity
at CPI Group (UK) Ltd

For Alessandra

As long as we desire, we can do without happiness:
we expect to achieve it. If happiness fails to come,
hope persists, and the charm of illusion lasts as
long as the passion that causes it. So this condition
is sufficient in itself, and the anxiety it inflicts is a
sort of enjoyment that compensates for reality ...
Woe to him who has nothing left to desire ...
We enjoy less what we obtain than what we hope
for, and we are happy only before being happy.

Jean-Jacques Rousseau, *Julie, or the New Héloïse*

CONTENTS

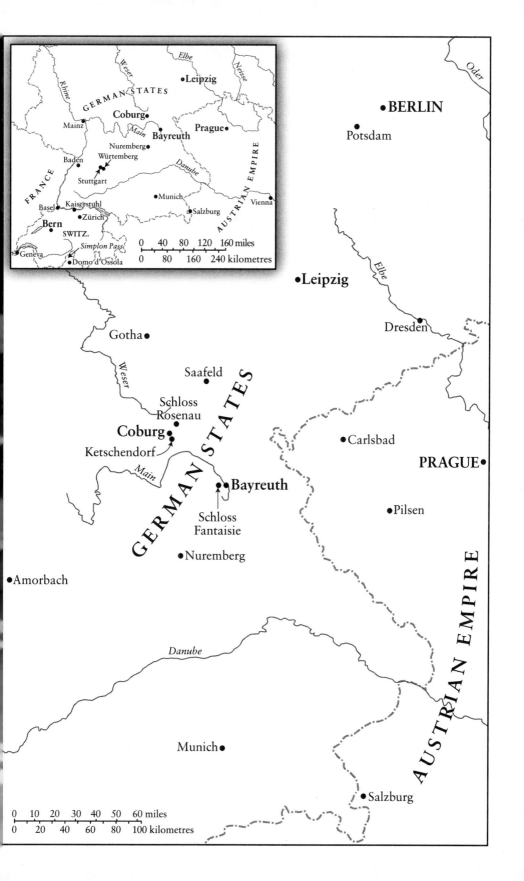

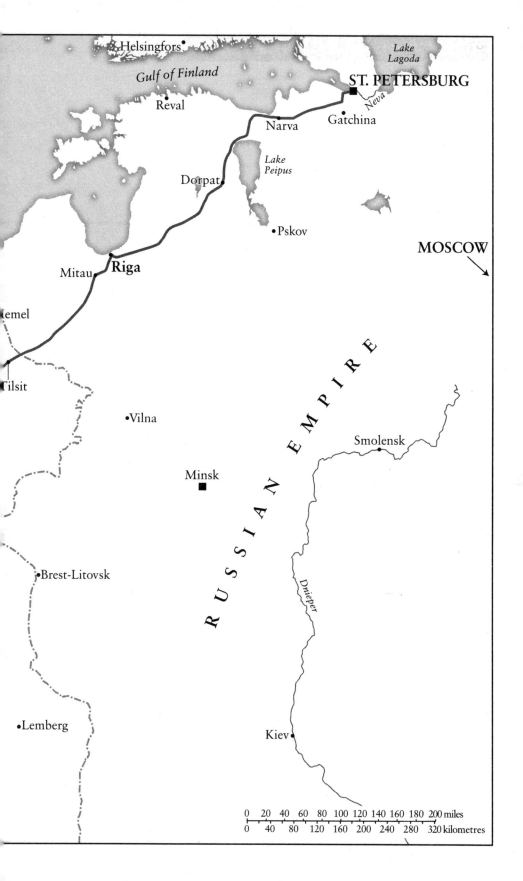

SAXE-COBURG FAMILY TREE

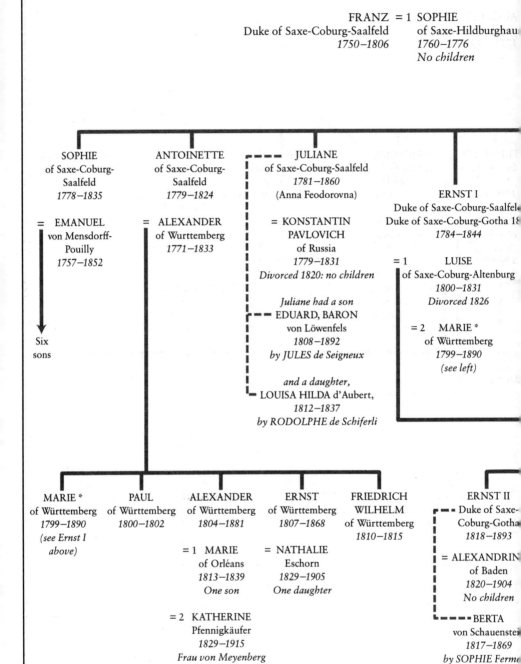

FRANZ = 1 SOPHIE
Duke of Saxe-Coburg-Saalfeld   of Saxe-Hildburghau
1750–1806   1760–1776
No children

SOPHIE
of Saxe-Coburg-
Saalfeld
1778–1835

= EMANUEL
von Mensdorff-
Pouilly
1757–1852

Six
sons

ANTOINETTE
of Saxe-Coburg-
Saalfeld
1779–1824

= ALEXANDER
of Wurttemberg
1771–1833

JULIANE
of Saxe-Coburg-Saalfeld
1781–1860
(Anna Feodorovna)

= KONSTANTIN
PAVLOVICH
of Russia
1779–1831
Divorced 1820: no children

Juliane had a son
EDUARD, BARON
von Löwenfels
1808–1892
by JULES de Seigneux

and a daughter,
LOUISA HILDA d'Aubert,
1812–1837
by RODOLPHE de Schiferli

ERNST I
Duke of Saxe-Coburg-Saalfel
Duke of Saxe-Coburg-Gotha 18
1784–1844

= 1   LUISE
of Saxe-Coburg-Altenburg
1800–1831
Divorced 1826

= 2   MARIE *
of Württemberg
1799–1890
(see left)

MARIE *
of Württemberg
1799–1890
*(see Ernst I
above)*

PAUL
of Württemberg
1800–1802

ALEXANDER
of Württemberg
1804–1881

= 1   MARIE
of Orléans
1813–1839
One son

= 2   KATHERINE
Pfennigkäufer
1829–1915
Frau von Meyenberg

ERNST
of Württemberg
1807–1868

= NATHALIE
Eschorn
1829–1905
One daughter

FRIEDRICH
WILHELM
of Württemberg
1810–1815

ERNST II
Duke of Saxe-
Coburg-Gotha
1818–1893

= ALEXANDRIN
of Baden
1820–1904
No children

BERTA
von Schauenstei
1817–1869
*by SOPHIE Ferm
de Marteaux*

= EDUARD
Baron von Löwen
1817–1869
(see Juliane abou

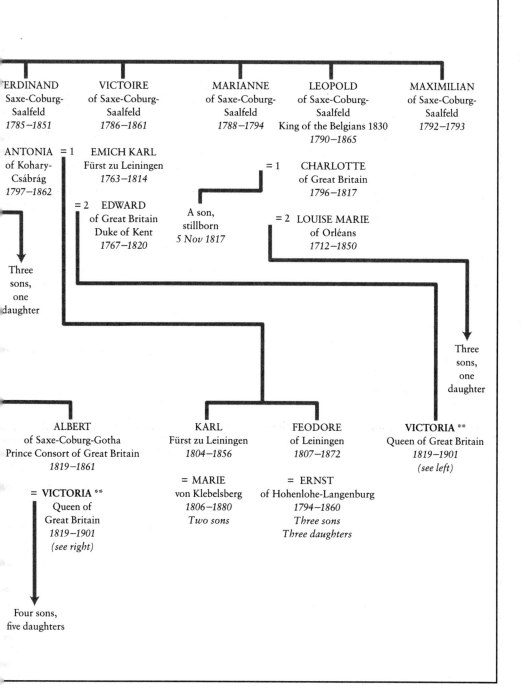

AUGUSTE
of Reuss-Ebersdorf
1757–1831

ERDINAND
Saxe-Coburg-
Saalfeld
1785–1851

VICTOIRE
of Saxe-Coburg-
Saalfeld
1786–1861

MARIANNE
of Saxe-Coburg-
Saalfeld
1788–1794

LEOPOLD
of Saxe-Coburg-
Saalfeld
King of the Belgians 1830
1790–1865

MAXIMILIAN
of Saxe-Coburg-
Saalfeld
1792–1793

ANTONIA
of Kohary-
Csábrág
1797–1862

= 1   EMICH KARL
Fürst zu Leiningen
1763–1814

= 2   EDWARD
of Great Britain
Duke of Kent
1767–1820

A son,
stillborn
5 Nov 1817

= 1   CHARLOTTE
of Great Britain
1796–1817

= 2   LOUISE MARIE
of Orléans
1712–1850

Three
sons,
one
daughter

Three
sons,
one
daughter

ALBERT
of Saxe-Coburg-Gotha
Prince Consort of Great Britain
1819–1861

= **VICTORIA** **
Queen of
Great Britain
1819–1901
(see right)

KARL
Fürst zu Leiningen
1804–1856

= MARIE
von Klebelsberg
1806–1880
Two sons

FEODORE
of Leiningen
1807–1872

= ERNST
of Hohenlohe-Langenburg
1794–1860
Three sons
Three daughters

VICTORIA **
Queen of Great Britain
1819–1901
(see left)

Four sons,
five daughters

ROMANOV FAMILY TREE

PETER III
Emperor of Russi
1728–1762

NATALIA ALEXEIEVNA = 1
1755–1776

PAUL I
Emperor of R
1754–180

ALEXANDER I
Emperor of Russia
1777–1825

= ELIZAVETA
ALEXEEVNA
(Louise
of Baden)
1779–1826

Two
daughters,
died young

KONSTANTIN
1779–1831
abdicated

=1 JULIANE
of Saxe-Coburg-
Saalfeld
1781–1860

=2 JOANNA
GRUDZIŃSKA
1795–1831

ALEXANDRA
1783–1801

= ARCHDUKE
JOSEPH
of Austria
1776–1847

ELENA
1784–1803

= FRIEDRICH
of Mecklenburg-
Schwerein
1778–1819

MARIA
1786–1859

= KARL FRIEDF
Grand Duke
Saxe-Weima
Eisenach
1783–1853

ALEXANDER II
Emperor of Russia
1818–1881

=1   MARIA
ALEXANDROVNA
(Maria of Hesse
& by Rhine)
1824–1880

= 2 EKATERINA
DOLGORUOVA
1847–1922

MARIA
1819–1876

= MAXIMILIAN
de Beauharnais
1779–1826

OLGA
1822–1892

= CHARLES
King of
Württemberg
1823–1891

ALEXANDR/
1825–1844

= FRIEDRICH-
WILHELM
of Hesse-Kass(
1820–1884

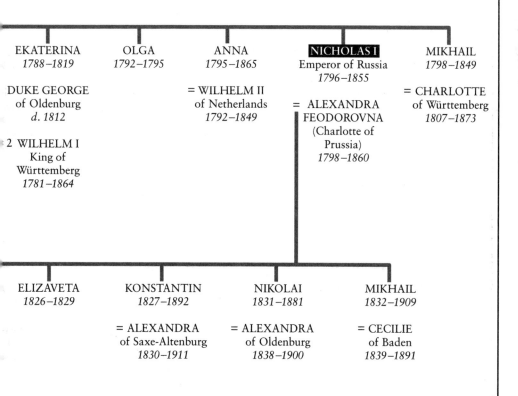

THERINE II
HE GREAT
ress of Russia
Sophie of
halt-Zerbst)
1729–1796

MARIA FEODOROVNA
(Sophie Dorothea
of Württemberg)
1759–1828

EKATERINA
1788–1819

DUKE GEORGE
of Oldenburg
d. 1812

2 WILHELM I
King of
Württemberg
1781–1864

OLGA
1792–1795

ANNA
1795–1865

= WILHELM II
of Netherlands
1792–1849

NICHOLAS I
Emperor of Russia
1796–1855

= ALEXANDRA
FEODOROVNA
(Charlotte of
Prussia)
1798–1860

MIKHAIL
1798–1849

= CHARLOTTE
of Württemberg
1807–1873

ELIZAVETA
1826–1829

KONSTANTIN
1827–1892

= ALEXANDRA
of Saxe-Altenburg
1830–1911

NIKOLAI
1831–1881

= ALEXANDRA
of Oldenburg
1838–1900

MIKHAIL
1832–1909

= CECILIE
of Baden
1839–1891

PROLOGUE

THE COBURG MARRIAGE

In May 1816, at the Prince Regent's Carlton House residence in London, an obscure German prince married the most sought-after royal bride in Europe – Princess Charlotte of Wales, second in line to the throne of Great Britain after her father, the Prince Regent. During the ceremony, held in the Crimson Drawing Room at 9 p.m., there had been barely stifled amusement – even to the bride herself – when, at the point when the couple exchanged vows, she heard her fairytale prince solemnly promise to endow her with all his worldly goods. For Charlotte knew full well that her new husband, Prince Leopold of Saxe-Coburg-Saalfeld, was the scion of a cash-strapped *'Pumpernickel-Staat'*,* 'a younger prince of Coburg [whose] whole income was only £200 sterling'.[1] All Leopold had in reality to offer his bride beyond his seductive good looks and his distinguished military credentials were his guile and ruthless ambition.

Nevertheless, the 'Coburg Marriage' – as it was dismissively referred to by the British aristocracy – was no mean achievement for an unremarkable German principality that in the political scheme of things had long been 'lost on the map of Europe' and on which the press

---

* In his 1848 novel *Vanity Fair*, Thackeray wickedly parodied the small-state trivialities of this German archetype: a dull little 'comfortable Ducal town' where everybody knew everybody and the highlight of the season was the marriage of the Hereditary Prince of Pumpernickel 'with the lovely Princess Amelia of Humbourg-Schlippensschloppen'.

had until then been entirely silent.[2] Leopold's marriage to Britain's favourite princess was an incredible coup for a minor European prince and brought the couple an annual allowance of £60,000 (over £6 million today), which was more than the entire annual revenue of his debt-ridden home country – a tiny, rural principality tucked away in central Germany. Its rulers could claim descent from one of the ancient European dynasties – the Saxon House of Wettin – that had once ruled much of the region, but successive divisions of the territory between the male heirs of the Ernestine branch[*] had fragmented the region into a complex tapestry of domains subject to periodic reshuffling. Saxe-Coburg-Saalfeld in fact comprised two small territories that were geographically separated: Coburg, the dynastic seat, lay in Upper Franconia just south of the Thuringian Forest while Saalfeld, which lay on the other side of the forest in the principality of Schwarzburg, was added through marriage and purchase in 1699.[3]

By 1801 the status and power of Saxe-Coburg-Saalfeld had atrophied considerably, leaving it shackled by debt and reduced to a combined military strength of only 150 musketeers and grenadiers and a militia of one battalion of 360 men.[4] Much of this debt had been the result of profligate spending and mismanagement of the Coburg coffers by successive dukes, who had ruled the region along old feudal lines.

During the terrible depredations wreaked across Europe in the Napoleonic Wars, Saxe-Coburg-Saalfeld was caught in the crosshairs, a perpetual victim of incursions by transient Napoleonic troops; for a while the ducal family had had to flee their capital for the safer location of Saalfeld. Nevertheless, Leopold and his two brothers Ernst and Ferdinand had 'exerted themselves, as far as they were able, for the emancipation of Germany' in the final push against Napoleon during 1813–14: Ernst with the Prussians in Berlin, Ferdinand with the Austrians in Vienna, and Leopold in service to Emperor Alexander I of Russia in Poland.[5]

---

[*]   In 1485 the ruling family of Wettins divided the territory between the eldest son Ernest (Ernestine branch) and his younger brother Albert (Albertine branch).

As the youngest son of a duchy that had adopted the law of primogeniture, and who was thus well down the pecking order below his two older brothers, Leopold needed to seek his fortune abroad and it was Russia that had set him on the ladder. His military record had been exemplary: enrolled as an honorary cadet in the Russian Imperial Guard at the age of five by Catherine the Great, Leopold's advancement thereafter, as the first German prince to join the Russian army, had been meteoric. In 1810 he had resigned under pressure from Napoleon but was reintegrated in the Russian forces by May 1813, after which he led his regiment of Russian cuirassiers in cavalry charges against French forces at the battles of Lützen and Bautzen in Saxony and scored his most significant military success at the battle of Kulm on 30 August. By this time Alexander I and his Prussian and Austrian allies had all acknowledged the merit of Leopold's services, and 'six or eight Orders were conferred on him', including the prestigious order of St Alexander Nevsky and the crosses of St George and Maria Theresa and the Iron Cross of Prussia for his role at Kulm.[6]

Prince Leopold was also present at the military engagement outside Paris on 31 March 1814 that saw the final defeat of Napoleon, an honour that brought him in the victors' parade into Paris itself and on to England that June with the allied sovereigns of Prussia and Russia.[7] When he arrived in London, Leopold, who couldn't afford a hotel and was staying above a grocer's shop in Marylebone, was already pondering a game plan that had been sown in his mind by the tsar.[8] Having had to abandon his 'fruitless passion' for Empress Josephine's 'pale, pensive and *spirituelle*' daughter, Hortense de Beauharnais, he found himself now in pursuit of 'a ruddy buxom girl, more German, perhaps, in her appearance than Leopold could have wished'.[9] For Alexander had apparently informed Leopold privately not long before they left for England that 'I intend for you to marry Princess Charlotte, the future Queen of England.'[10] Alexander's clever widowed sister, Ekaterina Pavlovna, Duchess of Oldenburg, who was then staying in London, took the plan to the next level. She befriended Princess Charlotte and contrived a meeting between the classically tall and dark Leopold and the boisterously endearing eighteen-year-old princess. This unwished-for encounter, as far as he was concerned, would soon turn the Prince Regent's own dynastic ambitions for his daughter upside down, as well as providing Russia with an important influence at the British court in the person of Leopold.

Charlotte had recently broken off her engagement to her father's choice of husband, the affable but dull Prince Wilhelm of Orange. She had reluctantly agreed to the engagement in December 1813 in the cause of a strategic Dutch–British political alliance, but had then been distracted by a short-lived passion for Prince Friedrich of Prussia. When this fizzled out, attempts were made to steer Charlotte back in the direction of the Prince of Orange but she had resisted this on discovering that, as wife of the heir to the Dutch throne, she would have to live in the Netherlands for most of the time. In any case, by the summer of 1814 the ambitious Leopold – whom even Napoleon had remarked upon as being 'one of the handsomest young men I ever saw' – had arrived at court and had begun to work his charm on her.[11]

By this time, Charlotte was growing increasingly rebellious, desperate for release from her father's stifling control; her liking for 'Der Leo', as she affectionately called him, soon turned to fascination and then to a very determined passion.[12] By early 1815, and despite the Regent's stubborn opposition, she had become convinced that of all the many suitors for her most eligible hand, Leo was the one who 'from his situation & everything I have heard of him is the most elagible [sic] connexion for me now ... I *delight* in Coburg because I am *quite satisfied he is really*, truly & sincerely attached *to me* & very much so desirous to the greatest degree to [do] all in his power to make me happy.'[13] Charlotte, who was notoriously headstrong and called the shots as the only legitimate child in line to the throne at that time, refused to give him up.

Leopold's German ducal credentials might not have been grand enough for the English royals, but at least he was from a ruling family, and no one could doubt the good prince's moral and intellectual character, his 'dignified gravity and unusual moderation', though privately the Prince Regent found his putative son-in-law cautious and pedantic, and later nicknamed him 'Marquis Peu-à-Peu'.*[14] But there was more to Leopold than initially met the eye: a cold intellect and logic lurking beneath the ingratiating façade, indicative of a determination to advance the interests and ascendancy of the Saxe-Coburgs in Europe.[15] For her own part, Charlotte had no intention of allowing this unequal royal match to diminish her: 'Do not imagine that, in marrying Prince Leopold, I ever can or will sink to the rank of *Mistress Coburg*. Entertain no such idea, I beg of you.'† She was already intimating her intention, when the time came, of seeing her German husband elevated beyond the role of mere consort, an aspiration nursed by Leopold himself. For, as the English diarist Henry Greville observed, he 'would do anything to be beking'd'.[16]

When news broke on 10 February 1816 that 'notice ha[d] been sent to the Court of Coburg of an intended union between the Princess Charlotte of Wales and Prince Leopold of Saxe-Coburg, third son of the reigning Duke', Leopold was so little known in England that even these basic facts were wrong. His father had died in 1806 and his brother Ernst was now on the throne.[17] The British aristocracy were contemptuous: 'He is after all but a petty Prince for the heiress to the British throne,' sneered Lady Charlotte Campbell Bury. Yet for all that, the Coburg marriage was 'the only genteel Topic of Conversation' in London society at the time.[18] It wasn't until November that anyone was the wiser, when Frederic Shoberl's *Historical Account of the House of Saxony*, containing a chapter on Saxe-Coburg-Saalfeld, was brought out for public consumption, outlining the prince's illustrious genealogy and career.[19]

*

Leopold arrived at Dover by packet boat from the Continent on 19 February 1816 for his wedding to Charlotte. Until the ceremony

---

* 'Marquess Little-by-Little'.
† Charlotte changed her tune later when she became so enamoured of her new husband that she took to signing herself as 'Charlotte de Saxe-Coburg'; it may also have reflected her desire to distance herself from her father, formerly Prince of Wales and now Prince Regent.

on 2 May he stayed at the Clarendon Hotel in New Bond Street, a respectable venue for 'single gentlemen'.[20] Public curiosity had been 'wound up to the highest pitch' by the time Leopold, dressed in his splendid general's 'regimentals' – having been newly elevated to that rank by the Prince Regent – gratified the eager throngs waiting outside Clarence House by making his appearance to the sound of their 'stentorian huzzas'. But the congregation for the wedding at nearby Carlton House was small by royal standards. Only fifty hand-picked dignitaries – foreign ambassadors, cabinet ministers and members of the British royal family and nobility – were in attendance.[21] No foreign royalty were there, nor even the bride's mother – from whom the Regent was estranged. Travel in the days before the railways was slow and difficult; Prince Leopold's scattered family was represented by the Saxon minister in London, who signed the marriage certificate, for nobody from Leopold's home country was present to witness this moment of triumph for the House of Saxe-Coburg-Saalfeld.

Not least among the absentees was Leopold's older sister Julie, for she it was who, through her own politically strategic marriage to Catherine the Great's grandson Grand Duke Konstantin in 1796, had made all this possible. For that union had brought exceptional honours and preferment not just to Leopold but to the whole family; more importantly, it had brought Saxe-Coburg under the protective wing of the Russian Empire. Julie, the beloved sister, sacrificed on the altar of dynastic expediency in a strange, foreign land at the age of only fourteen, had given a huge boost to the military careers of all three of her brothers, and with it the family's favour with the Romanovs. She had been the first of the seven Saxe-Coburg siblings – the surviving children of Duke Franz and Duchess Auguste – to wed; between 1796 and 1818 they achieved a spectacular succession of marriages that turned this obscure family into the king- and queen-makers of post-Napoleonic Europe, placing their progeny 'upon thrones, next to thrones, or behind thrones'.[22]

By the time of his marriage Leopold was already on the high road to international power and influence. Coburg, that insignificant 'archipelago of princes', as Catherine the Great's lover Prince Grigory Potemkin had once scornfully referred to it, achieved yet more dynastic success that same year, when Leopold's brother Ferdinand married the daughter and sole heir of the wealthiest man in the Austrian Empire.[23] A sister, Antoinette, was installed in the Russian court not long after Julie as the wife of Duke Alexander of Württemberg, brother of the German-born dowager empress. But it was the youngest sister, Victoire, who in 1818 scored the ultimate triumph by marrying Princess Charlotte's uncle and a son of King George III, the Duke of Kent. A year later she gave birth to a future monarch – Queen Victoria – who would bring the Saxe-Coburg story full circle in 1840 by marrying her first cousin, Prince Albert of Saxe-Coburg and Gotha.

It is not surprising therefore that few were aware then, as is the case even today, of the existence of the lost Saxe-Coburg sister, Princess Juliane Henriette Ulrike, who set in train the inexorable rise of the Coburgs. By 1854 Julie's story, such of it as was known even then, had reached the levels of myth: 'Who was this modern Iphigenia? – this Ariadne given up to the Minotaur? – this Andromeda whom no Perseus came to rescue?' thundered the *Dublin Weekly Nation* in an excess of indignant hyperbole. 'You'll search for her in vain in any list of the Russian royal family. For Heaven's sake, who was she?' For the world knew nothing of this 'poor doomed rosebud' who had been 'torn from the nursery' to further the Saxe-Coburg cause; nor of the high personal price she had had to pay in the cause of her mother Auguste's overweening ambitions in securing her marriage into the Russian imperial family. As historian Johann Heinrich Schnitzler observed: 'Such was the attraction of an imperial crown, that it overbalanced love of country, attachment to religious faith, and the apprehension which the state of things in Russia might then well cause.'[24]

Uprooted from her quiet and uneventful life in Coburg and abandoned unceremoniously, alone and friendless, in Catherine the Great's St Petersburg, Julie was stripped of her German birth name, which was supplanted by the alien, talismanic title of Grand

Duchess Anna Feodorovna of Russia, or the even more anonymising Grand Duchess Konstantin. But among her family she was always known as Jülchen – 'little Julie' – and the affectionate form of her name extended even to Queen Victoria, who spoke very fondly, and often, of her dear aunt 'Julia' and never referred to her by her Russian name. We shall use 'Julie' throughout this narrative, which charts the span of her difficult, elusive and often tragic life, much of it lived effectively as an exile, in avoidance of gossip and scandal.

CHAPTER 1

A PUMPERNICKEL STATE

When Princess Charlotte wrote of her forthcoming marriage to Prince Leopold of Saxe-Coburg, she noted that 'he seems vastly fond of his family who are exceedingly united.'[1] United they indeed were, by the straitened circumstances in which they had been forced to live thanks to the economic difficulties endured in that region from the late eighteenth century. Most people tended to use the abbreviated form 'Saxe-Coburg' rather than 'Saxe-Coburg-Saalfeld', which was one of five ducal houses of the Ernestine branch of the House of Saxony, the others being Saxe-Gotha-Altenburg, Saxe-Meiningen, Saxe-Hildburghausen and Saxe-Weimar-Eisenach.

These and other smaller states in the central region operated as little more than fiefdoms and prior to 1806 were governed by a plethora of knights, counts, margraves, burgraves, bishops, abbots, dukes and barons. Together they made up the German-speaking territories of the Holy Roman Empire that had ruled over much of central and western Europe since the ninth century. But their repeated political fragmentation had ensured that they shared little sense of a cohesive national identity until German nationalism took root after the defeat of Napoleon in 1815. For centuries these disparate German territories were thus embroiled in endless dynastic infighting over the division of the lands between their various heirs and control of the borders between them until the piecemeal introduction of the rule of primogeniture gradually brought the worst disputes under control; in Saxe-Coburg-Saalfeld's case this came in 1747.

After Napoleon's conquest of Germany in 1806 many of the smallest statelets were absorbed by the larger ones and faded into insignificance, thus greatly simplifying the political map. Saxe-Coburg-Saalfeld remained a third- or fourth-league state by status: below the imperial electorates like Hanover and the grand duchies like Baden and Hesse-Darmstadt, poorer than some bishoprics and imperial cities, but above the smaller principalities such as the junior Reuss line from which Julie's mother Auguste came.

The region in which Saxe-Coburg-Saalfeld was located languished as a patchwork of small duchies and principalities of limited wealth and little political clout, haunted always by the prospect of losing their autonomy through annexation, which preyed on the minds of Leopold's parents. Therefore, the five Saxe-Coburg states remained politically stagnant, always the clients rather than the peers of the larger powerful states such as Prussia, Hanover, Saxony and Württemberg, to whom, when their financial resources failed, they often hired out their armies and married off their daughters.[2]

Even in the 1840s the complex history of this region still defeated those attempting to present a succinct account for the British public when Leopold's nephew Prince Albert married Queen Victoria and questions were asked about his dynastic credentials. It was admitted that little was known about Saxe-Coburg beyond 'the simple fact that such a principality exists'.[3] The literary scholar and politician John Frederick Stanford was obliged to note that as with all the other German duchies, its early history was 'extremely complicated' and most people made no attempt to unravel it.[4]

Throughout the eighteenth century the German prince or duke had been, by and large, little more than a gentleman farmer, albeit on the large scale. Julie's Russian husband Konstantin would later remark disparagingly that his brother-in-law Duke Ernst II reigned 'over six peasants and two village surgeons'.[5] Princess Marie of Edinburgh (later queen of Romania), who grew up there in the 1870s, was rather more charitable. Coburg was 'a small town where *Gemütlichkeit* [warmth and friendliness] played a greater part than elegance ... a town of simple burghers, uncritical and loyal', with an 'old-world simplicity'.[6] The Coburg court or *Residenz*, which formed the microcosm of the Saxe-Coburg state, was, despite its old-world Teutonic charm, exceedingly narrow in its aspirations: pedantic, traditionalist and lacking political debate or cultural innovation. Its dukes 'cherished a blighting etiquette, and led lives as dull as those of the aged and torpid carp in their own stewponds'.[7]

In order to maintain their government and army, not to mention their personal lifestyle, Saxe-Coburg's rulers had squeezed the peasantry through heavy taxation to compensate for the limited revenue derived from local industry. Covering around 400 square miles and with a population of 57,266 (in 1812), Saxe-Coburg was about one and a half times the size of the Isle of Wight.[8] The land was fertile enough; located in a sheltered valley between two ranges of hills, it produced corn, flax, wine and rich pasture for fattening cattle. But the duchy's manufactures were modest, its best offerings being 'pots, hats, and peltry [animal skins]', as well as vitriol, potash, pitch and Prussian blue pigment.[9]

Saxe-Coburg had an imposing castle, the Veste, built on the site of a tenth-century fortress on a hilltop above a dense beechwood that dominated the landscape for many miles in every direction. But it was cold, comfortless and infested with rats and the ducal family found it too forbidding to live there.[10] Between 1543 and 1547 Duke Johann Ernst (1521–53) had drained the treasury to construct a grand palace – the Ehrenburg – on the site of a Franciscan friary in the town itself.* When Julie's grandfather the 4th duke, Ernst Friedrich (1724–1800), inherited the title in 1764 under the duchy's newly introduced law of primogeniture, he remained based in the better-known walled town of Coburg on the River Itz and kept the Saalfeld residence for official purposes only. His intention

---

* After he became duke in 1806, Julie's brother Ernst redesigned it into a splendid baroque palace.

was to enhance the duchy's prospects, but by then it was already in economic decline.

Life at the ducal court was parochial and socially limited, dominated by Ernst Friedrich's disappointed wife, the better-connected and imperious Sophie Antonia of Brunswick-Wolfenbüttel. Through family marriages to European royalty, including Emperor Peter II of Russia and Maria Theresa of Austria, Sophie had hoped for a more advantageous match for herself. In response, she 'ruled everything at Coburg', refusing to control her spending habits and propelling Saxe-Coburg into further debt.[11] As Prince Leopold himself later admitted in a glorious understatement, his grandmother had been 'too great a person for so small a duchy' and had treated it 'as if it had been an empire ... squander[ing] the revenues in a dreadful manner'.[12] It was the weak-willed Duke Ernst Friedrich's brother, Prince Friedrich Josias, who saved the duchy from the brink of insolvency and collapse by fighting with distinction for Maria Theresa's Hapsburg army in the Third Silesian War against the Prussians. Catherine the Great would later laud Friedrich Josias as the hero of the Coburg family. As a result, he was promoted to field marshal by the Hapsburgs and heaped with honours. His position also enabled him to secure Austrian help in the setting up of a Debt Commission in 1773 to administer the duchy's perilous financial affairs.[13]

Julie's genial father, Prince Franz Friedrich, eldest son of the 4th duke, left little mark on his time as hereditary prince for he suffered from poor health and had no political interests. He may have been the nominal head of the household, but he appeared utterly incapable of managing his finances, leaving those, plus the running of the household and child-rearing, to his wife. Instead, he devoted himself to patronage of the arts, to singing, good food and fine wine. His passion for art was a worthy enough enterprise, except that Franz spent well beyond his means in bringing together what is nevertheless considered to be the most important eighteenth-century German collection of copperplate engravings, Old Master prints and drawings, which forms one of the key collections at the Veste Coburg today. A typical eighteenth-century dilettante, Franz also amassed botanical specimens, coins, stuffed birds and minerals. Equally characteristic of his class and time was his engagement in numerous sexual dalliances outside his marriage, for which he became notorious in Coburg at large.

When Franz's wife, Sophie of Saxe-Hildburghausen, died of influenza in 1776 after only seven months of marriage, Franz already had a substitute waiting in the wings: Countess Auguste of Reuss-Ebersdorf. But she brought no fortune with her for she came from one of the smallest and least significant German principalities in Thuringia. At only 3 miles square and with a population of 1,200, Reuss-Ebersdorf was also the centre of the Moravian Brotherhood, a pietistic Lutheran community that had been established at Herrnhut in 1722 by refugees fleeing religious persecution in Bohemia. Auguste's great-aunt, Erdmuthe Dorothea, Countess of Reuss-Ebersdorf, had married the Brotherhood's founder, Count Nikolaus Zinzendorf. Her parents, Heinrich and Karoline, were devout followers of the movement, which is reflected in the very strict social and moral attitudes with which she was inculcated as a child.

In her later years Auguste, who was born in 1757, nursed a romantic memory of the 'lovely surroundings of my bright days', though she has left us no details of them. 'Only with my life', she wrote later, 'will the sweet memory of the father's house be extinguished.'[14] That household had nevertheless been an unremarkable, straitlaced and deeply religious one, where dancing and games were frowned upon and where Auguste had received the customary private tuition by governesses in art, French and geography, in preparation for a suitable marriage.[15]

Straitlaced or not, such a pious lifestyle did not get in the way of Count Heinrich of Reuss-Ebersdorf's sense of urgency in marrying off his pretty daughter at the first opportunity. So, when Auguste was eighteen, her cash-strapped father shrewdly invested in commissioning a painting of her posing as Artemisia of Caria – a queen of ancient Greece – lamenting over the urn containing the ashes of her dead husband, Mausolus. It cost 100 guilders and was painted by the fashionable German court painter Johann Heinrich Tischbein at Schloss Ebersdorf. It was then exhibited at the Regensburg Diet, the imperial legislature of the Holy Roman Empire, where Prince Franz of Saxe-Coburg had seen it and was immediately so entranced that he supposedly paid four times the asking price to secure the painting.[16] However, dynastic protocols at the time dictated that he contract a more politically strategic marriage to a relative – Princess Sophie of Saxe-Hildburghausen. After Sophie died Franz thus wasted no time in asking for the hand of Auguste. They were married at Schloss Ebersdorf on 13 June 1777. The brethren of the Moravian Church joined in the celebrations that day and played the Bach hymn 'Nun danket alle Gott'* on trumpets as the wedding group processed from the church.[17]

Little or nothing is known of the family life of Franz, Auguste and the seven of their ten children who survived into adulthood. While a few passing allusions survive regarding the sons such as Leopold – whose birth was greeted in 1790 with considerable rejoicing in the duchy – the arrival of far less politically valuable daughters was considered a drain on the family purse until they could be usefully married off. What we *do* know of the early years of the Saxe-Coburg children is entirely dominated by the forceful figure of Auguste. She was rather less beautiful than her Tischbein portrait suggested: handsome with piercing blue eyes, but with a distinctive long nose and determined chin (the nose was inherited most notably by her sons). She was small but made up for it with strength of character; she had a 'most powerful, energetic, almost masculine mind', in the words of her granddaughter, Queen Victoria.[18]

During the early years of Franz and Auguste's marriage the two great official residences – the Ehrenburg and the Veste – had become such a drain on the state purse that Duke Ernst could not afford to maintain them. In 1786 he transferred his family to a modest, four-storey townhouse on Steingasse, located directly to the side of the Ehrenburg Palace. Life here, where the family remained until 1800,

---

*   It is interesting to note that this was a favourite hymn of the couple's grandson Prince Albert, who asked his daughter Alice to play it for him when he was on his deathbed at Windsor Castle in December 1861.

was extremely plain by princely standards. The building was very old, dating back to 1464, and dilapidated, though some renovations had been made earlier in the eighteenth century. One large reception room for official business was located on the first floor and the family lived on the third floor. But how they lived there remains 'wrapped in obscurity', beyond the fact that their dire financial situation dictated a regime of strict austerity.[19]

All we know about the family's everyday life is that Leopold, born in 1790, and his brothers Ernst (born 1784) and Ferdinand (born 1785) were well educated with a view to their future advancement in the world. They received lessons in Christian doctrine and ethics, Latin, Russian, French, English, geology and history – a curriculum drawn up by Prince Franz and his advisors.[20] They were also encouraged in a study of natural history and geography by their mother, who collected botanical and ornithological specimens.[21]

In the historical record, the three good-looking Saxe-Coburg sons inevitably eclipse their four sisters, who were all born before Leopold: Sophie in 1778, Antoinette in 1779, Julie on 23 September 1781 and Marie Luise (better known as Victoire) in 1786. One other sister, Marianne, born in 1788, lived only to the age of six. We are told nothing of their lives as children but it is likely, given their mother's strict Moravian religious faith, that they received a fairly constrained religious-based education at home with governesses, although their cultured father certainly encouraged their musical and artistic gifts and the girls were taught to sing and play the piano. Even in 1818, all the British press were able to tell the public about the early life of Victoire when she married the Duke of Kent was that the four Coburg sisters had been educated 'under the immediate care and inspection' of their 'august and well-informed mother'.[22]

Only one aspect of these early days emerges with any clarity and that is the highly contradictory and forceful personality of their mother, Auguste. Her portraits all testify to a strong, if not ruthless, will that doesn't match the numerous fawning descriptions of her as 'an object of adoration among her children and grandchildren', a woman who 'by her wisdom and tender motherly care, created a family circle so happy and so well regulated, as is rarely to be met with on the thrones of Europe'.[23] Frederic Shoberl echoed panegyrics to Auguste in his 1842 account of Saxe-Coburg for the British market. The late duchess, he averred, had 'unite[d] all the softness of her own sex with the firmness of the other. Undaunted by the storms of fate she never lost sight for a moment of her destination as a wife and a mother. Amid the various pursuits to which her genius inclined, this extraordinary woman made the most careful education of her numerous family the business, the recreation, and the happiness of her life.'[24] But behind closed doors there are suggestions of tyranny, even cruelty, when it came to the treatment of her daughters.

In 1872 Queen Victoria produced her own saccharine memoir of her 'dear Grandmother', albeit written forty years after Auguste's death. But this misty view is strongly contradicted by other accounts.[25] Elsewhere, the Princess of Saxe-Coburg (she did not become duchess until 1800) has been described as 'ugly and tyrannical', a 'bigot' and a mercenary woman 'whose economy, parsimony, not to say avarice, were the only things about her deserving of praise'. Thus, a less gratifying view can be discerned of a martinet of narrow morality, with a sharp tongue 'whose presence caused a shiver' in her daughters.[26] Even her doting granddaughter Queen Victoria admitted that she herself had inherited Auguste's 'passionate nature' – an oblique admission, surely, of Auguste's intolerant personality. Victoria's half-sister Feodora concurred: 'the quickness of our tempers in the female line' went back to Grandmama Auguste.[27]

A fleeting memoir of the Coburg children has come to us from one of their playmates. Christina Stockmar, the daughter of Ernst Friedrich Stockmar, a Coburg merchant and financier, remembered them joining in games of hounds and hares and musical performances at the Stockmar summer residence at Glockenberg on the outskirts of the city.[28] But it is only in Auguste's voluminous journals that one occasionally catches glimpses of her true relationship with Julie. Her feelings for this daughter in particular swing from sweet, even adoring affection to painful recognition of her own past unkindnesses towards her, and include even occasional flashes of self-castigation, prompted by her Protestant sense of guilt. In her journal Auguste accused herself of 'having trouble enduring the small faults of her children and by her annoyance, of inciting them to impatience. She blames herself for criticising their preceptors instead of intervening to improve their influence and their education.' Even Queen Victoria had noted when her grandmother visited her in 1825, that she could not abide naughty children.[29]

The wounds of her early life must have run very deep, for Julie has left us no record at all of her childhood or of what seems to have been a difficult relationship with her domineering mother, although when Auguste died in 1831 she was engulfed by grief. Only a couple of her letters to Auguste survive in the Coburg archives, and for that matter Auguste's to her, perhaps because Julie is known to have destroyed much of her correspondence. But in 1805 Auguste made a revealing comment in her journal on how her daughter's 'unfortunate life has been plagued by hardships' and how she had learned in later years that during her early childhood Julie had been 'constantly provoked and ill-treated by a harsh governess' but, no doubt out of fear, had not complained. 'How often did I mistake your hurt and agitated feelings for wickedness and punished you for them,' Auguste admitted. The governess in question had left when Julie was ten and thereafter Auguste had kept her daughter close to her and educated her, for the most part, herself. But as a result, Auguste admitted, Julie had not enjoyed a 'carefree childhood' and, 'scarcely were you grown to girlhood, than fate tore you from my side, to destroy your life's happiness in every respect in that cold and foreign land.'[30] That land was Russia, but if anyone was the architect of Julie's fate there it was Auguste.

Queen Victoria has long been described as the 'Grandmama of Europe' thanks to her assiduous brokering of the marriages of her children and grandchildren, but in fact it is her own formidable grandmother Auguste who beat her to that accolade. As the acknowledged force behind her children's achievement of good fortune and social advancement through marriage, German sources look upon her as the *Stammutter des europäischen Hochadels* (ancestral mother of the European high nobility).[31] There was of course very good reason for Auguste and Franz to view their daughters as their golden ticket out of bankruptcy. Life in Coburg during Julie's formative years was never stable and the upheavals of the French Revolution of 1789 had severely affected any chance of Coburg's financial recovery. Ernst Friedrich Stockmar, the Coburg *Landkammerath* (counsellor of the Chamber of Provincial Finances), is said to have lent the ducal family considerable sums of money over the years, so much so that it was 'with positive terror' that he 'used to see the Court messenger approaching his beautiful snug house at the market-place in Coburg, carrying something under his arm'. He knew that such visits indicated that the duke or duchess were 'once more in great straits and on the point of borrowing from him, "on the pledge" by sending the messenger to him with something to pawn'. The visits became so frequent 'that they turned the poor old *Landkammerath* into a nervous hypochondriac during the last years of his life'.[32]

So dire was the situation that Duke Ernst and his heir, Prince Franz, had been forced to reduce their staff, already drab in their faded and threadbare liveries, and cut back on the number of dishes served at meals. The family rarely entertained and dressed modestly, so much so that, according to Christina Stockmar, 'none of the princesses had more than a single Sunday dress each.' On one occasion she remembered how Antoinette 'tore her Sunday dress on a gooseberry bush and was inconsolable in her dread of her severe mother' and she had come to her aid by cleverly mending the tear so that Auguste had never noticed it.[33]

At such a time of economic hardship, what could Prince Franz and his wife Auguste do, other than be 'watchful diplomats' and fall back on their most reliable commodities – their marriageable sons and daughters? Daughters were very valuable assets, especially if they were pretty – and compliant. All young German women from ducal families in the eighteenth century were groomed for such an eventuality, for in many cases the prosperity of their house depended on it.[34] For the most part, the lines of inheritance had been maintained through intermarriage with other German principalities of the same Lutheran faith. But Franz and Auguste would look far beyond that for their financial salvation.[35] The trafficking in princesses to Russia had already borne fruit with the marriages of Catherine the Great – originally Princess Sophie of Anhalt-Zerbst from a family of the Prussian minor nobility – to the Tsarevich Peter in 1745, and Princess Luise of Baden in 1793 to Catherine's eldest grandson and future heir to the Russian throne, Alexander.

Two years later, Catherine once more sent her emissary, the Baltic German diplomat Baron Andreas Eberhard von Budberg, on a secret mission to the German duchies to hunt for a suitable bride for her other teenage grandson, Konstantin, Alexander's younger brother. When Budberg arrived from Stockholm, where he had been serving as Russian ambassador, and knocked at the Coburg door, Auguste could not believe her good fortune. Budberg had, fortuitously, helped negotiate the marriage of Princess Luise. Would the pious Auguste be able to set aside her deep Protestant faith to contemplate the marriage of her teenage daughter to a Russian Orthodox Romanov and transform the impoverished fortunes of the Saxe-Coburgs?[36] 'I still see you as you were on your fourteenth birthday, fresh as a rosebud and naive as a child,' she wrote in 1805, recalling that fateful year. 'The anticipation for your future lay heavy on my heart . . .'[37]

But not *that* heavy, as it turned out.

CHAPTER 2

JOURNEY TO ST PETERSBURG

Given her country of origin it was natural that Catherine the Great would have a penchant for German brides for her children and grandchildren, so she demanded that detailed reports on prospective candidates, 'their moral character and the blood-relations of their parents' be sent to her.[1] She herself had endured such humiliating vetting and thought nothing of imposing it on others. She had married off her son and heir Paul (the only legitimate one of several offspring) to a German princess, Wilhelmina Louisa of Hesse-Darmstadt, in 1773 when he was nineteen. But Wilhelmina had died in childbirth only three years later. With indecent haste, Catherine immediately lined up a replacement: in fact she had had one who shared her own name and place of birth – Stettin (now Szczecin) on the Baltic coast of Pomerania – on the shortlist of German candidates the first time around. But as Catherine's first choice for Paul was only thirteen at the time, she had opted for a slightly older bride for him. Six months after the tragic demise of his first wife, when he was barely out of mourning, Paul was therefore steered by his mother into a union with another German teenager, Sophia Dorothea of Württemberg.

At seventeen years old, Sophia Dorothea, who, after conversion to Orthodoxy, took the Russian imperial name of Maria Feodorovna, came from a strictly moral family with strong militaristic ethics, but found herself married to an unattractive and eccentric husband.[2] Paul was in many ways a younger version of his quixotic and obsessively militaristic father, from whom Catherine had rapidly distanced herself after their marriage. But the steely Maria had made the most of what could have been a 'wretched fate' (as it was for some of her compatriots). She was strong and fertile and by 1795 had already more than fulfilled her dynastic duty by producing eight children. From the moment of their births, however, Catherine intervened and wrested control of Maria and Tsarevich Paul's first two male children, Alexander (born 1777) and Konstantin (born 1779), for she nursed great ambitions for them both. She brought them up at the Winter Palace in St Petersburg, along with their four eldest sisters, Alexandra, Elena, Elizaveta and Maria. The two younger sons, Nikolai and Mikhail, remained at the Gatchina Palace (bought by Catherine for their parents in 1783), located 30 miles south of St Petersburg, with their youngest sister Anna.

Catherine invested her hopes for the dynasty in her grandsons. She married Alexander off when he was still only fifteen years old, choosing a bride who was the niece of the queen of Prussia and from one of the most strategically important and powerful German states – Baden. Princess Luise and her sister Friederike made the long journey to the Russian capital in the late autumn of 1792, in terrible weather, unaccompanied by their mother despite being only thirteen and eleven years old. Of the two, Luise had won Catherine the Great's approval immediately with her angelic blonde beauty and thus became next in the line of sacrificial German lambs to the Romanov throne. Indeed, her mother before her had been a candidate for the hand of Tsarevich Paul, but, fortunately for her, when they travelled to St Petersburg to be vetted, her sister Wilhelmina had been favoured instead.

Like the other German brides before her, once engaged to Alexander and still only fourteen, Luise had been obliged to convert to Russian Orthodoxy. She took the name of Elizaveta Alexeevna on her marriage to Alexander in 1793. Although arranged, the marriage had initially been one of mutual attraction and affection. The German princess was irresistibly pretty, graceful and charming and had quickly fallen in love with her handsome husband. But what had seemed at first to be the perfect, harmonious union between 'Cupid and Psyche' did not remain happy for long. By 1795 Elizaveta had disappointed the domineering empress by failing to produce a son – or any children. Since the return of her sister Friederike to Baden after the wedding,* Elizaveta had found herself isolated and increasingly lonely, with only her maid of honour, Countess Varvara Golovina, to confide in. And Golovina had already noticed that despite the lovely grand duchess's many virtues, she would have 'liked the eyes of the Grand Duke to be upon her more often than on others'.[3]

With Konstantin the next in the line of succession – should Alexander fail to produce any sons – Catherine had been anxious to settle him while she was still alive, and with a suitably fertile bride, despite the obvious disadvantages of marrying him off while still so young and immature. And so, in 1795 when Konstantin turned sixteen, she had begun the search for yet another German princess, having already rejected an offer of one of the daughters of King Ferdinand IV of Naples – either Maria Amalia or Maria Cristina.† Catherine was appalled; there was a great deal of gene-weakening intermarriage in the Naples dynasty, she declared. She rejected this attempt to foist 'one of their little monsters' on the Russian imperial family in the most scathing of terms. The daughters were 'malicious, epileptic, deformed and ill-bred'; and worse, they were Roman Catholics: 'a Latin ... succession will never be accepted in my lifetime.'[4]

There seemed to be more than enough German brides to choose from, in Catherine's view, and as most of them were penniless they were less likely to be difficult. As diarist Charles François Masson observed in his *Secret Memoirs of the Court of Petersburg*: 'Young and affecting victims, whom Germany seems to send by way of tribute to Russia', were akin to those that 'formerly Greece sent ...

---

* Friederike's disappointment was mitigated by her subsequent selection as a bride for King Gustav IV of Sweden in 1797.

† As it turned out, the two rejects married well: Maria Cristina to the king of Sardinia and Maria Amelia to King Louis Philippe of France.

to be devoured by the minotaur'.[5] But for any German bride it was a rude and cruel awakening – after the degrading spectacle of the selection process – to be transplanted from a parochial *Residenz* to the all-powerful, pompous and corrupt court of the empress of Russia. For many of these young and innocent brides, Russia became a 'gloomy prison'; in Masson's cynical estimation the title of 'grand duchess of all the Russias' had 'hitherto been a title to be excluded from happiness'. Over the years, Catherine had sent for eleven German princesses to be vetted in this way: 'three princesses of Darmstadt, ... three princesses of Württemberg (who fortunately only got as far as Prussia before being turned back); two princesses of Baden and, in 1795, our three princesses of Saxe-Coburg.' Such brutal transactions meant that the rejects were summarily sent home, on a commercial 'sale or return basis' – as one contemporary observed – their hurt feelings compensated for by ribands, jewels and rubles.[6]

It is said that Baron Budberg's discovery of the three attractive Saxe-Coburg sisters had been something of an accident, for they had by no means been top of his list as being suitably prepared for such high marital status. In Catherine's scheme of things Budberg should have been headed for Prussia and the more prestigious duchies, but during his journey across Germany he apparently fell ill and had to stop off in Coburg to seek treatment and recuperate. It was there he discovered the existence of the three pretty teenage daughters of Prince Franz and Princess Auguste, and decided to look no further.[7] Budberg was relieved; he had expended considerable energy in 1793 trying to arrange a match for Catherine the Great's eleven-year-old granddaughter Alexandra Pavlovna to the new young king of Sweden, Gustav IV, which was still going through tortuous diplomatic discussions. He therefore sent an urgent letter back to the empress in St Petersburg alerting her to his fortuitous discovery and began preparing the ground for negotiations. What neither Franz nor Auguste knew, of course, was that unlike his handsome and most amiable brother Alexander, Grand Duke Konstantin was a quite different prospect. Despite having a few good qualities, he was already notorious at the Russian court for having a difficult personality and a reputation for unpredictable and often violent behaviour.

On 28 July (New Style (NS); 17 July Old Style (OS))* a letter from Catherine the Great arrived at the Coburg ducal court – in the first instance addressed not to Franz and Auguste, but, as protocol dictated, to Duke Ernst – in which she expressed her desire to make the acquaintance of his three granddaughters 'of whose amiable qualities and distinguished talents' she had heard tell from Baron Budberg. She asked that the three girls be brought to St Petersburg in the company of their mother for the current court season. At this stage no overt mention was made of the girls as bridal candidates but Catherine's euphemistic tone was clear: 'The welcome that awaits them there [in St Petersburg] will meet both the hopes of your highness and the intention in which I invite them.'[8] Catherine also sent the same courteous request in personal letters to Franz and Auguste, assuring them that her motive in extending the invitation was 'in my desire and in my resolution to consolidate by even closer ties the feelings of benevolence and affection with which I am ... the very affectionate cousin'.[9] In her letter to Auguste, Catherine was more explicit, explaining that once the princess had brought her daughters to the St Petersburg court to make her 'personal acquaintance', she hoped to 'fix the stay of one of them by an establishment in which the wishes of your highness seem to agree with mine'.[10]

Much as his wife was eager to accept Catherine's offer, Prince Franz took his time before replying. The duchy was in severe debt and there were many pressing reasons for seeking to secure an advantageous marriage for one of their daughters with Russia, but Franz was concerned about the requirement that whichever one was chosen would have to give up her Lutheran faith and convert to Russian Orthodoxy. He therefore wrote to the Coburg Consistory

---

* Russia at that time was still using the Julian or Old Style calendar, which had been replaced in western Europe by the Gregorian or New Style calendar by 1753. The Russian calendar was running at eleven days behind the European one and for the section of Julie's story relating to Russia both dates will be given where possible for the sake of clarity.

Court soliciting their advice on whether 'one of the princely daughters could, without damage to her conscience, or without losing her
eternal salvation, join the Orthodox church'.[11] During the ten days
of consultations with the consistory court and the ministry of the
City of Coburg, Franz also allowed his daughters an opportunity to
reflect on how they felt at such an outcome. When word came back
that the powers that be did not feel that adopting Russian Orthodoxy
would impinge on the daughters' 'inherent beliefs', Julie herself had
put in writing her feelings on the matter:

> I believe that it is truly a call from God ... if the Russian choice
> falls on me. Considering that I had nothing to do with this pro-
> posal and that my parents remained passive, I do not think I have
> the right to dismiss it on pain of committing disobedience ... I
> am convinced that its [Russian Orthodoxy's] doctrine does not
> differ at all in the principles in which my parents have instructed
> me and that until now I have held to be fair and consistent with
> my religion.[12]

We do not know how the other two sisters responded, but this is the
first we have from Julie and her words are astonishingly mature and
literate. Or was she careful to say what was required of her by her
domineering mother? Whatever the motive, on 26 August (15 August
OS) Duke Ernst was happy to grant his permission for the journey
to St Petersburg. Prince Franz wrote a gushing reply to the empress,
offering his 'admiration ... respect ... [and] gratitude' for her goodness and kindness and assuring her that his wife and daughters were
already preparing for their departure: 'Your Imperial Majesty can be
persuaded of the greatest eagerness on my part to hasten as much as
possible the happy moments when they will enjoy the happiness of
paying their respects to you.'[13]

In the meantime, a second emissary from Catherine arrived in
Coburg on 3 September to inspect the girls: Friedrich Melchior,
Baron von Grimm, another Baltic German in service to the empress
as the resident Russian envoy in Gotha, 60 miles north of Coburg.

He had travelled down to confer with Budberg at Catherine's behest, for she wished to be reassured of Budberg's opinion of the Coburg sisters. Grimm was well acquainted with Alexander and Konstantin and thought the former a paragon of teenage virtue: 'superbly attractive and a fine young man' who was modest and unaffected too. Konstantin's chaotic personality was quite different: he was physically awkward and not attractive. Catherine described him as *étourdi comme un hanneton* – 'as heedless as a cockchafer', a quaint description for which there is no modern equivalent.[14] Finding a suitable bride for him would be a challenge.

The following day, Grimm wrote to Catherine describing the gracious welcome he had been given by Julie's distinguished and pious uncle, Prince Josias, and how, on entering the gates of Coburg, he had encountered 'three nymphs on foot, led by their mother, who seemed to have come to meet us but who in fact walked off into a garden located at the city gates'. This was clearly a cleverly stage-managed form of introduction to her daughters by Auguste that was guaranteed to raise the baron's curiosity. 'We bowed to these Graces, of course,' he continued, 'and I told my travelling companion that if all the nymphs of this land look like this then we must regard this country as the Circassia of Germany.' But it was not until the following day that Grimm found out that they had met the three princesses who were to travel to St Petersburg.[15]

Writing back to Catherine on 4 September (24 August OS) after further inspection of these enchanting Three Graces, Grimm announced his own choice in an additional, enclosed note to her that was sealed for Catherine to read *after* she had made her own choice. Headed 'In Medio Virtus' – 'one must seek perfection in the middle' – it indicated that Grimm had selected the middle sister, Antoinette Ernestine Amalie, rather than Sophie the eldest or Julie the youngest. It had not been a difficult decision, he declared: 'Let no one say that I have sweated blood and water in making my choice, because it was the work of an instant, a sudden flash of inspiration, confirmed by a strict inspection lasting more than 120 minutes.' In short, as he announced somewhat dramatically, 'I came, I saw, I chose,' although he did, however, concede that the ultimate choice would be the empress's.[16] The women would be leaving Coburg the following Monday.

There is nothing to indicate that Baron Grimm apprised either Prince Franz or Princess Auguste of his choice, or whether indeed he even informed Baron Budberg, who was to escort the women to St Petersburg, but after only four days in which to frantically prepare for their long journey, at five o'clock on the morning of 7 September 1795 (27 August OS), Auguste and her three daughters clambered into the travelling coach that Budberg had commandeered to take them to Russia.[17] It was probably a capacious, well-sprung *berline de voyage* with upholstered velvet seating for six, drawn by six horses, with additional horses added en route, depending on the terrain. Seriously upmarket travellers might have opted for something more ostentatious such as an ornate grand carosse; either way, the family travelled more comfortably than in the standard bone-rattling and cramped stagecoaches that then served the post roads of Europe. Budberg most likely crammed into the carriage with them, as well as Auguste's lady in waiting, Baroness de Wangenheim from the Thuringian nobility. A second carriage – or more likely a wagon – brought a cook for preparing the family their favourite German meals and a chambermaid, as well as essential supplies for the journey.

The food at German post stations and inns could be notoriously bad. Many served 'nothing other than gingerbread with brandy wine or fatty black sausage with sauerkraut', and just plain black bread and butter and coffee for breakfast, so it was better to self-cater.[18] Servants would be hired en route, as and when needed, and a courier was sent on ahead to arrange the accommodation for each night and order supplies in time for the travellers' arrival.[19] Some of the women's personal luggage would have been carried under tarpaulin on the roof of their carriage but the rest, along with their bedding, collapsible travelling beds, cooking utensils and cutlery, was crammed into the second. It was quite normal for travellers to take their own travel beds with them on such journeys, for the coaching inns left a great deal to be desired.

By this period in the late eighteenth century, extensive travel had become commonplace in Europe among the wealthy and the aristocracy – particularly to spas for their health or on the Grand Tour, which was seen as an essential part of preparing young men for court and society. Numerous travelogues and guidebooks spoke – if not warned – of the extremely variable state of the roads and the terrible vermin-ridden post houses and inns, with many travellers opting to find private accommodation.[20] The journey Julie was making, while arduous, was thus by no means exceptional. It followed an ancient network of post roads, with stations every 6 to 12 miles in populated areas, that had been in use in Europe since Roman times, each controlled by the particular state across which they journeyed, with measurement of distances and currencies used constantly changing. The best of coaches travelling across central Europe at that time could not cover more than 60 to 70 miles a day, depending on the weather and the quality of the roads.* These became much worse once you had crossed the River Elbe out of East Prussia and into the Duchy of Courland. Further east miles per hour varied, according to the terrain, from 4 to 6, faster if the roads were frozen.[21]

St Petersburg was a very long 1,242 miles from Coburg – not counting detours to find overnight accommodation or allowing for roads being impassable and alternative routes having to be found. It therefore made sense for visitors to Russia from northern Europe to head for the coast and take the boat there, via the Gulf of Finland, and land at the naval port of Kronstadt outside St Petersburg. But in this case, most likely due to the time of year and the weather, the overland route was chosen. For the young Coburg sisters, who had

---

* Twenty years later, Louisa Adams, wife of US diplomat and future president John Adams, made a similar journey in reverse, from St Petersburg to Berlin, and then on to Paris, across war-torn Europe at the end of the Napoleonic Wars. Louisa wrote up her fascinating 'Narrative of a Journey from Russia to France in 1815' in 1836, which remains in manuscript, held in the Adams Papers, Massachusetts Historical Society.

lived such sheltered lives until then, the journey might not necessarily have been a daunting prospect but rather a novelty – a chance at last to see the world beyond Saxe-Coburg.

Prince Franz accompanied his wife and daughters on the first leg, the 157 miles from Coburg to Leipzig, the largest city in Saxony, before bidding them goodbye. Fifty years earlier, in January 1744, Catherine the Great had been lucky to have her father, Christian, as escort as far as Berlin in Prussia on her own arduous journey to Moscow from Zerbst in Saxony-Anhalt. However, in her *Memoirs* she tells us very little of how she and her mother Johanna (herself a princess of Holstein-Gottorp) had crossed the frozen flat terrain of Pomerania and East Prussia in the icy grip of a bitter cold winter, in a small convoy with a lady companion, a cook, major-domo and two maids in a second coach. At this time the post houses and inns offered very crude accommodation. Travellers complained of how desolate and uncomfortable they were. It was perfectly normal to find two or even three guests having to share the same bed, or even taking refuge on straw in the stables. In Catherine's case, she and her mother often had to make do wherever they landed up that night: even in the innkeeper's own rooms, along with 'his wife, their dog, hens and children – children especially, in cradles, in beds, on the stove, on mattresses – strewn any old how like cabbages and turnips'.[22]

Travelling further east, coaches then had to cross a marshy region. During the 1770s, Frederick the Great, king of Prussia, recruited Dutch engineers to drain the river valleys of the Elbe and the Oder to transform them into productive agricultural land. But at the time of Catherine's journey to Moscow, it was 'a patchwork quilt of stagnant pools and marsh, punctuated by areas of thick, waterlogged brush ... barely passable in spring and autumn, when flooding washed away the tracks that snaked across the marshes'. Coaches tended to hug the coast to avoid the worst terrain. 'Our journey was long, tiresome and harrowing,' Catherine recalled. Such was the cold during the six-week journey that she complained that 'my feet were so swollen that I was carried in and out of the carriage'.[23]

After she had said goodbye to her husband Prince Franz, Auguste kept a detailed journal of the places through which they travelled and the people they saw, following a route chosen by Budberg. Auguste expounded in particular on the joys of nature and the landscape and had an artist's eye for everything that attracted her attention. Baron Budberg, meanwhile, amused the Coburg sisters by telling them about Russia, its culture, history and geography. He regaled them with tales of former tsars such as Ivan the Terrible and Peter the Great and of his empress's great ambition to dominate and divide the world into two huge spheres of influence – one in the West, controlled from St Petersburg by her grandson Alexander; the other in the East, controlled from Constantinople by his brother Konstantin – hence his name.[24]

At Torgau, northeast of Leipzig, the coach crossed the River Elbe and, skirting south of Berlin, turned northeast across the Spreewald – the vast sandy delta of the River Spree – to cover the 95 miles to Frankfurt an der Oder. It was a boring expanse punctuated by pine trees in long stretches of sandy terrain and was hard going for the horses. Auguste noted that 'the undercarriage moves terribly slowly in the sand' and that they had to have eight horses, two by four abreast, and a postillion, while the other wagon had three sets of two horses abreast. Sometimes the going was so hard and the horses struggled so much that the family had to get out of the carriage and walk ahead, the deep sand filling their shoes.[25]

At Frankfurt there was the huge River Oder to cross – one of central Europe's longest rivers, on the border of East Prussia. For Auguste it was an unforgettable experience and reminded her of crossing the Rhine near Cologne.[26] Here they entered the Polish territories of Prussia at Küstrin (now Kostrzyn in western Poland), a strongly fortified town built to protect the eastern approaches to Berlin at the confluence of the Warthe and the Oder. Here again the land was low and marshy, but they soon left that dismal sight behind as the coach pulled further north, heading for Königsberg (now Kaliningrad) on the Baltic coast. Now the scenery was transformed into the vast forests of Landsberg (now Gorzów), which for centuries had provided the timber for shipbuilding at the important northern port of Stettin. Amid these extensive and magnificent forests of fir and pine the travellers' gaze was arrested by a series of lakes that gave the area the air of Switzerland. At last the going was good for the sandy surface had been removed and a road of granite stones had been laid with soil on top.

On the market square at Schneidemühl (now Piła) the travellers had been greeted by Polish villagers, whom Auguste found very 'picturesque', and a contingent of Hussars in colourful uniforms.[27] Auguste rarely says where they stopped at night, though she did recall one overnight stay at a farmhouse at Hoggenbruch where they slept in a kind of kitchen, which was so intolerably overheated that 'we could not stand it'.[28] Continuing their journey through northern Poland, the landscape suddenly opened up onto a beautiful lagoon and green meadows full of herds of cattle. Then on along the good straight road to Königsberg with the Baltic Sea in the distance. Auguste was delighted to see that local dignitaries turned out to greet the travellers as they passed through: 'We were treated like rare creatures in every town.' Sometimes even military bands played for them and it is possible that local gentry, out of respect for Auguste's rank, accommodated them at their manor houses. The girls used the journey to improve their French at every opportunity (that being the language of the Russian court) and Sophie drew many sketches.[29]

The 550-mile journey from Leipzig to Königsberg took fourteen days. Auguste and her daughters reached this historic northern seaport, formerly one of the great medieval trading towns of the Hanseatic League, in a cold cutting wind and rain. The last 3 miles had been sandy and Auguste had found the area 'unspeakably mournful'.[30] After passing through so many small, unremarkable towns and villages it was quite a moment to enter this, the historic and impressive 'metropolis of Prussia' and one of the largest cities in Europe.[31] When Frederick, Duke of Prussia, was crowned king of Prussia in 1701, Königsberg had become capital of the newly formed East Prussia. But while it had some elegant mansions, these were as nothing compared with what the travellers would see in Russia. For three and a half days they took a well-earned break in this fortified garrison town and major Baltic seaport. But Auguste did not warm to the place, finding its centre overcrowded and dirty.[32]

Only a few weeks before them, the French society painter Elisabeth Vigée Le Brun had travelled the same road from Königsberg to St Petersburg, to seek her fortune painting portraits of the Russian aristocracy after fleeing France in the wake of the revolution of 1789. She vividly recalled how 'the greater part of the land was fertile, but the sandy road was very troublesome'.

> We only managed one stop every seven hours, which meant that I often had to take my walk at night. Arriving in Königsberg from the direction of Marienwerder, one can see the sea, and close to the road, which is a very narrow one, the river Haff. I took ten days to travel from Reinsberg [in Saxony] to Königsberg and started out for Memel almost immediately. Far from any improvement, the route became much worse. Day and night we trundled over horrible sandy soil, running alongside the Haff so closely that half the carriage seemed to be leaning into the river.[33]

From Königsberg there were still another three weeks of coach roads; the next major stop would be Tilsit (now Sovetsk), 'a small but very neat town, situated in a fertile plain, on the river Memel', that traded mainly in corn and timber.[34] Once again the road was terribly sandy, and the carriage needed twelve horses to get them through. There was considerable danger they might break down under the strain and there were no inns where the travellers could have taken refuge until they got to Tilsit. It was as well they had brought their own beds and all necessary provisions with them.

From Tilsit the road took them 60 miles further north, still hugging the coastline and just inside the East Prussian border, up the Baltic coast to the busy port of Memel (now Klaipėda), across 'a desolate wilderness of sand and water', where the wind moaned 'with that strange unearthly sound which it has in lonely places, over tracts of snow or sand'. To the left were the cold waters of the Baltic, and 'everywhere else fields of sand and morass extend[ed] to the verge of the horizon.'[35] At this point some travellers opted to load their coaches onto a boat to take them up along the coastline, known as the Curonian Spit, rather than risk becoming stuck on the narrow post road bordered by sand dunes. But the Coburg coach opted for the longer route through the countryside. Here and there spectral pine trees thick with hoar frost pierced the winter gloom but it was a tedious and unforgiving landscape until at last they turned inland, crossing another border into Courland.* This duchy had, after years of conflict and territorial rivalries, only eight months previously been annexed to the Russian Empire by Catherine the Great, as part of the Third Partition of Poland. The post stations here were extremely rudimentary. They did not provide beds and only the most unappetising food, described by travellers as 'black and sour bread, rancid butter, insipid soup ... bad meat and execrable beer'.[36] The sight of Memel, with its church spire, citadel and windmills, must have been a welcome relief, but once again Auguste does not note where the family spent the night.

After another 160 miles, the carriages arrived at the rather uninviting town of Mitau (now Jelgava), southwest of Riga, which was a regular stopover point on the post road to Russia. From there the road became busier on the way to Riga, the capital of the Governorate of Riga (soon to be renamed Livonia) which eventually hove into view, situated on a large gulf on the Baltic Sea. With its steep pitched roofs and narrow streets, Riga reminded the weary Auguste of the towns on the Rhine and in the Netherlands; the houses were not particularly elegant and it was also a busy commercial port and trade centre. The Russian writer Nikolay Karamzin was impressed by its 'numerous shops, the streets thronged with people, the river covered with shipping of different nations, and the

---

* The Duchy of Courland has a complicated and confusing history and suffered centuries of conflict and territorial rivalry. Originally located in what was Livonia (which comprised parts of today's Estonia and Latvia), it became a vassal state of Poland in 1569. It was absorbed into the new Polish–Lithuanian Commonwealth created in 1726 until it was annexed by Russia in 1795.

exchange crowded', when he passed through in 1803.[37] Auguste and
her daughters took advantage of this to break their journey for a
few days to have some gowns made for their imminent arrival at the
court of Catherine the Great. Budberg advised these should be in a
traditional 'Moldovan' style favoured at court; they also obtained
furs, sable hats and thick Russian dresses for the cold of the Russian
winter.[38] While in Riga the sisters were delighted to be taken twice to
the theatre on Königstrasse, well known for its German repertoire.

There were still more bone-rattling roads to endure after Riga,
on the route to Dorpat (now Tartu), for as Elisabeth Vigée Le Brun
noted, the highways were unbelievably bad. Huge stones shook her
carriage violently. The inns had nothing to recommend them – they
were 'of the most rude order where it would have been impossible
to stay', so Vigée and her companions had been 'obliged to move
from rut to rut all the way to Saint Petersburg without any chance
of rest'.[39] For one German traveller the 'dreary road to Dorpat', after
leaving the fertile shore of the River Dvina, was a 'barren, monotonous wilderness'. To the left, in the distance, lay the 'magnificent
ocean' but the road itself took travellers across 'sand, marsh, heath
and forest ... in monotonous and unbroken order'. It was, he concluded, 'the most barren and ugliest district in Livonia'.[40]

After crossing the great triple-spanned stone bridge into Dorpat
and traversing the imposing Town Hall Square, the carriage rum-
bled on towards Narva. There were no stopovers here, on what
was known as the German Post (road), since all the wooden-built
coaching stations were run by Germans and had little to recommend
them. Respite came with arrival at the naval port of Narva, with its
imposing fourteenth-century castle built by the Teutonic Knights and
surrounded by magnificent forests. Until then, the travellers saw only
'solitary and uninviting houses, lying alone in the frowning forest,
and the inhabitants, muffled in their grey sheepskins' passing by.[41]

From there, Auguste and her daughters did not, however, head
straight for the Russian capital, but for a few hours' stopover at the
palace at Strelna, the final stop on the post road into St Petersburg
from Peterhof. Approaching Strelna, the party sensed with growing

excitement Peter the Great's gleaming new city, for they could see its skyline in the distance. Elisabeth Vigée Le Brun had revelled in how the road now was 'bordered on both sides by some charming country houses, surrounded with tastefully arranged gardens, rather in the English style. The inhabitants have turned the marshy land to their advantage, ornamenting their gardens with summerhouses and pretty hillocks, canals and small streams.' But as evening descended, 'even before sunset, fog rises from the ground, so thick that everything seems covered by its dense black pall'.[42]

At the end of their arduous forty-day journey the travellers drew up outside the palace at Strelna, without fanfare, at midday on Saturday 17 October (6 October OS) 1795.[43] How different from Catherine the Great's own reception in 1744, when she crossed the Russian border by sleigh in deep snow as Sophie of Anhalt. On that occasion, she and her mother had been met by an official party of a regiment of light horse, a brass band and court officials bearing welcome gifts of sable furs to keep out the cold for the remainder of their journey by sledge to St Petersburg, where they had been entertained by fireworks and with elephants paraded in front of the Winter Palace. After this the women were whisked at breakneck speed in a convoy of sleighs to meet the Empress Elizabeth and the putative groom, her nephew Tsarevich Peter, in Moscow.[44]

In 1795, however, the Saxe-Coburg princesses had had rather an ignominious start to their Russian experience. Strelna, begun by Peter the Great, was described at the time as a 'vast building of brick stuccoed, built upon piazzas, and surrounded with undulating woods and pleasure-grounds'.[45] But despite these wonderful gardens and a commanding view of the Gulf of Finland, the palace itself was in a very sorry, unfinished state, for Peter had abandoned its completion in favour of his more magnificent palace at Peterhof. Although Strelna was later gifted to Grand Duke Konstantin by his father, in 1795 he only had a small hunting lodge there. As Auguste noted in her journal, the palace was 'threatened with collapse because it has been uninhabited now for many years'. It must have been a cheerless and anticlimactic welcome but at least the women had a few hours in which to rest and prepare themselves. For, according to the protocol explained to them by Baron Budberg, they must present themselves to the empress of Russia at the Winter Palace between seven and eight that evening.[46]

CHAPTER 3

'THE LARGEST AND MOST BRILLIANT COURT IN EUROPE'

We can only speculate on what might have been Julie's response to the great northern capital city of St Petersburg, founded by Peter the Great in 1703 on the windy shores of the Gulf of Finland. But it must have come as something of a shock after the insular world of the Coburg court. Peter's choice of location at the point where the mighty River Neva empties into the Gulf was intended to open up Russia to the West, both politically and commercially. By placing his capital on the sea route across to northern Europe, he established Russia as a powerful naval force, with its base at the island of Kronstadt. But it was far from ideal: the new capital was built at the mouth of a low, swampy, sandy area with only a thin scattering of birch trees and brushwood. It bred disease and was constantly threatened by flooding, not to mention the perpetually dark and looming skies of rain-soaked autumns and the snow and ice of a sub-zero winter that would freeze the Neva solid for as much as six months of the year.

After a brief rest and time to change from their travelling clothes, Auguste and her daughters left Strelna at 5 p.m. on 17 October (6 October OS). The 'sun was just going down on the loveliest and brightest autumn day', as they headed down the post road into the capital. The view was magnificent, featuring 'an uninterrupted line

of sumptuous palaces' with grounds stretching down to the Gulf
of Finland, all of them 'built in every variety of chaste, fanciful,
and imitative architecture' on the right-hand side of the road, and
with the fields and trees leading to the gulf on the other.[1] Auguste
noted with amusement the presence of a very colourful Chinese
house alongside an Italianate villa with all kinds of pillars, next to
a summer house looking as though it had been transported there
'from Leipzig'. The grandly positioned Naryshkin mansion 'with
grounds stretching right to the bay' and an English terraced garden
was particularly impressive – a beautiful oasis in the surrounding flat
marshy landscape. It was, of course, a mere country seat in Russian
aristocratic terms, for the family owned another impressive palace
in St Petersburg.[2]

It was, however, the sight of St Petersburg in the distance, 'spread
out like the wings of the imperial eagle', that took the breath away,
projecting the sense of a metropolis of 'vast and grand dispositions'.
After a long and gruelling coach ride winding along the inhospitable
shores of Prussia and traversing the wild and uncultivated plains of
Livonia, eighteenth-century travellers to Russia were 'struck with
astonishment and rapture at finding again, amid a vast desert, a large
and magnificent city, abounding in the sociality and amusements,
the arts and the luxury', which one traveller had supposed to 'exist
no where but in Paris'.[3]

On first arriving, many were left speechless by the city's dazzlingly
white and elegant Palladian buildings, the gilded onion domes of
its churches, its imposing granite quaysides on the Neva, all of
which 'lifted the spirits as one approached by road'.[4] St Petersburg's
straight, broad and often very long streets, intersected by spacious
open squares; its fine monuments, institutions and academies; and
everywhere the meandering presence of numerous canals, gave it
the air of a Russian-style northern Venice on the grand scale – not
as beautiful perhaps, but certainly more extraordinary. The French
writer Madame de Staël was utterly seduced by the sight of the
turrets and golden spires when she arrived in 1812: 'You arrive in
one of the finest cities in the world, as if, with a magic wand, an

enchanter had made all the wonders of Europe and Asia start up from the middle of the deserts.' All in all, St Petersburg presented 'a wonderful picture of what power and genius can accomplish'.[5] By the end of the eighteenth century it was drawing in many visitors and had become part of the European Grand Tour. Traveller James Brogden noted that many of its public buildings and palaces were 'built upon a much more magnificent scale than any buildings I am acquainted with in London'.[6]

As their coach drew into the Admiralty Quarter, the travellers were presented with the Russian equivalent of Paris's Quartier du Palais-Royal: the vast, imposing, stuccoed brick façade of the Imperial Winter Palace. Catherine the Great had made it the heart of St Petersburg, the palace occupying the 'space of a small town ... in which luxury and wealth have established their seat ... the centre of amusement and business, the brilliant resort of pleasure and fashion'.[7] In front of it to the south stood an enormous parade ground, Senate Square, edged by a crescent of handsome government buildings; behind lay the granite quays of the Palace Embankment and the River Neva.[8]

The Winter Palace, where the Coburg party were commanded to appear, was occupied by Catherine and her court during the coldest months, after having spent the summer season from May out at the more salubrious environment of her blue and gold rococo palace at Tsarskoe Selo. The Winter Palace had replaced an earlier wooden building begun by Empress Anna in the 1730s and had been considerably embellished and extended by Empress Elizabeth in the mid-century. Many thought that this newer, imposing size was excessively large and heavy. In 1764 Catherine had added her own Small Hermitage to the east of the original palace, and then another building known as the Old – or Great – Hermitage (on the site of an earlier building erected by Peter the Great), for housing her huge art collection, was constructed over a period of ten years from the 1770s. Finally, Catherine had added the exquisite Hermitage Theatre in the 1780s.

Many travellers at the time had plenty to say about the arresting sight before them and Auguste, of course, was fulsome in her descriptions in her letters to Franz. Even though it was 'already completely dark' when she and her daughters arrived, what they saw of the city as their coach crossed the Fontanka Bridge over a branch of the River Neva seemed like fairyland. 'All that could be seen were long rows of lanterns, like an illumination, dancing before our eyes,' she said, and then, with a flourish, their escort suddenly announced: '*Le Palais!*'[9] Auguste admitted that 'my knees were trembling as I climbed from the carriage. The thought that the destiny of one of my daughters would be decided here struck my soul so powerfully that I do not know how I went up the tall steps on the arm of the Marshal of the Court, Prince Bariatinsky.'[10]

After entering the Winter Palace, the women were conducted up a grand marble flight of stairs and then through several suites of rooms known as the 'Golden Enfilade' that were used for balls and assemblies. They were full of paintings, statuary, furniture and artefacts collected by Catherine over the past thirty-three years in her ever more voracious hunt for the best of European fine art. Auguste tells us that she and her daughters then entered a brightly lit antechamber, surrounded by pages, runners and footmen, where 'Mesenzof' (probably Budberg's adjutant Mezendorf) was standing at the door and 'I suppose it was he who said sotto voce to me in passing "L'Impératrice est Là!"'[11]

The Russian court at the end of the eighteenth century was legendary for a richness and splendour that 'surpassed description'. 'It retains many traces of its antient Asiatic pomp, blended with European refinement,' wrote William Coxe in 1784.[12] The best time to see it on display was when the empress made her appearance at around seven in the evening, surrounded by 'an immense retinue of courtiers'. 'The costliness and glare of their apparel, and a profusion of precious stones, created a splendour, of which the magnificence of other courts can give us only a faint idea.' Court ladies bejewelled to the hilt and wearing the latest fashions from Paris and London, complemented by 'lofty headdresses' and an excess of rouge, must have given the Coburg party the most withering of sneers at the sight of their modest provincial German dress. The male courtiers too were veritable peacocks, their garments covered in diamonds, elaborate buckles, buttons and gold epaulettes – and all of this splendour softly reflected in the warm light of hundreds of candles.[13]

As ruler over 29 million subjects and renowned across the Western world for her fearsome intelligence, her cultured mind and political acumen, during her reign Catherine had consolidated her empire and increased its wealth; with her reform of the laws she had won the respect of many of her international contemporaries. The prestige of her name throughout the world at the end of a reign that had now lasted a third of a century was reflected in territorial gains that extended Russia's domains from the Baltic in the north to Siberia and the Pacific in the east and the Black Sea in the south. After the ruthless partitions of Poland in 1772, 1793 and – the year of Julie's arrival – 1795, Catherine had turned her ambitions towards Asia Minor, initiating expansion into the Ottoman Empire during the Russo-Turkish War of 1768–74. This had brought her territories in Moldavia, Ukraine and Crimea. But she still held to one remaining ambition: to retake Constantinople and place an Orthodox Russian on the throne – her grandson Konstantin. Whoever his future bride might be, she too would have to be prepared to rise to these grandiose imperial heights.[14]

Always a handsome woman and a commanding presence despite her relatively small stature, the empress, in this the final year of her life, had grown portly, although her complexion still seemed fresh and her eyes as bright blue as ever. But she was now sixty-six and suffering from high blood pressure as well as being prone to swelling and ulceration of her legs. She also needed spectacles for reading.[15] Nevertheless, she still had enough vigour to rise early, at six, light the stove in her room and prepare herself strong coffee. She paid little attention to her toilette during an ordinary working day dealing with state business and writing letters, dressing simply in a loose silk gown. But when it came to court occasions Catherine loved her diamonds – of which she had a prodigious collection – and she rouged her cheeks and lightly powdered her hair.[16] Her receptions were noted for their magnificence and good taste and she was adept at entertaining foreign visitors and guests, having a reputation for courtesy and for putting visitors at their ease.

As one of the enlightened despots of her age, when it came to marrying her son and grandsons Catherine acted ruthlessly in the dynasty's best interests. The sooner these young boys – Alexander and Konstantin, on both of whom she doted – were married and produced children of their own, the safer for the Romanov throne. Alexander, now almost eighteen, was tall and physically striking and cultured. He was polite and attentive to ladies – if not something of a flirt – and seemed not just the perfect marital catch but also a romantic tsar in the making. Catherine even now was secretly plotting to remove her weak and feckless son Paul from the succession, exile him to Lithuania and bypass him as heir by ordaining that Alexander should succeed her.

Alexander's brother Konstantin was very much still 'an unlicked bear cub', as Catherine herself said, and was unruly and confrontational.[17] His rowdy behaviour would need to be curbed and his manners knocked into shape for him to fulfil the grand ambitions she had for him. She was relieved that the Coburg princesses had finally arrived: 'I have been so tired all these days by Constantin and everything to do with him beyond all the everyday battles', she admitted to Baron Grimm, 'that I have not had a moment to myself.'[18] She was eager to resolve the question of Konstantin's marriage as speedily as possible.

Auguste's account is unclear about where precisely she and her daughters were received by the empress. Was it in the Small Hermitage perhaps? That same evening she tells us they attended a concert there, which would pinpoint this as the venue.[19] In any event, Catherine received the Coburg women 'with the utmost graciousness and friendliness', despite their being ogled by her courtiers, who, 'impelled by curiosity, crowded near the door through which the foreign Princesses were to enter'.[20] Their arrival was, however, rather less striking than had been that of the two princesses of Baden three years earlier, as court diarist Charles Masson noted. Be that as it may, the unsophisticated Auguste was impressed. The empress was a woman of considerable presence, of a strong build and seemed to be 'uncommonly well':

> She is exactly as I imagined fairies when I was a child. Her face is large and perfect. One would think her less than sixty. Neither her hair nor her eyebrows are blackened, but grey. She still has a lot of hair and has it dressed in a way befitting her years. She wears a striped scarf with two enormous diamonds on her head. Her facial features are unusually kindly. Her mouth is still extraordinarily beautiful, her nose not large but well-shaped, and a pair of blue eyes just as they should be ... She applies rouge but only a little. She must never have put white [lead] on her face or her skin would not be so fresh. Her gait is noble, as is her whole manner, and amazingly light for her age. She is the personification of dignified age.

More to the point, Auguste could not help noticing that, as Catherine cast a close eye over her three young daughters, 'her gaze lingered on Jülchen'. '*Mais, ce sont des beautés!*' the empress exclaimed with pleasure.[21]

This may have been the empress's initial impression of the three sisters but courtier Prince Adam Czartoryski could not help but find it 'painful to see this mother offering her daughters like goods for sale, and watching anxiously to discover on which of them would fall the eye of the empress and the handkerchief of the Grand-Duke Constantine'. During the elaborate court engagements that served as the backdrop to the selection process, he and his friends tried not to notice the cold-bloodedness of this ritual inspection, for the daughters were pretty and amiable and 'worthy of respect' rather than being sized up as might be 'slaves to inhabit the harems of Turkish pashas'.[22] Many at the imperial court found it all rather infra dig and noted with disdain the 'antiquity and bad taste' of the Coburg women's dress, which appeared totally unsuitable for the splendours of their surroundings.[23] With their provincial lack of sophistication, they became the object of pity, if not scorn.

Countess Varvara Golovina, Elizaveta Alexeevna's lady in waiting, noted Auguste's embarrassment that she and her daughters' modest appearances did not reflect 'the largest and most brilliant Court in Europe'.[24] When Elizaveta Alexeevna had arrived here from Baden, she had been put into panniers and elaborate court dress with her hair powdered for that first all-important appearance. Catherine soon noticed her guests' discomfort and, mindful of how she herself back in 1744 'had arrived in Russia poor', the next day sent her guests 'two baskets of all kinds of rich silk stuffs', and half a dozen of her own tailors to measure them up for new and more appropriate clothing.[25]

For the duration of their visit the Coburg family were accommodated in specially prepared, plush apartments in what Auguste referred to as the 'Potemkin Palace', a short distance away on Bolshaya Millionnaya Ulitsa – so close in fact that it was linked by a corridor to a series of galleries leading into the Hermitage.* Here they would take their meals with their small entourage, comprising Baron Budberg, an imperial chamberlain – Prince Golitsyn – and two silent but attentive young gentlemen of the bedchamber, 'Golovkin and Prince Apalinsky'.† The next day, Sunday 7 October (18 October NS), they attended church (though whether it was a German Lutheran one or the Russian Orthodox one in the Winter Palace we do not know), after which Catherine came to see them with Alexander and a sheepish and blushing Konstantin.

This visit gave the sisters their first clear glimpse of the putative bridegroom. He seemed perfectly agreeable: well spoken, courteous and more mature than his sixteen years. He was rather small in

---

*   Auguste is probably referring to the Potemkin apartments at no. 22 Millionnaya, built in the 1730s and once occupied by Catherine's favourite, Count Potemkin. The building was originally part of the Winter Palace but was destroyed by fire in 1837 and replaced by the New Hermitage during the reign of Nicholas I.

†   Count Fyodor Golovkin (1766–1823) and Prince Alexei Apalunsky, according to Julie's Swiss biographer, Alville.

stature – though Auguste assumed he was still growing – with 'a round, full face which, leaving aside the snub nose, is attractive; a pair of dark blue eyes full of fire and reason, almost dark eyebrows and eyelashes' and a 'very small red mouth' which was 'pleasing when he laughs' and revealed 'nice teeth'. Auguste had already noted that both young grand dukes looked extremely attractive, with their 'sinewy bodies' so well displayed in their infantry uniforms that they 'would stand out as handsome among a whole corps of officers'. In her opinion they were far superior in appearance to the blasé court dandies.[26] She also perceptively noted that Konstantin was 'a soldier body and soul'; his bride would discover the downside to this fixation to her cost, and only too soon. For now, Auguste announced to her husband Franz in a letter home that she would be 'heartily glad' to accept whichever girl 'the lot falls to' to marry him.[27] Before leaving them, Catherine presented the four Coburg women with the Order of St Catherine – a star and cross lavishly inlaid with diamonds and hung on a red riband, that aside from being presented to grand duchesses of the Romanov family was also given to a few chosen members of other ruling houses and high nobility. She also invited them to attend her again at the Small Hermitage that evening.

For this second official court appearance the women donned the Moldavian costumes they had had made for them in Riga. These would have comprised a sleeveless *sarafan* or full-length tunic, over a white long-sleeved chemise, with a high ornamental headdress known as a *kokoshnik* hung with a long veil. At 6 p.m. they made their way from their apartments through several galleries of paintings and works of art in the Small Hermitage, and into 'a small and friendly' reception room where they met the empress's granddaughters and were formally introduced to Grand Duke Alexander and his wife Elizaveta Alexeevna. Alexander was a perfect Adonis, thought Auguste: 'handsome as a picture, tall in stature, of elegant but manly build, with a kind and gentle face'; in short, 'much better looking than his brother' with more regular features. As the older brother he appeared more self-confident and worldly than Konstantin and had an effortlessly charming manner, if not inclining to 'a little indolence'.[28] The two brothers had a close relationship, it was clear, and Konstantin seemed to have Alexander's complete trust. The empress clearly took great delight in their young sisters – her granddaughters Alexandra (twelve), Elena (eleven), Maria (nine) and Ekaterina (seven) – who were all 'absolutely delightful', as was Elizaveta – a 'pretty delicate blonde' who reminded Auguste of the Duchess of Meiningen.

Countess Golovina noticed how quickly her mistress and Julie struck up a friendship, so much so that Julie referred to her as Elise and we shall use that form of her name hereafter. She delighted in being able to gossip in German with the Coburg sisters about friends and family back home, whom Elise still keenly missed.[29] Indeed, starved of sympathetic company at court, she had eagerly antici-pated the arrival of the Coburg princesses. Elise recorded their first uncertain steps in a letter she wrote to her mother Princess Amalie, in Baden, a couple of days later. She thought Auguste, who was only thirty-eight at the time, looked past fifty. Sophie, her eldest daughter, was good-looking except for a 'disagreeable mouth'; the blonde second sister, Antoinette, was the least attractive. It was Julie with her chestnut hair and bright eyes and a mischievous air who was definitely the prettiest and most animated of the three.[30] Elise found them all good company and Auguste revelled in her good impression of her daughters: 'My children get along with all the Grand Duchesses as well as if they had been together all their lives,' she told Franz. Elise was already eagerly making 'a thousand plans' about what she and her new sister-in-law would do in the future.[31]

The following day, 8 October (19 October NS), brought first sight of Catherine's only son and heir, the Tsarevich, Grand Duke Paul, who with his German wife Maria Feodorovna travelled into St Petersburg from his home at Gatchina to inspect the prospective Coburg brides.[32] Auguste had been aware, even from the distance of Coburg, that Paul had a difficult relationship with his mother – who had usurped the throne of his father, Peter III, in 1762 (Peter had died not long afterwards in suspicious circumstances). The Tsarevich was well known for being excessively neurotic, despotic and unpredictable. But despite his patent alienation from his mother, Grand Duke Paul was kind and friendly with the Coburg visitors and complimented the girls on their beauty. He sang the praises of his son Konstantin, telling Auguste that he would not like to be in his shoes, having to 'choose between these three beauties'. He was impressed with how well they were coping with what must be a stressful situation.[33]

In the evening of that same long and enervating day, the Coburg princesses were paraded at a ball at the Hermitage. Auguste was surprised to find that courtiers were allowed to sit in the empress's presence – 'where and how they liked'. The young Russian grand duchesses were the centre of attention, all of them demonstrating what graceful dancers they were. Alexandra and Elena in particular impressed Auguste as they showed off their dainty feet dancing a *minuet à la reine*, a *cosaque* and an *Allemande figurée*. With their impressive, nymph-like lightness of foot they '[stood] out in stark comparison with the affected court ladies'. After the empress retired to bed, Alexander and Konstantin escorted their guests to supper where once again the young grand duchesses were eager to chat with the Coburg sisters, until the night's entertainment ended at midnight.[34]

Prince Adam Czartoryski recalled that during their stay, numerous other entertainments were laid on for the German visitors. There were 'fêtes, soirées, balls, and promenades every day', as well as visits to the Italian operetta at the Hermitage, all to provide ample opportunity for Konstantin to scrutinise the three bridal candidates at close hand.[35] But for the time being, however, he seemed indifferent. Granted, he went through all the required motions of royal *politesse*, his grandmother no doubt having commanded that he rein in his usual 'knavish' behaviour. To those who knew him he appeared, at this time, uncharacteristically reticent. The more cynical observers such as Charles Masson and others at court noted how Konstantin studiously projected an image that ran entirely counter to his real reputation. He feigned an air of extreme modesty and shyness verging on reluctance. Privately, however, he complained that the Coburg princesses were unsophisticated and coy, that they 'were too German to please him, and he preferred Russians'.[36]

If he had had any choice in the matter, Konstantin would have preferred not to get married at all, thought Countess Golovina, but he knew he would have to submit to his imperial duty whether he liked it or not.[37] Catherine the Great was eager for him to make his choice so that she could welcome one of the Coburg princesses into the family: 'The Crown Princess of Saxe-Coburg is a beautiful woman worthy of respect,' she told Baron Grimm in a letter of 9 October (20 October NS), 'her daughters are pretty. It is a pity that our suitor can choose only one, as it would be good to keep all three.' Contrary to Grimm's wishes, Catherine had opened his sealed note recommending Antoinette but was confidently predicting that 'our Paris will give the apple to the youngest: you will see that it's Julie who wins.' This was already the consensus at court, she told him: 'About two hundred people who've seen them so far have opted for only one: Julie. The mischievous Julie will win out over her sisters, you'll see,' Catherine insisted.[38]

An apocryphal story persists that Catherine had come to this decision the very first day the Coburg party had arrived. She had apparently been watching at a window with Konstantin when the sisters alighted, in disorderly manner, from their carriage in the courtyard below, in a moment of comedy akin to the arrival of Cinderella's two Ugly Sisters at the ball: 'The first got entangled in the unwonted Court train and fell to the ground. The second, taking warning from that catastrophe sprawled out on all fours. The third and youngest, the pretty little Juliana, hardly fourteen, took her train up in both hands and gracefully sprang to the ground.' 'That's the one! She will do for our wild Constantine,' Catherine had exclaimed, to which he had supposedly grumpily replied: 'Very well, then, if so it must be, I'll wed the little ape.'[39]

When Elise, as Princess Luise of Baden, had arrived in St Petersburg for her own bridal inspection in 1792, she had had to endure six weeks of socialising and endless card games with the empress before a stiff and punctilious Grand Duke Alexander had finally presented her with a note announcing that he had been 'authorised by his parents to tell me that he loved me' and asked her to marry him.[40] Such were the ways of Russian imperial match-making. It took his brother Konstantin eight days to finally make up his own mind. In the meantime, the Coburg princesses had dined with Elise several times, and had spent the evenings dancing at the Winter Palace, socialising and attending a masked ball. On Monday 22 October (2 November NS) they had visited Madame Vigée Le Brun's studio to see her paintings and had spent the rest of the day together until changing for their attendance at court that evening. By now Elise had become completely enamoured of her fellow German visitors: it was 'as though we had spent our whole life together', she told her mother.[41] The three Coburg sisters had by then struck a chord at court too, where they were being referred to as the *tri blagosloveniya* – the three blessings – or *die drei Schönheiten*.

Empress Catherine, however, was beginning to find Konstantin's failure to make a decision a strain; as a woman of considerable intellect and sophisticated tastes she had also wearied of the obsequious Auguste's constant attentions and sentimental chitchat. Catherine suggested she take some rest, no doubt wishing a break from her company. Left to her own devices for a couple of days, Auguste revelled in living in the lap of Russian imperial luxury – albeit temporarily – and threw herself into all the trips and entertainments offered her, such as a drive along the quayside of the Neva to take in the view and a tour of the art galleries in the Hermitage. She visited the Russian chapel at the Winter Palace to hear the liturgy: 'the beauty and solemnity of the singing of over a hundred men's voices cannot be put into words,' she told Franz. There was also an entertaining evening watching a comedy at the Hermitage Theatre, translated from Russian into German by the empress herself, and a whole day spent marvelling at the interiors of the Tauride Palace built by Prince Potemkin, as well as a visit to the Smolny Convent, now a school for the daughters of the poor nobility.[42]

For many of these excursions, Konstantin, again uncharacteristically meek and tongue-tied, dutifully escorted Auguste and her daughters, along with Alexander. He described the paintings and their provenance in impeccable French as Auguste stopped to admire works by the Swiss-German artist Angelica Kauffman, by Raphael, Rembrandt and Rubens, and proceeded on through rooms stuffed with *objets d'art* of marble, bronze and other precious stones. She swooned at her punctilious Russian escorts ('There cannot be many men to equal the two brothers, the Grand Dukes, so close to the throne,' she told Franz) and invited Konstantin to tea in their apartments. But even on this occasion, he 'still could not bring himself to chat with the girls', engaging instead with Baron Budberg, of whom he seemed very fond.[43] Auguste concluded that by setting themselves apart from the mass of courtiers with 'an icy politeness', Alexander and Konstantin had kept 'their lovely souls pure', but the Empress Catherine should take the credit for having ensured their careful upbringing and education. Once again she noticed how Konstantin insisted that 'his only wish is to go on a campaign', to serve his country. 'He said this with such an honest, good face,' she added. Could there possibly be a more admirable, upstanding, cultivated young man? 'What will not these two men one day achieve!' she gushed. 'The Empress looks on them with bliss.'[44]

As the days passed, Auguste noted that slowly but surely Konstantin was becoming entranced by Julie, particularly when she played the piano and sang, and he was now joining the family every evening for dinner. But while he flirted self-consciously with her sisters, speaking to them in 'comically broken German', he remained restrained and serious with Julie.[45] But finally, on the evening of Wednesday 24 October (4 November NS) and much to the collective relief of the parties concerned, Konstantin ceased prevaricating. Auguste excitedly wrote to tell Franz that their Jülchen was a bride-to-be: 'Everything is decided, and everything as you expected. Jülchen's star has prevailed.' A nervous Konstantin had come to Auguste at six o'clock that evening and 'in a trembling voice' had said: '*Madame, je viens vous demander la main de Madame votre fille.*' They both had wept, as Auguste impressed upon the grand duke how she was entrusting him with the happiness of her child, adding, significantly, that 'with her very sensitive nature he could make her both extraordinarily happy and unhappy'. She was 'placing her fate in [his] hands'.

When Julie was brought into the room to be told this momentous news, there followed a storybook scene, as described by Auguste. Her daughter wept quietly, her mother proudly noting that 'I have never seen her look prettier' as her new fiancé kissed her hand and in impeccable French asked if she might come to love him one day. 'I know I don't deserve it yet, but I will try to become worthy of you,' he told her. Julie burst into floods of tears when her mother exclaimed if only her father could see her right now, upon which Konstantin grasped both her hands and promised that he would take her to Germany as soon as the empress permitted, and that she would soon see him again.[46] Shortly afterwards Grand Duke Alexander arrived, to express his joy 'at his brother's happiness' and to reassure both Auguste and Julie that Konstantin was 'truly in love'; and that he had sat up half the previous night with him discussing his momentous decision. 'Julie will be very happy with this family,' Auguste confidently wrote to her husband afterwards; she would be leaving her daughter behind in Russia 'with an easy mind'.[47]

So it was that the wrong sister drew the short straw. Julie's younger brother Leopold would later admit that 'clever, amiable' Antoinette – as Budberg had already rightly concluded – would have been a much better choice for the wayward Konstantin. Antoinette, the older sister who would later be so critical of Julie's desperation to escape the misery to which she had been condemned, would, according to Leopold, 'have suited that position wonderfully well. I know much of all this from Constantine himself ... How strangely ... do things often come to pass,' he mused.[48]

CHAPTER 4

'JÜLCHEN'S STAR HAS PREVAILED'

As a Romanov grand duke, third in line to the throne after his father and brother (should Alexander produce no male children), Konstantin had had the freedom to reject several brides already suggested to him. Julie, on the other hand, had no say in the matter. The weight of family expectation obliged her to gratefully accept Konstantin's proposal, knowing how important a marital alliance with Russia was for the prospects of her cash-strapped parents and the Duchy of Saxe-Coburg itself. During the visit, Catherine had inspected the Saxe-Coburg family tree, prepared by a certain Baron Thümmel, that Auguste had presented to her. She was interested in ascertaining the suitability also of Auguste's sons in the Russian marriage stakes: 'Tell me if the second son of this Duchess is good in face, heart and mind,' she instructed Baron Grimm. 'I am going to make a note of all the cadets in Germany and when I have a complete list of them, I will choose as many as I need for brides.'* Russian brides, as she and the impoverished German duchies knew, would 'make their husband's fortune'.[1]

---

* By 'cadets' Catherine intends the younger sons of royal houses, other than the male heir to the title, who would not be available to marry and live in Russia. Auguste's second son, Ferdinand, was ten at the time; his elder brother, Ernst, eleven, was heir, and Leopold, the youngest, was still only four years old.

By now Catherine had clearly noted an impetuous strain in Julie, remarking of the match that 'everyone weeps and laughs by turns at this interesting couple ... They are two mischiefs together.'[2] For the time being it seemed endearing. But if Julie was naturally high-spirited in her innocence, what kind of man was the sixteen-year-old Grand Duke Konstantin whom she was marrying, behind the superficial simpering shyness and formal stiff courtesies he had shown her? The impressions of his contemporaries do not paint a flattering portrait of him and Catherine the Great herself had noted her grandson's uncouthness and bullishness, even as a small child, describing him as 'a little vulcan'.[3] She had been determined that Konstantin should not be exposed to his father Paul's eccentricities, and maintained tight control over his and Alexander's education at the Winter Palace. The two boys' early childhood was spent under the watchful eye of a governess, Sofya Benckendorff as well as, in Konstantin's case, a Greek nurse, but soon these were replaced by male staff, headed by the obsequious but ineffectual Count Nikolai Saltykov.

Catherine's instructions to Saltykov were most particular: the boys were to eat simple food, wear plain and unrestrictive clothing; there would be no feather beds; lots of exercise to encourage strength in both body and mind; an avoidance of unnecessary medicines; and most important of all, no tears or tantrums were to be tolerated.[4] This regime worked, in principle, with Alexander, who proved to be compliant and studious, but it soon became painfully apparent how difficult it would be to impose the empress's careful educational, cultural and spiritual plan on Catherine's little 'Kostik'. Nevertheless, she had it all mapped out: the brothers must learn to be kind, obedient, truthful, courageous and courteous. They were to show compassion for all 'dumb creatures' – 'birds, butterflies, flies, dogs, cats' – and were forbidden to torture them. None of the boys' lessons should last longer than half an hour, she stipulated, and should end 'before they get bored'.

She believed that children should not be forced to learn, but in contradiction of that, she imposed a wide-ranging curriculum.

Alexander and Konstantin would be taught Russian, French, German and Latin. Konstantin would focus also on Greek, with his future imperial role in mind, while Alexander would study English. This was in addition to tuition in geography, history, astronomy, mathematics, civil laws and even the art of war. Physical exercise was also an important element of their education: riding, fencing, swimming, wrestling, archery and 'everything that gives strength and agility to the body'.[5] Catherine thought of everything; she even stipulated that in her view art and music were less important for she could see no logic in any father wishing his son to become a poet.

One might imagine that, given this expansive and enlightened curriculum, the empress's two beloved grandsons would be moulded into paragons of wisdom and virtue. For Catherine's educational ethos was based very much on the principles of the Enlightenment thinker John Locke, who advocated the encouragement of the child's natural curiosity and his receiving an education suitable to his station in life. She was also influenced by the views of Swiss philosopher Jean-Jacques Rousseau, who, like Locke, believed in the fostering of the child's natural talents and goodness as the key to education, and eschewed learning by rote and enforced study. Catherine also greatly admired Rousseau's advocacy of the training of young children in manual and physical work so that they should be in harmony with nature, and from a very young age the two boys were taught to be 'gardeners, butchers and carpenters'.[6]

Catherine hired precisely the right man to see their education through to its successful culmination, under Saltykov's supervision: a Swiss national, a man of the Enlightenment and of great integrity named Frédéric-César de La Harpe. Born in the canton of Vaud, La Harpe had originally trained as a lawyer but his republican support for Vaud's independence from the domineering Bernese adminis-tration had forced him to go abroad. He went to Russia where he was recommended to Baron Grimm as a French tutor; after being introduced to Catherine the Great in 1783, La Harpe had secured the empress's admiration and confidence sufficiently – despite his polit-ical views – to present to her a paper on his theories on education.

Catherine was impressed and elevated La Harpe to Saltykov's deputy, under the strict understanding that he was not to share his political views with his pupils.[7]

Despite this, while instructing the boys in the duties of the sovereign La Harpe made a point of instilling in Alexander and Konstantin the horrors of tyranny and the nobility of republicanism, but it is doubtful whether any of his fine principles took root in Konstantin's erratic mind. Indeed, it proved to be a serious misjudgement for Catherine and her chosen team of tutors to try to educate two such different boys together; the failure to separate them would have fatal consequences in terms of Konstantin's later behaviour. For Alexander studied diligently and did well and he and La Harpe developed a close and instinctive relationship; but with Konstantin, who was nineteen months younger, the battle to contain his erratic behaviour was relentless. When his pupil reached seven and a half, La Harpe reported on the struggle to educate him.

The boy had a good heart and natural talents, he conceded, but these were outweighed by his aversion to paying attention to anything for more than a few minutes at a time. He was encountering extreme difficulty in trying to curb his impulsive and often uncontrolled behaviour. Konstantin was extremely obstinate and would often become violent – 'throwing books, maps, paper and pens on the floor' in fits of rage, stamping his feet, gnashing his teeth and behaving in ways 'that would infuriate even the most patient person in the world'.[8] La Harpe endured such tantrums on many occasions and they wore him ragged: 'only those who witnessed these scenes know how much they tested my patience, and what it cost me to maintain due composure in these critical moments,' he declared. At times Konstantin's rough behaviour even caused physical harm: once during a game of forfeits with Catherine's 'old gouty courtiers' he had broken the arm of 'the feeble count Stackelberg, by rudely jostling against him, and throwing him down'.[9]

Five years later, in another report to Saltykov, La Harpe concluded, with considerable regret, that despite his best efforts, Konstantin's stubbornness had 'acquired the character of such intemperance that it is no longer possible to indulge and endure it'.[10] Only recently he had bitten La Harpe's hand in class. The young grand duke's elevated imperial position meant that his quivering tutors were all obliged to indulge and flatter him and answer to his every whim. La Harpe was the only one who dared tell Konstantin that his behaviour was unacceptable, but his endless reprimands fell on deaf ears and Catherine forbade the use of corporal punishment.[11] Yet Konstantin was not entirely oblivious to the pain and hurt he caused with his verbal and physical insults. He made endless apologies for being such 'an ass' to the harassed La Harpe, begging his forgiveness and promising to improve. In a despairing admission of his shortcomings written to General Saltykov, one can clearly hear the self-disgust. It is the cry for help of a troubled young man: 'At twelve years old I don't know anything; I can't even read. Being rough, ill-mannered and defiant is all that I aspire to. My knowledge and diligence are worthy only of an army drummer. In a word, nothing will come of me in my whole life.'[12] It was thus inevitable that the brighter and placid Alexander should receive the lion's share of his tutors' and his grandmother Catherine's love and attention; for even she admitted that 'Alexander is an Angel, but Constantine is a Fury.'[13]

The neglect that Konstantin suffered thanks to the preferential treatment accorded his brother and the inability to understand or support his troubled personality certainly caused lasting emotional damage. It encouraged him to lash out like the unloved child he was. With alarming clarity, as early as September 1789 La Harpe had predicted in the boy of twelve the kind of adult he would become: a military man, a machine, who believed that 'education, reasoning, feelings of honour' were harmful to strict discipline and who was trained to 'swallow insults silently'.[14]

Even as a child, Konstantin had only ever been happy among soldiers and marching in line with them, or playing with firearms and indulging in war games. As a name-day gift his father had presented Konstantin with two detachments of soldiers – one cavalry, one infantry – and thereafter his main amusement had been in endlessly drilling them on the parade ground at Gatchina. When he was berated by his tutors for failing to apply himself to his studies and exhorted to emulate his brother, Konstantin's response had been a simple and obstinate one: 'He's the tsar; but I am a soldier. What should I learn from him?'[15]

This behaviour became more marked after Alexander's marriage in 1793, when their father put the two brothers into military training under his precise instruction. Konstantin's education came to an abrupt halt, with his military passion now consuming all his interest. By the spring of 1795 the brothers were being forced to attend parades and Prussian-style drills four or five times a week out at Gatchina, where Paul spent most of his time in deliberate avoidance of his mother, further inflaming Konstantin's 'military monomania' and with it 'the same eccentricities, the same passions, the same severity and the same turbulence' that he would share with Paul, along with his unattractive looks.[16]

This constant shuttling between the hedonistic St Petersburg court of Catherine and the militaristic austerity of Gatchina, observed the historian Nikolai Shilder, was the difference 'between Athens and Sparta' and must have had an unsettling effect on both brothers.[17] The martinet side of Konstantin's personality that was being encouraged by his father did not bode well for any future bride. Tellingly, when she stopped off at Gatchina on her way home to Coburg, on 8 November (28 October OS), Auguste had found 'the ambience here very different from St Petersburg'. Everything was 'stiff and silent' in the old Prussian manner, she complained; the officers of Grand Duke Paul's entourage were forced into old-fashioned Prussian uniforms of the time of Frederick the Great and looked like 'figures cut out of an old family scrapbook'.[18]

By 1794, La Harpe was once more feeling the pull of his republican sentiments and clashed with Catherine when he discovered her plans to sidestep Paul and ensure that the throne passed straight to Alexander on her death. La Harpe resigned and returned to Switzerland in support of the campaign for independence in Vaud. From here he maintained contact with his two former charges. Konstantin hoped one day to visit his old tutor in Switzerland with his new wife, but all La Harpe's efforts over thirteen years to knock some sense into his pupil had been futile, as Konstantin told him: 'Once a donkey, always a donkey; however you wash a donkey's head you only waste the soap. You can't make a donkey drink when he doesn't want to. Farewell.'[19]

On 26 October 1795 (6 November NS) Catherine the Great and her grandson Konstantin both wrote formal letters to Prince Franz in Coburg asking for his consent to Konstantin's marriage to Julie. In her letter in French, Catherine spoke warmly of the three daughters, and how hard it had been to choose one above the others, for they were all 'blessed with fine qualities', and would make any husband happy with whom they should share their lives.[20]

In the final euphoric days of her visit to St Petersburg, Princess Auguste of Saxe-Coburg had of course had no inkling of the troubled personality to whom her innocent fourteen-year-old daughter was soon to be consigned in marriage. Beguiled by one lavish reception after another laid on to celebrate the match, she had no reason to doubt the favourable impression she had gained of her future son-in-law. And indeed, Konstantin did genuinely seem pleased with his choice; even his sister-in-law Elise noted that for once 'he was very loving and very happy'. Already knowing something of Konstantin's contradictory personality, however, she wrote to her mother on 26 October (6 November NS) somewhat cryptically that his joy and love were 'manifested by a thousand madnesses', suggesting a degree of erratic behaviour in that joy.[21]

Elise had by now become greatly attached to the Coburg women; they were, she went on, 'a charming family'. Auguste was 'sensible and sensitive', and the daughters were 'excellent children'. She was so used to their company that she had to admit that she was 'really seriously annoyed that they are leaving'.[22] She was going to miss the many pleasant evenings when they had come to dine, after which they had played music together and Sophie, who was a keen artist, had sketched. But now that the engagement had been announced, the empress made clear to Auguste that it was time for her to go home.

As the family packed for their departure Elise nursed an increasing sense of dread on Julie's behalf, knowing the heartache and sense of abandonment that were in store for her. For she too had been through that awful experience only two years previously.

Meanwhile, on the evening of 25 October (5 November NS), Catherine laid on a spectacular masked costume ball for 7,000 at the Winter Palace to honour her guests before their departure. That morning she sent servants to Auguste with extravagant gifts of jewellery: a diamond necklace, earrings, several pearl bracelets with gold clasps and a huge diamond ring, as well as jewellery for her two daughters and flowers for their hair; Julie was made a special gift of a diamond bracelet.[23]

More importantly, in terms of the desperate straits of the Saxe-Coburg treasury, Catherine also presented Auguste with a promissory note for the extraordinary sum of 60,000 rubles – or 46,270 thalers,* which was equivalent to several times the income of the entire principality, as well as the annual income of Prince Franz.[24] It was to be given to her by Baron Budberg, who was escorting them home, when they arrived in Leipzig; her two daughters were to be given 50,000 each. Auguste's lady in waiting, Baroness Wangenheim, was also gifted 3,000 rubles and the servants who had travelled with them to Russia were not forgotten either. More importantly, Catherine bestowed Julie's brothers – Leopold, who was almost five, and eleven-year-old Ernst – with regimental honours, enrolling them as honorary captains in Konstantin's regiment of St Petersburg Grenadiers.[25] Konstantin took great delight in presenting Auguste with sabres, sashes and aiguillettes to take back to Coburg for them. These would be the first of several Russian military preferments that would greatly enhance the brothers' status in the Napoleonic Wars to come.

That evening Auguste was stunned by the enormous variety of

---

* It is very difficult to quantify the value of thalers in terms of today's money. One 1958 source on the Saxe-Coburgs gives 12,000 thalers as equivalent to £1,800. Four times that would be £7,200, which today would have the spending power of approximately £827,000.

costume on display at the opulent ball at the Winter Palace. Her girls wore traditional German national costume for the occasion, but this seemed drab in comparison to the array of merchants' wives from the different provinces and regions of the Russian Empire in their elaborate national dress and wearing towering golden *kokoshniki*. She marvelled at the sight of Turks, Armenians and Tatars wearing all kinds of exotic fabrics, at Cossacks from the Don 'richly and elegantly dressed and presenting a fine picture with their long beards'.[26] For her the Russian men were much more 'superior in looks', with their strong features and black eyes, than their women, who she felt 'have too much red and white make-up and blacken their eyebrows a lot'. She and her daughters circulated in the brilliantly lit halls of the palace from 6 p.m. until midnight, admiring the attentiveness shown the empress, who was 'constantly surrounded by people from all nations and classes'.[27]

During those final days in St Petersburg, Auguste had of course worried a great deal about leaving her young daughter behind in Russia, admitting in a letter to Franz that she had 'cried secretly for a week'. Julie had also been 'excessively affected' at her mother's imminent departure and wept the whole night before she left. But Auguste knew already that her daughter had a valuable ally in Elise, who was 'uncommonly fond of Jülchen and very much a friend to her'.[28] She also comforted herself that Julie's care and preparation for her marriage would be supervised by a mature woman whom she felt she could trust: 47-year-old Countess Charlotte Lieven. A Baltic German, she was the widow of Baron Otto von Lieven, a major-general in the Russian army, and was a mother herself of fourteen children.* She had been recommended to Catherine the Great by Count Browne, the governor general of Riga, in 1783 as governess to the five daughters and two younger sons of Grand Duke Paul and Maria Feodorovna. Alexander and Konstantin both revered her, as

---

*   One of Lieven's sons, Christophe, became a noted diplomat and would marry Countess Dorothea von Benckendorff. During her husband's ambassadorship to London between 1812 and 1834 Princess Lieven became one of the most influential social and political figures of the period.

did their father, and Lieven enjoyed a position of considerable respect and favour at the Russian court.

At eleven o'clock on the morning of 27 October (7 November NS) grand dukes Alexander and Konstantin arrived to escort the Coburg princesses to their carriage. For Elise, the farewell between Julie and her mother was agony to watch – like reliving that with her own mother. Afterwards she had gone and hidden in a corner and 'wept like a baby'.[29] Indeed, everyone had wept – even Alexander – at the leave-taking; except, that is, for the empress, who was relieved to see Auguste go. As Countess Golovina had noted, despite her best ingratiating efforts, Auguste had failed to 'win the Empress's affection' and during her stay she had rarely spent time with her in private.[30] Be that as it may, Auguste had garnered the prize of a prestigious connection to Catherine the Great by marriage. She may have lost a daughter, but she left Russia convinced that Catherine, the 'good fairy', had waved her magic wand; that her son-in-law was kind and unspoilt and would treat Julie well. She also returned to Coburg enjoying a now more elevated position among the royals of Europe, in the knowledge that her daughter was only three steps from the Russian throne, should Alexander produce no sons.

After a night's stopover at the Catherine Palace at Tsarskoe Selo and a brief visit to dine with Grand Duke Paul and Maria Feodorovna at Gatchina, the travellers settled in for the long journey home. It was arduous, with winter well set in, as their coach rolled through 'birch forests covered in hoar frost' that looked 'like sugar-coated sweets'. Snow alternated with heavy storms and rain, and the rivers were swollen, but before they reached Riga a messenger caught up with them bearing a letter from Julie, reassuring her mother that although she had been 'extremely sad and downcast on the first day ... everything possible had been done to raise her spirits' and Elise 'had shared in her regrets like a sister'.[31]

On 26 December (15 December OS) the Coburg ladies arrived in Berlin, where they were met by Auguste's sons Ferdinand and Ernst and spent a few days being entertained with balls and dinners by Friedrich Wilhelm III, his wife Luise and the Prussian royal family.

Their long Russian adventure finally came to a close when they entered Coburg at year's end – 31 December 1795 – to considerable rejoicing and celebration of Princess Auguste's triumphant Russian marriage-brokering.

Back in St Petersburg, while she did not as yet enjoy the same status as the married Grand Duchess Elizaveta, Julie would live and share meals and lessons with the two young grand duchesses, Alexandra and Elena, until her wedding.[32] Her German life was over; she was now to be thoroughly Russianised in preparation for her new and imperial status as a Romanov grand duchess.

CHAPTER 5

'ALEXANDER IS AN ANGEL, BUT CONSTANTINE IS A FURY'

Shortly after Princess Auguste of Saxe-Coburg-Saalfeld happily set off back to Coburg, confident in having secured a glittering dynastic coup with the marriage of her daughter into the Romanov family, Julie began discovering the rigours of her new life. On 1 November (12 November NS) she wrote home describing how her time was 'so planned out' that she barely had time to write letters. She rose at six, breakfasted at seven with Madame Lieven and Konstantin and immediately was plunged into a lesson in how to recite the Russian Orthodox catechism in Old Church Slavonic at her conversion ceremony. Arduous sessions of religious instruction followed from 8 to 11 a.m. with a rather frightening priest who spoke to her in 'a highly edifying German and to God's misfortune, I can understand not a word'. Without Madame Lieven's assistance 'I would not know what he said.' Konstantin had laughed at how she stumbled over the Russian word *arkhimandrit* for priest, and even now she struggled in her letter, writing it as *Agrimandrit, Archipek* and even the irreverent *Arschimandrit*.[1]

After her gruelling lessons, Julie would have her hair done and be dressed for court attendance on the empress. Konstantin seemed enraptured with his bride and wrote to La Harpe in Switzerland, telling him the happy news. 'I am now in the sweetest state of life,' he declared, 'I am promised to the princess Julie of Saxe Coburg. I'm sorry you haven't seen her; she is a very good person. I love her with all my heart.'[2] On the surface, he appeared to be the model bridegroom; but even before the wedding, behind closed doors, Julie was already being exposed to unnerving signs of his erratic behaviour. She had been given rooms in Konstantin's suite in the Winter Palace, where sometimes he insisted on joining Julie for breakfast with a drum and a trumpet and made her 'play marches on the harpsichord, which he accompanied on these two noisy instruments'. Such contrary behaviour smacked of an earlier tsar – Peter III, Konstantin's grandfather – for he too had behaved in similar eccentric fashion towards his young bride Catherine, holding parties in their rooms and ordering his servants to wear masks and dance while he played his violin. According to Countess Golovina, these musical breakfasts were 'the only proof of affection' that Konstantin gave his bride-to-be in the weeks before they were married. More often than not he was rough rather than affectionate, despite his professed love for his fiancée, and he sometimes caused Julie physical pain, twisting her arm and biting her.[3]

Julie was no doubt bewildered by this behaviour as well as being unused to the rigid protocols of the Russian court after her quiet and informal family life in Coburg. She had been provided with an entourage of ladies to prepare her for the wedding under the watchful eye of Madame Lieven but preferred to spend as much of her time as she could with Elise, whenever the latter was free of her official duties as Alexander's wife. For she was a kindred spirit and knew what it felt like to be alone and friendless at the Russian court, as she had been when she first arrived in Russia from Baden. Elise relished Julie's company as a fellow German and found her 'a charming child ... good, loving, confident. I could not have wished for a better companion and friend,' she told her mother. 'She is cheerful and funny too, she will give me back my old happiness.' She had noticed that Julie had about her 'a determined little air that suits her very well', but it also warned of an independent spirit that would refuse to be cowed.[4]

At the Winter Palace, Julie and Elise grasped every opportunity to be together, gossiping about fashion and the social round of balls, sharing their interest in music and poetry and all the news from home. There would be daily discussions about what to wear and how to style their hair; hours spent sitting together reading and sewing, and also time outside walking in the gardens and enjoying the sledging parties organised by the empress, who greatly enjoyed them herself. Elise was deeply touched by the affection Julie displayed towards her and was amused by the sweet naivety with which her future sister-in-law used a familiar German word – *heimlich*, meaning, at that time, 'cosy', 'homely' – to express her delight at things. Elise's private sitting room was so *heimlich*: 'it's one of her favourite expressions,' Elise told her mother. 'I even have earrings that she finds *heimlich*. This word is used for everything: she finds balls and salons *heimlich*. She is so funny.' Funny, yes, but this touching unworldliness also underlines how vulnerable and impressionable Julie was.[5]

In between times, her tuition for her future role at court continued in Elise's company: there were drawing lessons, dancing lessons with Monsieur Picque, music with Monsieur Sarti, as well as Russian lessons with writer and statesman Ivan Muravev-Apostol on Mondays and Thursdays. As an admirer of the principles of Rousseau, Muravev-Apostol had previously tutored Alexander and Konstantin and encouraged Julie to read the Swiss writer. At lunchtime she usually ate with the younger grand duchesses, while Elise took hers with Alexander.

In the evening, when resident at the Winter Palace, the imperial family would convene in the Diamond Room on the second floor, so called for being where the crown jewels were kept in glass cupboards. This venue was used during the winter season for small receptions and court assemblies and was connected on one side with Catherine's bedroom and private apartments.[6] Here, close members of the imperial family and those officers on duty in the entourage would gather for cards or the word game *secrétaire*, or sit together looking at engravings and prints, while the empress sometimes did embroidery or sat with her favourite, Prince Platon Zubov, playing chess or the French card game Boston.[7] Catherine also loved to play blind man's buff, or the sleight-of-hand game 'hot cockles' with her smaller grandchildren; supper was served at nine though she never ate it, before retiring to bed at ten.[8] It was a quiet and unchallenging routine, the stiflingly warm room heated by huge porcelain stoves to keep out the harsh northern winter.

French plays and Italian operas performed at the Hermitage Theatre were a welcome addition to family entertainments, and many in the court enjoyed the snow hills erected in the grounds of the Tauride Palace.[9] These daily family gatherings, as well as balls, dinners, receptions and visits conducted by the various members of the imperial family, were all catalogued in slavish detail in the official *Tseremonialnyi Kamer-fur'erskii zhurnal* ('Ceremonial Court Journal'), but in Julie's case, despite her being listed among those in attendance around Catherine, references are disappointingly unrevealing, beyond testifying to the rigid court duties to which she was obliged to adhere.

Throughout that winter of 1795–6, as arrangements went ahead for the wedding in February, the two young German princesses took centre stage as the great beauties of the Romanov family (even Catherine's lover Count Zubov could barely take his eyes off them during family evenings in the Diamond Room). Elise, a pale, blue-eyed gentle blonde, was soft-spoken and had an angelic face that belied her innate wisdom; in contrast Julie, a striking brunette with large intelligent brown eyes, was bold and more outgoing but, in her naivety about the ways of the world and the Russian court, tended to impetuosity. She was grateful for Elise's quiet presence, her advice and mentoring in the intricate niceties of Russian court life. In turn Elise valued Julie's warm personality and trustworthiness; she watched over her and as a result their friendship rapidly deepened. In many ways Elise, despite her youth, became an important surrogate for Julie's missing mother. Another German speaker now also offering Julie her protection and guidance was Madame Maria Andreevna de Renne. Originally from Livonia and the wife of a general in the Russian army, she had been in service at Catherine's court for many years before being specially assigned to Julie's care. Renne would prove to be a kind and loyal friend to Julie until her death in 1810, as too would her daughter Caroline, who also joined Julie's entourage.

It wasn't until 2 February 1796 (13 February NS) that a manifesto was issued by Catherine's court announcing the engagement of 'our beloved grandson' Grand Duke Konstantin to a princess of Saxe-Coburg-Saalfeld. That same day, Julie's conversion ceremony – and her official 'Russianisation' – took place in the Grand Church, located in the eastern wing of the Winter Palace. Built in the rococo style between 1741 and 1762 by Empress Elizabeth, it was used, among other things, for the conversion ceremonies of foreign princesses marrying into the Romanov family. On that day, a nervous Julie entered in a dress of gold brocade, decorated with diamonds and flowers, and formally renounced her Lutheran faith, made her confession and was baptised into the Russian Orthodox faith, surrounded by long-bearded priests in ornate robes reciting in Old Church Slavonic. The whole imperial family, attired in splendid court dress, was gathered in the church to witness this, after which the empress took Julie by the hand and led her to the sacred icons of the Holy Mother of God to bow down, pay homage and kiss them.

Such extravagant rituals were totally unfamiliar to Julie's Lutheran upbringing and while the ceremony was no doubt impressive, it must have been a bewildering experience. Prince Adam Czartoryski, who with his brother Konstanty had been a gentleman of the chamber at the Russian court since 1795, noticed how alien and theatrical the whole Byzantine ritual had seemed, in comparison to the simplicity of Protestantism:

It was painful to see the young princess advancing in a dress of cloth of gold laden with diamonds like a victim crowned with flowers, to bow her head to images which were in no way sacred to her, to submit to the exigencies of a ceremony which was opposed to her convictions and her sentiments. It was evident that she did this simply out of deference, knowing opposition was useless, and without attaching the slightest importance to the ceremony.[10]

There seemed something 'barbarous' – pagan even – about the whole proceedings to the Catholic Pole Czartoryski. He was forcibly struck by the worrying sacrificial-lamb element to the whole affair – the sight of a 'young princess, endowed by nature with gaiety and charm, accepting the new religion without foreseeing her destiny – which, however, it was easy to guess at'.[11] At her conversion ceremony, Julie was further distanced from her German heritage by being given the Russian imperial name of Anna Feodorovna and the titles of Grand Duchess and Imperial Highness, by which she would henceforth be known in Russia.*

On the following day, she and Konstantin were formally betrothed and exchanged engagement rings at the Winter Palace and Julie was awarded a personal allowance of 30,000 rubles a year. Konstantin also presented her with a 'bouquet with diamonds and emeralds of 19,000 rubles' as well as several more pieces of lavish diamond jewellery.[12]

On 6 February (17 February NS) Empress Catherine wrote separate letters to Prince Franz and Princess Auguste in Coburg, informing them of the engagement and assuring them how greatly she valued these new ties that now bound their two families so closely together. To Auguste in particular, she reiterated the promise of her personal attention: 'The marks of tenderness and affection that I gave to the young princess and to Your Serene Highness were visible proof and a guarantee of the care that I will take to ensure her wellbeing and contentment.' The wedding day was set for 13 February (24 February NS), but in the event, Julie developed a

---

*   The adoption of this name has sometimes created confusion in contemporary sources in its variant forms and spellings, with Julie variously referred to outside Russia as Grand Duchess Anna/Anne Fyodorovna/Feodorowna/Pheodorovna, as well as Grand Duchess Constantine. This latter usage sometimes leads to confusion with Konstantin's second wife, who was also referred to in this way after he remarried in 1820.

painful toothache and high temperature; her face swelled up and the wedding had to be postponed until the 15th, a Friday. Many superstitious Russians at court saw this as a bad omen for the marriage.[13] That morning at eight o'clock, as Julie heard five cannon volleys outside, she was taken to the empress's apartments to be dressed in her wedding gown by Catherine and her ladies. They helped her into a traditional, elaborately embroidered and bejewelled court robe edged in ermine, placed a jewelled *kokoshnik* on her head, and then draped her in a long strawberry-coloured velvet train that was also edged in ermine. (Brides did not wear white at this time in Russia, as the colour was regarded as sacred and not appropriate for weddings.)

Thousands of troops stood in formation outside on Palace Square and in the surrounding streets as, to sounding trumpets and rolls of drums, the imperial procession made its way to the Grand Church, where foreign ambassadors and government ministers and their wives were already assembled to witness the ceremony being performed by Catherine's own personal confessor. Standing in silence on either side of the gilded marble pillars as they passed were three squadrons of the Guards, the most handsome of them hand-picked for the occasion, with their swords unsheathed and pointing to the ground. The procession was led by the most important dignitaries of Catherine the Great's court, two masters of ceremonies carrying their official sceptres of gold topped with imperial Russian eagles, and the grand master of the Order of Malta.[14]

Empress Catherine in her imperial mantle and wearing the small Romanov crown, with six courtiers holding her long, heavy train, headed the imperial family, followed by Grand Duke Paul and Grand Duchess Maria with their entourage, Grand Duke Alexander and Elise and finally the bride, Julie, her train carried by four chamberlains, and alongside her the groom, Konstantin. Other grand dukes and duchesses followed, as well as the ladies in waiting, including Countess Renne, and other courtiers.[15] No members of Julie's family were present.

The Russian Orthodox setting must have been overwhelming for her, so strange and unfamiliar in its ornateness, with the powerful voices of a magnificent choir, the gleaming icons, the flickering candles and the air heavy with incense. The three-hour ceremony was conducted with the entire congregation standing, the bride and groom holding lighted candles through the long chanted liturgy, weighed down by their heavy court robes and with the nuptial crowns held over them – Konstantin's by Count Shuvalov and Julie's by Prince Zubov.[16] The service was completed by a prayer of thanksgiving and the traditional singing of the '*Mnogoletye*' ['Many Years'], upon which the cannons on the Peter and Paul Fortress across the Neva boomed out, as well as volleys of fire from the troops outside. Church bells all over St Petersburg began to peal out in celebration and would continue to be rung for three days.[17]

After the ceremony a grand dinner was celebrated in the magnificent St George's Hall, designed by Italian architect Giacomo Quarenghi, with pink marble columns and gleaming parquet floor, one of the largest state rooms in the palace, which also served as the throne room. The newlyweds dined with the imperial family under a canopy close to Catherine's throne, the food served on plates of gold and Japanese porcelain, to the singing of choirs.[18] That evening the whole frontage of the River Neva was illuminated with lanterns glittering on the Peter and Paul Fortress, the Admiralty Fortress, the Winter Palace and the Marble Palace. Catherine retired to her rooms at 8 p.m. but a full dress ball was held late into the evening, before Alexander and Elise conducted the bride and groom to what was to be their new home – the Marble Palace. Located a short distance from the Winter Palace along the embankment it was Catherine the Great's wedding gift to them. Here – according to Russian tradition when welcoming someone into their new home – Alexander and Elise presented Julie with bread and salt on a golden platter. Julie then went to the bridal suite to await the arrival of her bridegroom; but an hour passed, and he did not come. When he did finally arrive some time later, it is said that Konstantin threw himself on the bed and fell into a deep sleep.

Whether or not Julie's sexual initiation took place that night, it is difficult to imagine what the fourteen-year-old's first experience must have been like, and how little prepared she was for it, either physically or emotionally. Brought up in a very sheltered family and entirely ignorant of what was to come, she might well have recoiled in fear and horror at her first sexual encounter.[19] Nor for that matter was her bridegroom prepared, for during their education Catherine the Great had ordered that her two grandsons be kept in ignorance of sex and reproduction by their tutors, intending to organise their sexual initiation herself (presumably with courtesans) before they were married. When the boys had begun asking innocent questions about pistils and stamens during botany lessons, these had been abruptly curtailed.[20] Konstantin's ignorance of sexual matters, given his quixotic personality and the totally masculine, militaristic world he had until then inhabited, might well have made Julie's wedding night a frightening ordeal, though how much Countess Lieven, who prepared her for the marriage bed, had intimated to her is not known.

A story is told that the reason for Konstantin's lateness that night was due to the fact that he had been busily engaged in violently berating a soldier on guard for some petty infraction of duty, and when he did arrive in the bedroom, it was in a bad temper.[21] Such an incident confirms Adam Czartoryski's observation that 'the princess was given to a youth barely entering manhood, but with a violent temper and savage caprices', for he knew that those bad habits had 'already furnished many a topic of conversation' at court. Rumours circulating later alleged that 'on the morning subsequent to their Royal Highnesses' nuptials, the Grand Duke was seen at five o'clock manoeuvring a regiment of soldiers in the courtyard of his palace. Of course this preference of Mars to Venus and Cupid, could not have been very flattering to the bride – it was a measure calculated to beget not only eternal hatred, but the utmost contempt.'[22]

Charles Masson shared Czartoryski's view of the young grand duke. He was astonished at Konstantin's 'vulgar tricks' and how he had abandoned his bride in preference to drilling his soldiers. 'I do not know whether this military mania announces a good general,' he wrote, 'but sure I am that it is a proof of a very bad husband.' Indeed, as Masson also noted, not long before his marriage Konstantin had been reported to Catherine for cruelly drilling his personal detachment of Grenadier Guards to exhaustion and in a fit of rage had caned the major who commanded them. Catherine had put him under house arrest and taken his soldiers away from him until after the wedding.[23] Perhaps his anxiety to be back with his soldiers following the wedding was a response to this.

Whatever transpired that first night, Julie was now thrown into days and days of exhausting festivities marking the occasion of her marriage, which left her little time to reflect on it. The following day, Saturday 16 February (27 February NS), the couple dined with Catherine and there was another grand ball and supper at the Winter Palace that evening. Sunday was a rest day, but on the Monday there were more entertainments when a signal from five cannons announced a public holiday for the citizens of St Petersburg. Roasted oxen were prepared on two elevated pyramids decorated with gilding, ribbons and flowers, and red and white wine was freely available from two fountains.[24]

That evening, Catherine dined at the Marble Palace with Konstantin and Julie. She prided herself on her magnanimity in gifting the young couple this splendid palace, for she believed there wasn't a finer mansion in St Petersburg with richer and more tasteful furnishings. Built of grey-pink granite and marble, it had been designed by the architect Antonio Rinaldi for Catherine, as a gift for her then favourite Count Grigory Orlov. But he died in 1783 before it was completed and Catherine bought it from Orlov's heirs for 1.5 million rubles. She had recently paid for renovations to the interior decorations, setting aside 118,528 rubles for the palace to be upgraded for the use of the couple and by guests who had come for the wedding, with furniture brought over specially from the Winter Palace.[25]

After a couple of days' respite on 19 and 20 February (1 and 2 March NS), the marriage celebrations were resumed with another dinner, and a ball given by Julie's new in-laws, Grand Duke Paul and Grand Duchess Maria. Then, on Saturday 23rd, it was Grand

Duke Alexander's turn to host a dinner and ball. The high point of this week of extravagant celebrations was a grand masquerade held at court on the Sunday.[26] Catherine wrote to Baron Grimm of how some 8,540 people had taken part, at which she and her court were delighted to see Elise, Julie and all the young grand duchesses and their ladies perform a traditional Russian folk dance – the *plyaska* – to Russian music. Everyone in St Petersburg was still talking about it the following day: the grand duchesses had all looked ravishing and were superbly dressed. The evening had, however, been spoiled by an eruption of Konstantin's boorish behaviour.

The *pièce de résistance* of these displays of imperial extravagance came on Wednesday 27 February (9 March NS) with a firework extravaganza on the Neva embankment opposite the Winter Palace, orchestrated with military precision by Pyotr Melissino, a Greek-born general of the Russian Artillery. The centrepiece of his design was a representation of the Temple of Minerva, surrounded by palms and laurel trees, in the centre of which was a pedestal bearing the initials of Konstantin and Julie. Above them was a brilliant firework representation of Catherine's initial and imperial crest with rays of light emanating from it over the entire scene.[27] Catherine had to admit she was relieved when it was all finally over, writing to Grimm that she was glad that the Russian Orthodox 'Great Fast' – Lent – was almost here and there would be a respite from so much excess for the next seven weeks.[28]

Throughout those long, exhausting days of courtly display, the cultivated and highly observant Adam Czartoryski had cast his jaundiced eye over the proceedings, from Julie's conversion to the Byzantine ritual of the Russian Orthodox wedding and through all the sumptuous dinners, balls, fireworks and entertainments. To his mind 'all these noisy diversions, splendid as they were, did not inspire mirth.' For him, 'a sinister veil of sadness' had 'hovered over the ceremony and the fetes which followed it ... It was a mournful spectacle, this handsome young princess, come from so far to adopt a foreign religion on a foreign soil, to be delivered up to the capricious will of a man who it was evident would never care for her happiness.'[29]

Privately, and in ways which no doubt humiliated his bride further, Konstantin had spoken to his cronies at court about his honeymoon and his bride's sexual initiation with what Czartoryski found to be 'an unexampled want of delicacy'. Indelicacy certainly appears to have been Konstantin's chosen metier, for he wrote to La Harpe about his marriage in crude terms at around the same time, bragging of how he had 'saved' himself for his wedding night and how glad he was that 'I hadn't stuffed that bitch S— or Z—' (in reference probably to two courtesans) – as the young 'mischievous turks' had urged him to do.[30] His life among military men had clearly coarsened Konstantin and fuelled an innate misogyny.

Countess Golovina was already entertaining serious doubts about Julie's suitability for the role that she had taken on. The grand duchess 'had a very pretty face', she conceded, but she had neither 'grace of movement nor education, and she had a romantic little head that was the most dangerous to her because she was totally lacking in knowledge and principle'. True, Julie had 'a kind heart and was naturally quick-witted', but 'not possessing any virtues likely to safeguard her against temptations, she was surrounded by dangers on every side, while the atrocious behaviour of [her husband] contributed further to bewilder her ideas.' The suggestion here is that the vulnerable and too-trusting Julie might all too easily be led astray. There certainly seems to have been a degree of jealousy in Golovina's comments about Julie in her *Memoirs*, for she clearly took umbrage at being displaced from her position as Elise's close confidante by Julie, who, she complained, 'came every morning to fetch the Grand Duchess Elizabeth for a walk in the garden'.[31]

Grand Duke Alexander was also expressing his concern, almost from the moment the couple were married. He had noticed how his brother Konstantin's behaviour was becoming ever more extreme and confided as much to La Harpe a week after the wedding. 'He often causes me grief,' he told him, 'he is more hot-headed than ever, very wilful, and what he wills often does not coincide with reason.' In particular, Konstantin's increasing absorption in military exercises and manoeuvres at Gatchina and Pavlovsk, leaving Julie a 'military widow' for hours on end every day, had seriously alarmed Alexander. 'The military life turns his head,' he complained to La Harpe, 'and he is sometimes brutal with the soldiers of his company.'[32] At the Marble Palace, according to the foreign minister, Count Rostopchin, Konstantin had set aside a room as a place of punishment where any of his soldiers who displeased him could be locked up; it was said that he 'maltreated them pitilessly, imprisoning officers on account of a button placed too high or too low'.* Within the first few weeks of marriage, Julie too found herself exposed to Konstantin's abrupt behaviour and to 'manifestations of affection very much more like ill-treatment than love', as Countess Golovina had predicted.[33]

Aside from the companionship of dear Elise, consolations were few and rare, the most precious being the receipt of a letter and unexpected Christmas gifts from her father Prince Franz in late February. It brought her 'extraordinary joy'; his presents were 'more dear to me than all the jewels that the Tsars can give me', Julie told him. They reminded her so powerfully of home and standing 'by you at the Christmas tables'. Her tone in this brief letter of 21 February (3 March NS) appears superficially cheerful: in the first week of her marriage, she hadn't had a single dull hour, she told Franz. She knew that married life would not be without its 'unpleasantnesses' – a valiant attempt to conceal her true horror at what she had already experienced – but she was sure hers would be happy. Konstantin, she insisted, 'has the best character and the heart of an angel', though, Julie added somewhat tellingly, 'he is a little hot-tempered.'[34]

Konstantin bored easily: when he wasn't playing at soldiers, he took sadistic pleasure in firing a small cannon at rats deliberately let loose in the *manège* of the Marble Palace; the spectacle turned Julie's stomach.[35] Knowing her terror of rats and mice, Konstantin

---

* Konstantin was infuriatingly dogmatic with regard to the continued use of the old-fashioned periwigs and uniforms that his father had insisted on. He resisted the suggestion made later by General Kutuzov of doing away with these tiresome trappings, which Kutuzov said obliged soldiers to get up early 'to curl each other's braids and apply powder and grease' (Mikaberidze, *Kutuzov*, 171).

played a cruel trick on her one day by ordering a quantity of mice to be procured, and, 'having them confined in a box, which was purposely placed in a large room, on pretence of some business, he conducted the Grand Duchess in to the chamber, opened the door of the said box, let loose the mice, retreated himself, locked the door, and laughed most heartily at his spouse's hoppings and jumpings, and screams and entreaties, while he was joined by his officers, who also enjoyed the fun by peeping through the key-hole.'[36]

This was nothing new; Konstantin had once celebrated Alexander's name day by ordering 'hundreds of live rats ... to be fired out of a cannon'; he also liked to 'witness hens *dancing* on large plates of heated iron' or observe the 'desperate efforts of cats in a hot Russian stove'.[37] We do not know whether Julie was witness to all this despicable cruelty to animals, but stories of Konstantin's sadistic streak, of how he was 'known to knock out the teeth and even the eyes of his soldiers, and to test their discipline by marching them into the river up to their chins before ordering the about-turn', were legion.[38] The violence extended to Julie: on one occasion Konstantin came for his wife and took her into the great entrance hall where a line of huge blue Chinese vases stood and picked her up, dropped her down into one of them and proceeded to fire his pistol at it, to his wife's utter terror.[39]

There are moments in contemporary descriptions of Konstantin's erratic and often violent behaviour that are very disturbing and suggest what today might be deemed manifestations of a personality disorder. Julie was clearly the victim of domestic violence but for the most part contemporary eyewitnesses resort to euphemism when describing the 'unpleasantness' that she was already experiencing in the marriage. There certainly is no hint of this in a letter Catherine the Great wrote to Franz and Auguste at that time, telling them how happy she was to confirm that 'our young people seem to live in the greatest intimacy and are very happy with each other.' Perhaps she was fooled by what seemed the first flush of love and hoped that Konstantin was now a reformed character; but given Catherine's astute personality it seems more likely she was inwardly praying that the eccentricities in her grandson's personality did not manifest themselves during the delicate marriage negotiations. For now, Konstantin seemed perfectly content, writing to his father Paul of how much he loved his 'dear and good' wife. 'I used to be a joker, with no knowledge of any woman, but now I am totally occupied with my dear Julie.'[40] Maybe he did love Julie in his own erratic way, but Julie was already having doubts. For, as courtier Charles Masson had warned about the fate of German sacrificial brides to the Romanov dynasty, 'if love embellish not by his illusions the abode of weariness and constraint in which you dwell, it will soon become to you a gloomy prison.'[41]

According to Countess Golovina, one of the two Czartoryski brothers, Konstanty, appeared to have fallen for Julie and she in return had '[taken] a fancy to him', though we do not know to what lengths that 'fancy' actually took them – perhaps no more than innocent flirtation.* But Julie was already feeling trapped and desperate. She confided her feelings about Konstanty to Elise, who had 'tried to reprove her and to save her from herself', in response to which Julie 'would cry and talk of her husband's tyranny', his capricious and violent behaviour and how he often kept her confined to her rooms. Elise, as it turned out, was the least equipped to offer advice, for she had become bored with her effete husband and was now seeing a great deal of Konstanty's 26-year-old brother Adam, even though he was a close friend of Alexander's.[42] Her marriage had, as yet,

---

* Adam Czartoryski and his brother Konstanty were born in Warsaw in 1770 and 1777 respectively, the sons of Prince Adam Kazimierz Czartoryski, a leading family of Polish nobility with estates in Podolia. When an insurrection took place in Poland in 1794 the family's lands were confiscated by Catherine the Great. The two brothers were sent to St Petersburg to plead for their return, were made officers in the Imperial Guards and appointed gentlemen of the chamber. They were both popular at court and developed close relationships with the Romanov grand dukes Alexander and Konstantin. Adam was appointed aide de camp (ADC) to Alexander in 1797, shared the young grand duke's liberal views and became a good friend, later serving as a diplomat in his government. Konstanty – Julie's supposed lover – like his brother was appointed ADC in 1797 to Grand Duke Konstantin and developed a close relationship with him when Konstantin later served as viceroy in Congress Poland.

produced no children, and Empress Catherine had made plain her disappointment. Both partners, despite their affection for each other, were beginning to stray: at the end of December 1796 Alexander fathered an illegitimate son, the product of one of several transient liaisons he would engage in over the next few years.

At the Russian court, gossip was brewing not just about Julie and Konstanty Czartoryski but also that Elise was having an affair with his brother Adam, and that Alexander himself seemed to be facilitating it. All that whispering and gossiping, coquetry and reading of romantic French novels together behind closed doors was drawing the two sisters-in-law into a web of romantic intrigue that certainly was beyond Julie's limited life experience and that she was ill-equipped to deal with.[43] Both women longed for love, but circumstance had seen them taken from their homeland as innocents and married to men from whom they were both becoming increasingly estranged. No wonder that in their precious hours together during the summer months when the court moved to the Catherine Palace at Tsarskoe Selo, they had secretly read a copy of Rousseau's romantic 1761 novel *Julie, ou La Nouvelle Héloïse* lent to them by one of Catherine's ladies in waiting, Countess Ekaterina Shuvalova. It had been an international bestseller for decades, especially among female readers, and was undoubtedly *the* most popular romantic novel of the eighteenth century, along with Goethe's equally melancholic *The Sorrows of Young Werther* (which no doubt both these German princesses had also read). Indeed, the European public had 'learned how to fall in love' while reading *Julie*, a sentimental story of passionate, forbidden love, based on the medieval legend of Abelard and Heloise.[44] Such subject matter was guaranteed to fire both impressionable teenage grand duchesses' romantic imaginations. In the words of Rousseau: 'As long as one desires one can do without happiness: one expects to achieve it; if happiness fails to come, hope persists, and the charm of illusion lasts as long as the passion that causes it. This condition suffices to itself, and the anxiety it inflicts is a sort of enjoyment that compensates for reality.'[45]

For now at least, Julie, like her namesake heroine, was living in anxious hope of an as yet intangible romantic happiness to come. But she already knew that it would not be found in the arms of her husband.

CHAPTER 6

'A LIFE OF BRILLIANT MISERY'

As 1796 progressed Julie's daily humiliations at the hands of her husband continued. Konstantin's bad behaviour even tried Catherine the Great's patience and a crisis point was reached in August–September during an important state occasion for which the empress had been preparing for some time.

That June, having married off her two eldest grandsons, the ageing Catherine's preoccupations with her own mortality had turned her attentions to the first of her five very marriageable Romanov granddaughters, Alexandra Pavlovna, who was now almost thirteen.* The bridegroom Catherine had had in mind for some time was Gustav IV Adolf, the king of Sweden, currently under the regency of his uncle Charles, Duke of Södermanland, until he reached his majority in three months' time. Three years earlier, Catherine had dispatched Baron Budberg to Stockholm to initiate negotiations for the match, which had initially been favourably received, though put on hold as both parties were very young.

Now he had turned seventeen, in August 1796 Gustav was brought to St Petersburg by his uncle, accompanied by a considerable suite. They were to meet with Catherine and his prospective bride at the Tauride Palace, where Catherine was resident during

---

* Alexandra is often referred to, French style, as 'Alexandrine' in letters in French written by members of the imperial family, such as Grand Duchess Elise.

the autumn. To honour the visit she had arranged a whole series of extravagant balls, dinners and receptions; but, as Charles Masson noted, 'all the pomp of the Russian empire, which was sedulously exhibited to [Gustav's] view, seemed in nowise to dazzle him'; Gustav seemed strangely unmoved if not sullen.[1] Catherine, however, was greatly taken by the tall, stately and courteous young king and was painfully aware of how, in contrast to her troublesome second grandson, Gustav displayed 'a certain gravity, that bespoke his rank, never forsook him'; others, however, would see it as a worryingly melancholy streak.[2] Despite this, the young Grand Duchess Alexandra was instantly smitten with him and he appeared to be equally so with her.

No sooner had the official festivities begun than wayward Konstantin soured the atmosphere with one of his wearisome outbursts. At a reception held for King Gustav by the procurator general, Alexander Samoilov, the grand duke had behaved in a 'disorderly, dishonest and obscene' manner, embarrassing his hosts and using profane language in earshot of their Swedish guests. At several other public events for the king, Konstantin had also shocked foreign dignitaries with his bad-boy behaviour; for example, at a review of the Corps of Cadets attended by Gustav, escorted by Alexander, Konstantin had disgraced himself by 'running and bawling behind the soldiers, imitating them in a burlesque manner, threatening them, and even beating them'. Catherine was appalled to be told of this and wrote a despairing letter to Count Saltykov, saying that she could not understand 'how such a vile *sansculottisme** ha[d] taken root in him'.[3] She went on to tell Saltykov that in his role as Konstantin's governor and still effectively in charge of his upbringing, he should join with the imperial family in 'calming down this scatterbrain' before he did serious damage not only to his own rank and position but to the Russian monarchy's reputation. She insisted that she did not 'intend to indulge Konstantin'

---

* Catherine here uses a reference to the '*sans-culottes*' – the poorer working classes of the French revolutionary movement as a means of alluding to Konstantin's rough and ready, uproarious behaviour.

any further and Saltykov must 'tell him from me and in my name that he should refrain from slander, foul language and debauchery from now on, if he doesn't want me to make an example of him'.[4]

The empress was furious, for it appears that in one of his foul-mouthed outbursts that evening at Samoilov's, Konstantin had said to King Gustav: 'Do you know what my grandmother is? She is the biggest whore in the city' (original sources refrained from printing the entire word). When this got back to her, Catherine had threatened to have Konstantin arrested, only for him to promptly fall sick with a high fever. Catherine said it was poetic justice – out of fear of the punishment she would mete out to him. She hoped it would teach him a lesson.[5] For the time being Konstantin appeared to repent; but for Julie, living with such a volatile and unpredictable personality must have been terrifying.

In addition to all the problems with Konstantin, Catherine ultimately had to deal with the failure of the marriage negotiations with the Swedes. Despite the young couple appearing to be 'mutually enchanted' the Swedish courtship had, as in the early negotiations, foundered on the thorny issue of religion. The Metropolitan of Russia had relished the idea of seeing a 'queen of Sweden of the Greek religion', and preparations had gone ahead for the formal betrothal to be held at 7 p.m. on 21 September (2 October NS), on Gustav's assurance that Grand Duchess Alexandra would not be prevented from practising her own religion. The whole Russian court assembled in their ceremonial robes, with Alexandra looking lovely in her bridal gown and attended by her sisters and Catherine taking centre stage 'in all her pomp'.

Much to everyone's extreme consternation and dismay, Gustav did not appear.[6] It turned out that shortly before the ceremony he had been presented with the marriage contract, which for some reason nobody had bothered to examine in detail until then. It included the stipulation that the bride should retain her religion and have her own private chapel and clergy at the palace in Stockholm. The pious young Gustav announced that he could not possibly comply; while his bride could hold to her beliefs in private, he refused to countenance any outward manifestation of her observation of the 'Greek religion', which he deemed to be 'idolatrous'. He felt it would be an 'insuperable bar to their happiness'; Alexandra must agree to 'profess the religion of the country'.[7] Conversion of the Russian grand duchess to Lutheranism was of course out of the question for the Russians, and Gustav would not have it any other way. He retired to his apartments and locked the door.

The empress was deeply shocked at this unexpected demolition of the mighty dynastic Russo-Swedish alliance she had been plotting and almost collapsed with the shame and grief of it. She may in fact have suffered a slight stroke, for according to an eyewitness 'every limb shook, and her face underwent sudden and violent convulsive changes'.[8] Certainly it was a sign that many felt had presaged her approaching death, if not accelerated it. Poor disappointed Alexandra, who had stood in the chapel waiting until ten o'clock that night, was grief-stricken and hysterical and promptly fell sick. Two days later the court was due to celebrate Julie's fifteenth birthday with a ball. It went ahead, in the awkward presence of Catherine and Gustav, observing royal protocols to the letter, but nobody was inclined to dance.[9] Gustav remained in St Petersburg for a few more days while desperate efforts were made to retrieve the situation and balm was poured on the empress's humiliation and indignation. But a week later he left; it was only then that Catherine discovered that during the many occasions that Gustav and Alexandra had been seen 'murmuring together in undertones', far from whispering sweet nothings to his putative bride, he had been lecturing her on theology and trying to persuade her to convert to Lutheranism.*[10]

Catherine never recovered her health after the debacle of the failed Swedish marriage. Her final days were increasingly filled with a mounting horror of the eventuality of her unstable son Paul

---

*   On 6 October 1797 after a peremptory 'courtship' Gustav married Elise's kind and gentle younger sister Friederike Dorothea of Baden. But the marriage was a troubled one; Gustav was deposed in a coup in 1809 and the couple divorced in 1812.

as tsar, for she looked upon him as her eccentric husband Peter's shadow and dreaded that he would turn the once mighty Russia into a 'Prussian province'.[11] In secret she planned to disinherit Paul, leaving instructions in her will that the throne should pass directly to Alexander. But she failed to persuade her grandson to endorse her plan for his succession in preference to his 42-year-old father.[12] In reality, Alexander wished rather the reverse: he had no desire to become tsar but, having absorbed the spirit of his tutor La Harpe's French republicanism, cherished the vague romantic notion of granting Russia a constitution and going to live with Elise in obscurity in either Germany or America.[13]

The mounting disappointment that the empress now felt in both her grandsons increased the strain she was under during her final days as she struggled to secure the future of the Russian throne. With no sign of any radical improvement in Konstantin's behaviour, in October she took drastic action, summarily removing him and Julie from the Marble Palace and bringing them to live with her at the Winter Palace where she could better keep an eye on him.* Shortly afterwards, 'death took Catherine by surprise.'[14] At nine o'clock on the morning of 5 November (16 November NS) she was found by her footman collapsed in her water closet, apparently felled by a stroke several hours earlier. She was laid on a leather mattress on the floor, her body too heavy to lift onto the bed. Tsarevich Paul was sent for and arrived from Gatchina at 8 p.m. with his wife and entourage. The whole tenor of the palace was immediately transformed; it was now invaded by Paul's officers, 'dressed in a manner so novel and grotesque that they seemed the apparitions of a former century, or ghosts from another world'.[15]

The doctors bled the empress and applied clysters (enemas), but after thirty-six hours in a state of almost total paralysis, Catherine died at 9.45 p.m. the following day, having been given the last rites. Julie and Elise were witness to it all, standing around the

---

* The Marble Palace was leased soon after to the last king of Poland, Stanisław August Poniatowski, who had abdicated the throne in November 1795.

deathbed through that long, exhausting day with their husbands and other members of the imperial family and entourage. For the next four weeks, in accordance with Russian Orthodox practice, Catherine's embalmed body, her face uncovered, lay in state in the magnificently decorated Great Hall of the Winter Palace, 'stretched out on a ceremonial bed surrounded by the coat of arms of all the towns of Russia', with a gold crown on her head and the 'Imperial mantle covering her to the chin'. The corpse was watched over by ladies and gentlemen of the court.[16] But it was not a pretty sight: Catherine's body had been badly embalmed and 'soon appeared quite disfigured: her hands, eyes, and the lower part of her face, were black, blue and yellow,' recalled Charles Masson, 'all the riches that covered her corpse, served only to augment the horror it inspired.'[17]

In the meantime, Paul sent Catherine's favourite Count Zubov packing and confiscated most of the estates and thousands of serfs he had acquired through her patronage. Within hours he had the palace filled with portraits of his late father. He ordered that Tsar Peter's coffin be disinterred from its resting place in the Annunciation Church of the Alexander Nevsky Monastery and his pitiful remains (a few bones and shreds of uniform) transferred to a new ornate coffin. At Paul's insistence, on 2 December (13 December NS) the whole court processed on foot behind Peter's coffin the 3 miles or more from the monastery all the way up the long straight Nevsky Prospekt to the Winter Palace, where it was placed on a bier alongside Catherine's in the Great Hall. On 5 December the imperial family then followed both coffins – Paul ensuring that his father's coffin, led by 'a Horse Guard dressed from head to toe in gold armour', went first, ahead of Catherine's, led by a guard wearing only iron armour.[18] This mournful procession, following behind a bare-headed Tsar Paul in the winter wind, and all in deep mourning, crossed the Troitsky Bridge to the cathedral of the Peter and Paul Fortress on Zayachy Island. 'They had to walk through the snow and suffered terrible cold from the palace to the fortress, which is some distance away on the other side of the Neva,' recalled Elisabeth Vigée Le Brun, who watched it all from the window of her lodgings overlooking Palace Square. By the time they arrived, the women were 'half dead with cold and fatigue'. Inside the cathedral a joint funeral service was conducted after which the coffins were interred in white marble tombs.[19]

The death of Catherine seemed to have a profound effect on the emotional and impressionable young Julie, who of late had grown thin and frail and collapsed during the interment ceremony at the Peter and Paul Cathedral. People were already noticing a stark contrast with the vivacious young woman who had arrived at court the previous year.[20] It was a mercy that Julie had Elise for moral support, though after Catherine's death Konstantin had at first locked her in their apartments and had forbidden her to join her friend. Elise was greatly distressed by this: Julie had been 'my only consolation, as I hers', she told her mother. Eventually, Alexander had taken it upon himself to go and liberate Julie from her 'prison'. It brought such comfort: 'Just imagine, mama, how at times like this, a person whom we love so much is a great help. We wept, we grieved together.'[21] Catherine's death had been a terrible experience; they had not slept for days.

Both grand duchesses found it hard to adjust to Tsar Paul's new regime. Elise was shocked at how, long embittered by his mother's involvement in the murder of his father, Paul was entirely fixated on resurrecting Tsar Peter's legacy, rather than offering a single kind word for the empress-mother whom he clearly had hated. She expressed her disgust at how she and Julie had been obliged to kiss the hand of the new emperor at his coronation, and to witness everyone 'promising to be the slaves of a man who at that moment I detested'. It was distressing to 'see him there in the place of the good Empress, to see him with such a satisfied air'.[22] Elise talked of the many unwelcome changes at court in long letters to her mother in Baden; in those very few letters of Julie's for this period that survive, we have no word about her own reaction. But from all that Elise says, Julie clearly shared her sister-in-law's despair. The days of the old empress's warm affection had gone: 'You have no idea of the dreadful emptiness there has been, of the sadness, of the bleakness felt by everyone, except for the new majesties,' Elise wrote.[23]

Although the Romanov family were plunged into six months of official mourning for Catherine, 'never was there any change of scene at a theatre so sudden and so complete as the change of affairs at the accession of Paul I,' observed Adam Czartoryski. 'In less than a day costumes, manners, occupations, all were altered.'[24] Paul now ordered the court to be transferred from the Winter Palace – as well as the Catherine Palace, the summer residence at Tsarskoe Selo – to two palaces beyond St Petersburg: Gatchina and Pavlovsk, the summer palace he had built during 1782–6 on the Gulf of Finland. This residence was mainly used by his wife Maria Feodorovna, who modelled it on Marie-Antoinette's Trianon, in contrast to Paul's Prussian-style Gatchina, which was not to her taste. She had also developed an aversion to the beautiful Catherine Palace at Tsarskoe Selo, despite the fact that it could comfortably accommodate the entire court. On Maria Feodorovna's orders the Catherine Palace was promptly 'abandoned and despoiled of its most beautiful effects', which were crammed into the smaller palace at Pavlovsk.

Most of Paul's time meanwhile was focused on Gatchina, which he effectively turned into an army camp and would become the microcosm of his militaristic new Russian state.[25] But here at least Alexander and Elise had apartments on the upper floor of the middle section of the palace, with Konstantin and Julie's apartments alongside and sharing the same entrance, thus ensuring that the two sisters-in-law remained in regular close contact.

On the day of his accession Paul had appointed Konstantin colonel of the Izmailovsky Lifeguards and Alexander to the Semyonovsky Regiment. With his new appointment Konstantin's military mania accelerated; it also meant that he and his brother were obliged to permanently wear the old-fashioned Prussian uniforms of high buttoned tunics, thigh boots and gauntlets that Paul favoured. So dramatic was the transformation, so retrograde, that someone remarked that the two brothers looked 'like old portraits of German officers walking out of their frames'. At Gatchina Paul's fanatical pleasure in 'parading his battalions of Holsteiners, in shortening their periwigs, or in altering the patterns of their coats' rubbed off on Konstantin, who admitted that much as he loved the parades and drills with all his men lined up in their fine uniforms, he didn't like war itself – 'because it spoils [the look of] the troops'.[26]

After spending the hottest summer months near the cooler sea air at Pavlovsk, Tsar Paul transferred to Gatchina during the autumn until the end of the year, where his day would start at seven o'clock with an early morning ride in the park with his two sons and his entourage, followed by hours studying the finer points of military science and taking part in tedious manoeuvres.[27] When he wasn't absorbed in military matters Paul marked all the protocols of imperial birthdays, anniversaries and religious festivals with obsessive exactitude, down to the correct number of genuflections and kissing of hands when greeting dignitaries.[28] It was a closed world, set in a time warp of obsolete military discipline and honour. At army parades and manoeuvres, 'important events unfolded in miniature, the rise and fall of fortune, failures and successes, which brought people either horror or unspeakable joy.' Officers could be summarily moved to other regiments straight from the parade ground for the slightest infringement or error, so much so that it became a habit for them to 'keep several hundred rubles of banknotes in their breast pockets' so as not to be left without money 'in the event of a sudden exile'.[29]

The Gatchina world of 'parade mania' had a deleterious effect on Alexander, making him deaf in one ear from the cannon fire, but its influence on his younger brother was far more marked. Konstantin allowed himself eagerly to be sucked into the rude and crude talk of army life there, into card games, vodka-drinking and sexual profligacy. This brutal, dehumanising world of endless square-bashing, corporal and other summary punishment, sticks and ramrods, hardened his naturally cruel personality. 'An officer is nothing but a machine,' he had once told La Harpe. 'Education, reasoning, feelings of honour and straightforwardness are harmful to strict discipline.'[30] The once frivolous life both brothers had enjoyed at court during the reign of their grandmother was now gone; the 'Grand Dukes were nothing better than corporals,' Countess Golovina remarked bitterly. Alexander wearied of this rigid militaristic regime and the additional burden of his appointment by Paul as military governor of St Petersburg; his brother, however, revelled in it all.[31]

At some point in the year before her death Catherine the Great commissioned the French painter Elisabeth Vigée Le Brun – who, since setting up her studio in St Petersburg in the autumn of 1795, had been very much in demand, commanding high prices for her work – to paint the portraits of her grandsons' wives. So sought after was Vigée at the Russian court that Count Rostopchin complained that she was charging 1,000–2,000 rubles for portraits 'which you would pay two guineas for in London'.[32] Catherine had already commissioned Vigée to paint her two oldest granddaughters, Alexandra and Elena, not long after she arrived, though she had been rather critical of the finished work. For Vigée had painted the two enchanting young girls side by side in gossamer Greek-style gowns, with bare arms and wearing wreaths of flowers on their heads. Catherine was appalled by what she considered to be an inappropriate style of dress for grand duchesses and Vigée, much to her dismay, had been ordered to repaint the dresses in the prevailing court style.[33] Nevertheless, Catherine commissioned her again, this time to paint Elise in October 1795, just as the Coburg visitors arrived. Vigée had found Elise a most beguiling subject – utterly ravishing and with a perfect oval face. She painted her with roses in her hair standing by a table with a bowl of flowers, wearing conventional court dress and presented the work to Catherine on 2 November (13 November NS); but the second, more informal, portrait she painted soon after – for Elise's mother at the grand duchess's request – of her wearing a violet shawl and leaning on a cushion, is far lovelier.[34]

Elise had taken Julie and her family to visit Vigée at her studio during their stay and in her memoirs, Vigée says that she began work on Julie's portrait at around the same time as Elise's. It is dated 1797 on the back and was therefore not completed until after Catherine's death. Although Vigée did not find Julie as 'outstandingly beautiful as her sister-in-law, but still very pretty', she was struck by 'the most lively exuberance [that] shone through her features'.[35] But she could also see that she was unhappy and was aware that her husband 'took after his father' and had 'the same tendency to fly into terrible rages'.[36] From letters she wrote to her father Franz, Julie was clearly intending to send a portrait of herself home to Coburg, for on 21 September 1798 (2 October NS) she told Franz that Duke Alexander of Württemberg (who was about to marry her sister Antoinette) would be coming on a visit and 'should be bringing you my portrait which has been promised for so long'.[*] She did not specify who had painted it and added that Württemberg

---

[*]   The portrait referred to is likely to have been the best-known one, of Julie wearing a red shawl with a white feather in her cap, which is now in the Pushkin Museum in Moscow. However, it was originally located in the Herzoglisches Schloss Museum in Gotha and is listed in its 1890 catalogue, which confirms the painting's original presence with the Saxe-Coburg family. It was probably relocated to the palace at Gotha after 1826, when Ernst I, Julie's brother, took up residence there after the duchy was reconstituted as Saxe-Coburg-Gotha. The portrait was originally thought to have been destroyed by bombing during the Second World War but it now appears that during the Soviet military occupation of Thuringia at the end of the war, it was confiscated as 'war reparations' and taken to Russia. It was rediscovered in the early 1990s, languishing unidentified, in a storage room at the Pushkin Museum. Thankfully, Prince Albert had had a copy of it made in Coburg by William Corden the Younger in 1844, which hung in Queen Victoria's bedroom at Windsor and is now in the Prince and Princess of Wales's apartments at Kensington Palace, and there is a second copy by an unknown artist also in the Royal Collection. There seems to be no chance of the original ever being returned to Gotha.

had deemed it 'a poor likeness'. Julie disagreed, explaining that she had been 'unwell and very pale' at the time.*

Julie's worsening health may well have been partly down to her no longer having the protection of the Empress Catherine, who until then had been a restraining influence over Konstantin. Much of the winter of 1796–7 passed in preparation for Paul's coronation, to be held in Moscow the following April, which imposed on the court an exhausting round of ceremonials dressed in heavy state robes, for which the emperor and empress demanded the most slavish adherence to Russian Orthodox ritual. Certainly, the last thing Julie needed in the spring of 1797 was to have to travel the 437 miles south to Moscow for the coronation, which was to be held on Easter Day, 5 April (16 April NS), at the Kremlin's fifteenth-century mother church, the Cathedral of the Dormition. At the time Julie was plagued with bad headaches and dizziness. But, as Countess Golovina explained, 'as illness was a great offence in the Emperor's eyes, she fought against her sufferings,' only to catch a chill on the journey south.[37]

After five days on the road, Julie and Konstantin arrived on 15 March (26 March NS) and took up their apartments in the Arsenal, whereupon Julie had to drag herself through many tedious court rituals and church services. One small pleasure came in the publication of the score for a 'Grande Symphonie' – a special

---

*   In early 1796, in anticipation of Julie's elevation to Russian grand duchess by her marriage, her father commissioned an engraving of her by the Bavarian court engraver, Heinrich Sintzenich, in Leipzig. It is not known who executed the original portrait from which he worked. But it is reminiscent of Vigée in its styling and dress. Could the engraving have been based on a now lost second half-length portrait of Julie that Vigée said she had painted at around the same time? The engraving was dedicated to Julie 'with the most humble reverence' by Sintzenich, who possibly himself hand-coloured the copy that is featured in the plate section of this book. But the puzzle remains: was this colourised version a copy of an original portrait? The only other known copy of the engraving is in Duke Franz's collection of engravings at the Veste, Coburg; see https://www.bavarikon.de/object/bav:BSB-CMS-0000000000002648 Vigée is thought to have executed sixty-seven portraits while in Russia but some have proved impossible to trace and some have been lost or destroyed. See Nikolenko, 'Russian Portraits'.

pianoforte piece for the coronation by the German music publisher Johann Julius Hummel, bearing the dedication 'A *Leurs Altesses Impériales Mesdames Les Grandes Duchesses de Toutes les Russies Elisaveta Alekseevna & Anna Feodorowna*', an obvious piece of self-promotion, directed at two German grand duchesses who were excellent pianists, that was aimed at raising Hummel's profile at the St Petersburg court.[*]

Through all the rehearsals and attendant ceremonies in the run-up to the coronation, Paul 'behaved like a child, delighted with the pleasures prepared for him'.[38] But his courtiers did not share in his enthusiasm; many became 'overwhelmed by fatigue', their tiredness exacerbated by the imposition of heavy and ornate court dresses, the ladies being forced to wear the cumbersome old panniers of an earlier era.[39] At one of many interminable church services held in the presence of their majesties, this time at the Petrovsky Monastery, Count Golovkin was not alone in noticing how ill Julie seemed, and how she 'suddenly turn[ed] pale'. He barely managed to catch her from falling onto the hard stone floor and had to lay her down on an old marble tomb to recover.[40] Golovkin later heard that a few days before, Grand Duke Konstantin had marched into Julie's bedroom with some drummers of the guard first thing in the morning when she was still asleep and had ordered them to sound the reveille; the noise had frightened her half to death.

Despite her obvious frailty, Julie was forbidden the least infraction of imperial protocols. Her fever escalated and she developed pneumonia. They bled her. Paul went to see her, thinking that she was malingering, and was irritated to discover she was genuinely seriously ill. 'I am sorry to see you suffering so,' he told her. 'I admit that up to the present I thought it was one of the little ways you had got into in the past reign, and which I am determined to extirpate,' an allusion presumably to his conviction that Catherine had indulged Julie's sickliness.[41] Somehow, on 5 April, Julie managed to get through the

---

[*]   It was not, however, Hummel's original work, but adapted from a 'Sinfonie périodique' in D major by a Bohemian composer of Italian descent, Antonio Rosetti.

protracted coronation ceremony at the Cathedral of the Dormition, immediately after which the new tsar announced the introduction of a Family Charter in which he instigated the rule of primogeniture in the masculine line, putting an end to the possibility of another woman like his much-hated mother ascending the throne – except in the unlikely absence of any males in the direct line.[42]

This single act changed everything for Julie: now, should Alexander and Elise fail to produce any male children, the crown would pass to Konstantin and then any sons that he and Julie might produce. She must surely have pondered the distinct possibility that she *could* one day become empress of Russia. As too must her mother Auguste back in Coburg. But Julie's father Prince Franz had other more immediate preoccupations. Coburg was perpetually broke and the only one of his children he could appeal to for financial help was his married daughter Julie. Letters she wrote to her father in 1797 testify to the considerable pressure, if not harassment, Julie was subjected to by Franz on this score. On 24 January (4 February NS) she wrote to say she had sent him 1,000 ducats,[*]

> may they be of some little use to you. It makes me really unhappy that I cannot give you more. I feel your sad situation, best Father, and would gladly help you. If only I could dispose as I wished of all the money I had to use for the coronation toilette ... How many poor people one could have made happy with this sum of money, with which one can scarcely get a robe. Such a dress costs 3,500 roubles, and one must have several. It really is a sin to waste the money which one could have spent so much more usefully.[43]

Franz said that she should look on any money she sent as a loan but

---

[*] These were the new 1797 gold ducats, mimicking the Dutch ones, issued for Paul's accession. The reverse bore a quotation in Russian from Psalm 115: 'Ne nam, ne nam, a imeni tvoemu' ('Not to us, not to us, but to Thy name'), which was the motto of the Knights Templar. Paul had been given the title of a protector of the Order of St John that year. It's impossible to place an equivalent value on them in today's terms, though the gold content at melt value would be over £160 per ducat today.

the kind-hearted Julie insisted that he treat it as a gift, that it would be 'shameful' of her to do otherwise, when she knew she would be receiving more money from her allowance.[44]

By October of 1797 Franz was still pressurising Julie for help, asking her to lobby the tsar for preferments and pensions for his various associates in Coburg.[*45] Such demands must have put a huge burden on the sixteen-year-old, at a time when her health was in serious decline and when she was longing to see her parents again. On 8 April 1797 (19 April NS) Grand Duchess Elise had told her mother that 'poor Anne [sic] has been ill for three days; she has a high fever. She is so weak that she cannot stand upright.'[46] But not long after the coronation, in early May, Tsar Paul set off on a tour of Russia with his two sons and Julie and Elise found themselves obliged to accompany the empress on a five-day visit to the Polish territories, during which Maria Feodorovna was difficult and demanding and insisted they both sleep in her bedroom. A few days later the women arrived back at Pavlovsk and were joined there at the end of the month by Paul, Alexander and Konstantin. It was a miserable time, the two grand duchesses finding themselves the constant butts of Paul's petty rules and regulations and witnessing his unpredictable moods – 'more changeable than a weathervane' as Elise put it, turning from kindness one minute to bouts of unjustifiable cruelty, especially towards his officers.[47] Worse than this, to Elise's mind, were the constant petty humiliations that Paul inflicted on Maria Feodorovna with his blatant attentions at court to his mistress, Ekaterina Nelidova, one of the empress's own ladies in waiting. Julie must, surely, have noticed the worrying similarities between father and son; it did not bode well for her life with Konstantin.

If Catherine the Great had favoured her older grandson Alexander over his younger brother, the tables had been smartly turned with Paul's accession. It was Konstantin who was now indulged. When he celebrated his eighteenth birthday on 27 April 1797 (8 May NS),

---

* Julie's incomplete identification of various people, combined with her tendency to misspell names mentioned in this regard, has made it impossible to identify them so far.

Paul gifted him the palace at Strelna – where Julie, her mother and sisters had stayed that first night in Russia. Alexander was given the more modest palace out at Oranienbaum.

In addition to the palace itself, Konstantin's domain at Strelna included the surrounding estate and villages and the 149 serfs who lived and worked on it. As Princess Auguste had noted two years previously, the palace had been in a state of neglect for some time. Konstantin set about restoring it: trees were cut down, stagnant ponds cleared and the park was decorated with sculptures, obelisks and pavilions. But what comfort was that to an increasingly lonely and sick Julie? She would now be expected to spend some of the summer here with her husband, separated from Elise, and subjected to Konstantin's eccentricities without redress to her friend or the concerned protection of Grand Duke Alexander.

In the autumn of 1797 after Julie had endured the tedium of being in close proximity with the empress Maria Feodorovna at Pavlovsk, the court transferred to Gatchina for the equally tedious round of autumn manoeuvres demanded by Tsar Paul. Adam Czartoryski did not remember the palace with affection. It had recently been enlarged and 'looked like a prison'. 'It is built on a perfectly level plain, without trees or fields. The park had a sombre and melancholy air; the sun seldom shines there, and it was so cold and rainy that we had no temptation to walk. Military parades or manoeuvres in the morning, and the French or Italian theatre in the evening, did but little to relieve the prevailing dullness.'[48]

It grated on the nerves to have to listen to the constant background beating of drums and shouted orders, the rattle of boots and sabres during drills and parades.[49] In November the court returned to the Winter Palace and official court mourning for Catherine the Great came to an end. In his determination, thereafter, to divest himself of Catherine's legacy, when Maria Feodorovna gave birth to her tenth child – a son, Mikhail – in January 1798, Paul began construction of a new home. He chose the site of Empress Elizabeth's wooden and now dilapidated Summer Palace, which was demolished at maniacal speed. Its imposing neoclassical replacement, known as the

Mikhailovsky Castle, would eventually be his new son's residence; Paul would lavish vast amounts of money on its construction but he would not live to see it completed.

The only happy diversion that winter of 1797–8, and one which revived Julie's plummeting spirits, were the balls held at the Winter Palace, from six in the evening for a couple of hours, at which Alexander would lead the grand dukes and duchesses into the ballroom with Julie, followed by Konstantin escorting Elise, to open proceedings with a French minuet. Paul never took part in the dancing, nor did his wife, who preferred to sit and play cards.[50] With Julie's familiar vivacious charm once more re-emerging, people began to talk of her as '*L'Etoile du Soir*' – 'The Evening Star'. Her beguiling personality did not go unnoticed by her handsome brother-in-law, who seemed to be paying her a lot of attention and was forever kind and courteous. Had Alexander fallen for Julie? Since his teens he had seemed perpetually susceptible to beautiful women, as Prince Leopold later recalled. Alexander's solicitous and charming behaviour towards women was hard to resist; while remaining emotionally cool he had an extraordinary gift for pleasing them and making them fall in love with him and there already were many unable to resist his charms. But Alexander lost interest once he had conquered – in reality, he was much closer to his sister Ekaterina.

It had certainly become noticeable at court that the relationship between Alexander and his wife was rather detached. Elisabeth Vigée Le Brun could see it and also that Grand Duke Konstantin had become 'very jealous of Alexander' for openly exhibiting much affection and kindness towards his sister-in-law. Elise, for all her undoubted charms, 'was no more fortunate in holding a husband's heart' than Julie was with Konstantin. According to Vigée, who appears to have had an ear to the gossip at court, this had 'led to some dreadful quarrels' between Konstantin and Julie, and she was 'furious that he should suspect her of being intimate with his brother'. Any inappropriate behaviour on her part in the full glare of the court would have been noticed and the last thing Julie needed was to alienate her only other ally – Elise. Yet doubts were cast on the true nature of her relationship with Alexander, creating an endur-ing enigma.[51] One thing was clear: whether it was to Alexander or elsewhere that Julie looked for the affection she craved, Konstantin's cruelty and neglect was, with remorseless inevitability, driving her away from him.

CHAPTER 7

'She Has Come Back to Us After All'

Despite the well-known rumours about Alexander's wandering eye, there were very good reasons why Elise and Julie should remain united in friendship and not allow gossip at court to undermine their relationship, for they constantly had to contend with the threatening presence of a mother-in-law who patently disliked them. Since the coronation, there had been no let-up in the empress's bullying and her demands on the two young wives, whom she treated like ladies in waiting in the most humiliating fashion. It only strengthened the bond between Elise and Julie, and the *Kamer-fur'erskii zhurnal* testifies to their daily walks, dinners and public engagements together.

Maria Feodorovna seems never to have warmed to either of her daughters-in-law, especially Julie; she was jealous of their beauty and popularity and was also highly censorious of anything that either of them said or did, or even wore, of which she did not approve. 'That is not proper' was, according to Countess Golovina, the empress's favourite catchphrase.[1] It is said that some of her antagonism towards Julie was down to a long-standing 'hereditary enmity between the House of Württemberg and the Coburg House'.[2] But more recently, Maria Feodorovna had bitterly resented the marriage of Gustav of Sweden to Elise's sister Friederike after her own daughter Alexandra's rejection – for she had nursed a consuming ambition to see her daughters become queens.³ (Alas, she would not live long enough to see her youngest daughter Anna Pavlovna become queen of the Netherlands in 1840.) Maria Feodorovna clearly favoured her two much younger sons Mikhail and Nikolai over Alexander and Konstantin. Konstantin in fact told Julie's brother Leopold years later that his mother had not wanted 'the "ménages" of the two older brothers to succeed', in other words, produce heirs, as she wished the Russian throne to pass to the younger brothers, specifically Nikolai.⁴ She was perhaps preoccupied too that her ambitions would be thwarted, with the news in November of 1798 that Elise, after five years of marriage to Alexander, was at long last pregnant. But was the child his?

Sensing the two sisters-in-law's growing favouritism of the Czartoryski brothers, who initially had been appointed as aides-de-camp to the two grand dukes, Tsar Paul had deliberately put some distance between them, appointing Adam to his daughter Grand Duchess Elena's entourage and Konstanty to that of her sister Grand Duchess Maria.⁵ It is said that this was a result of someone having gained access to letters hidden in Julie's desk which may well have been compromising with regard to her and Elise's closeness to the brothers. Many years later a French servant confessed that it was he who had stolen them and that he had put them back after they had been read – but by whom?⁶

Could the meddlesome Maria Feodorovna have instigated the theft, hoping to find compromising material that would discredit Julie? Prince Leopold certainly believed that the empress had had a hand in the 'domestic squabbles' that seemed to punctuate her marriage to Konstantin and asserted that 'without the shocking hypocrisy of the Empress Mother, things might have gone on' (that is, the marriage might have survived). Leopold believed that, for all his faults, Konstantin 'admired his wife extremely; and with an amiable husband, generous-hearted as she was, she would have been an excellent wife'. The trouble was that Konstantin was incapable of being an 'amiable husband' for very long before, Jekyll and Hyde-like, he switched back to the tyrannical monster and libertine he had become.[7] Elisabeth Vigée Le Brun likewise conceded that the grand duke could at times be 'obliging and kind' – but only with those who 'had discovered the path to his heart'.[8] The one person who achieved this was not Julie – who knew only 'his foul temper and violent nature' – but Konstantin's sister Anna Pavlovna, to whom he remained extremely close. His letters to her over many years after she married and left for the Dutch court reveal a man more than capable of being 'understanding, sympathetic, generous, candid, honourable and witty'.[9] But for now Konstantin was adding to Julie's misery with open acts of infidelity and highly promiscuous behaviour that was putting her health at serious risk. As Countess Golovina recalled: 'Having no longer any occasion to fear his father's anger, he formed intimacies unbefitting his rank, and gave little suppers in his rooms to actors and actresses, the result being that the Grand Duchess Anne, who was unaware of his conduct, was attacked by a complaint from which she suffered for a long time without knowing its cause.'[10]

Golovina seems to be alluding here to some kind of venereal infection. Julie had not as yet conceived a child. Could her failure to do so have been the result of the irresponsible and libidinous Konstantin having infected her; or was it that, being small and underweight – as contemporary descriptions attest – she may not yet have had her first period? A withering article published in the *London and Paris Observer* in 1826 was scathing in its condemnation of Konstantin's sexual profligacy and of the injury he had done to his own health 'by indulgence and excess'. It hinted darkly at 'degrading and barbarous action . . . in terms which we shall not transcribe in our pages'. To do so, the editor wrote, 'would overpower the feelings of most of our readers'.[11]

Such a scenario was all too common at the time: innocent, monogamous wives were frequently and unwittingly infected by promiscuous husbands with gonorrhoea – or worse, syphilis. If the latter, Konstantin would have been infectious for up to five years, which, while not preventing conception, might have triggered miscarriage. The record is not explicit but there are very clear indicators from Julie's later letters, and those of her family and friends, that she suffered long-term health problems. Lassitude and a general sense of debility were certainly symptomatic of venereal infection, perhaps reflected in the fainting fits that Julie often suffered; but the infection, if it was syphilis, would not appear to have progressed beyond the latent stage to the fatal tertiary one, for as we shall see she was later able to conceive. More concerning, however, is a lifetime's trouble with her eyes – which she frequently referred to in letters and is a well-known symptom of syphilis infection. Julie may well have realised or been told, privately, that her husband was the source of her health problems. Either way, she was desperately looking for an escape. She longed to see her parents again and had in fact planned a visit to Coburg the previous year, but her plans had had to be abandoned, for whatever reason. Most likely Konstantin or Tsar Paul himself had forbidden it.

With her health once more in noticeable decline, Julie became reclusive; she rarely joined the imperial family for meals and was frequently absent from church services. Elise confirmed this in a letter to her mother at the end of January 1799. Julie had 'spent the greater part of the winter shut away in her room, suffering from a thousand different ailments. The poor little thing, she doesn't even dare risk going outside, without getting cold in one way or another.'[12] Yet Julie did not betray a word of her suffering in her letters home. Franz was still busy badgering her for money in every letter that arrived from Coburg. But Auguste had certainly become aware of her daughter's ill health, having learned this at second hand from Julie's lady in waiting, Madame de Renne. Renne's reports of Julie's febrile emotional state and her complaints of perpetual physical weakness greatly alarmed Auguste. She begged Renne to supply her with all the details of her condition 'that I might show [them] to a physician very skilled in female complaints who is here [in Coburg] at present', for she knew that 'there are so few doctors who take the trouble to study our ailments and know how to treat them.'[13]

In response, Madame de Renne arranged for Julie to consult with the court doctors – who concluded that she was suffering from physical and mental exhaustion and 'could only be radically cured

by a course of the waters in Bohemia'. Countess Golovina revealingly
noted that Konstantin seemed to recognise that he was the cause of
his wife's ill health and was duly chastened. He 'tried in a thousand
ways to correct the injustice he had done', but 'Grand Duchess Anna
was full of indignation' and determined to get away to Coburg, for
good if possible.[14] Her spirits lifted once the doctors recommended
that she take the cure at Carlsbad (now Karlovy Vary) and plans were
made for her to travel there in the spring. By the beginning of 1799
she had confided all this to Elise, convinced that her Coburg family
would undoubtedly take her side and protect her. Once safely back
home, the emperor and empress would be informed that nothing
in the world would make her return to her hateful husband.[15] Elise
was hugely relieved: 'She will see her parents again. Ah! That alone,
I think, will bring her back from the gates of death ... I am certain
that the change of air, the exercise of the voyage, a thousand other
things will do her great good.'[16]

Alexander, who was let in on the secret, like his wife was very
solicitous of Julie's welfare and offered to help. Elise and Julie discussed how they would be able to correspond avoiding the censor
when she had left Russia. For they were faced with a major problem:
the tsarist secret police had become notorious for their perlustra-
tion of letters in and out of the country. Foreign minister Count
Rostopchin had long since been ordered by Tsar Paul to open all
of Elise's and Julie's letters to Germany, which might well explain
Julie's reticence in her brief surviving letters home, and there was no
point in resorting to subterfuge such as invisible ink. Instead, they
would have to send letters via intermediaries travelling to and from
Germany. However, none of their correspondence has survived, suggesting that they had agreed to destroy each other's letters as soon
as they had received and read them.[17]

It was war in the end that provided Julie with the perfect escape.
In January 1799, after French revolutionary forces led by Napoleon
had rampaged across the cities of northern Italy and he had seized
Milan, Tsar Paul joined a military coalition with Austria and

Piedmont-Sardinia to drive them out while Napoleon was away on campaign in Egypt. The distinguished 69-year-old Russian field marshal Alexander Suvorov was appointed in March to lead a Russian expeditionary force of 60,000 men to join the Coalition forces in Piedmont and Lombardy. Eager to be involved, Konstantin asked his father's permission to go on campaign with Suvorov, as a volunteer. He bade farewell to his parents and Julie after a church blessing at the Kazan Cathedral and left St Petersburg on Friday 11 March (22 March NS), to follow Suvorov to the Russian army's headquarters in Vienna, travelling as 'Count Romanov'.[18]

Knowing how desperate Julie was to grasp this opportunity to go and see her family, one of Paul's close advisors, Nikolai Kotlubitsky, took pity and advised her that the best strategy would be to feign an air of great sadness that evening at dinner with the emperor. Julie did so, and when asked by Paul what was wrong, told him how melancholy she was about the departure of her dear husband and how badly she needed to visit her family, whom she had not seen for some time. The ruse worked; Paul gave his permission for Julie to leave Russia for Coburg.[19] She did so the following day, Saturday 12 March, accompanied by a large and conspicuous entourage of servants in a convoy of fifteen vehicles, as befitted a Russian grand duchess. Her entourage included Madame de Renne, Renne's daughter Caroline – whom Julie always called Renette – Ivan Tutolmin as major-domo, his wife and a lady in waiting, Countess Ekaterina Vorontsova.[20] Only Alexander and Elise were privy to Julie's intention of never returning. Elise, already anxious about the imminent arrival of her first child, was utterly distraught at the prospect of the 'inexpressible void' that this would create.[21]

We do not know when exactly Julie arrived back in Coburg, but Elise told her mother in a letter of 15 April (4 April OS) that she would be arriving there any day now. However, it was a bad time to be returning home: Saxe-Coburg's population might be small but it was becoming increasingly disgruntled and restless with the wilful mismanagement of state finances, heavy taxation and the crushing indebtedness of the ducal house. This had been further stretched by expensive renovations to the Ehrenburg Palace while the ducal family lived at their old house on Steingasse.[22] Auguste travelled out to meet Julie at Leipzig but by the time the women reached Coburg, Konstantin had arrived, unannounced, from Vienna, supposedly displaying his concern for his sick wife.[23] Mercifully, he left for Italy again on 1 June (21 May OS) and soon after Julie and her parents travelled 125 miles east to Carlsbad for her to receive treatment. The press reported the arrival of 'Countess Romanov' with a 'numerous entourage', in time for the opening of the summer season on 15 June and noted the considerable attention she attracted, thanks to her 'exalted rank'; while there she sat for one of the most fashionable German portraitists, Johann Friedrich August Tischbein, a brother of the Tischbein who had painted her mother in 1775.[24]

Carlsbad was at the time the 'most aristocratic watering-place in Europe', situated at the bottom of a valley along which wound the River Tepl. Beneath the town were located numerous caves and hollows of boiling, vaporous waters, so hot they could boil an egg.[25] The water with its naturally occurring chemicals – sulphate of soda (Glauber salt), carbonate of soda, salt, bromine and potash – was drunk by patients, as well as used in mud and douche baths. No doubt Julie would have visited one or other of the principal bath-houses – the Mühlbäder or the Sprudelbäder, or the vapour-baths on the right bank of the Tepl, where streams of vapour were admin-istered in the form of a douche. The waters at Carlsbad had become renowned for curing liver and abdominal disease, such as cirrhosis, gout, rheumatism, dropsies (oedemas) and pulmonary complaints. They also were recommended for chronic uterine inflammation, endometriosis, amenorrhoea and other women's health issues. There is no specific recommendation of their use for venereal disease and we can only guess at what Julie's actual physical ailments were.

Patients at Carlsbad were treated with up to eight cups of the spa waters, administered every fifteen minutes, between five and nine in the morning, which they 'emptied by degrees' while 'pacing up and down the covered colonnade to the sound of soft music, a band being stationed in the neighbourhood of the well'.[26] The empress had written to Madame de Renne on 10 June (21 June NS) telling her that Emperor Paul was convinced 'that the doctors will immediately find the "Eger Water" is beneficial to the grand duchess' – a reference to the famous thermal baths at Eger in Hungary – and that they were 'very pleased to know that you hope to bring the good dear Grand Duchess back to us fresh and healthy. God bless her.'[27]

Julie's presence in Carlsbad was noted on the occasion of the historic Jeu de l'Arquebuse, a grand annual medieval-style tournament at which fireworks and illuminations were displayed.[28] By July she was seen at another fashionable Bohemian spa, Töplitz (now Teplice in Czechia), 60 miles northeast of Carlsbad. It was a most beautiful and restful spot, with numerous parks and gardens, where bands played throughout the day. It also had a busy social scene. Louisa Adams, wife of US diplomat John Adams, who was having treatment at the thermal baths there at the time, was introduced to Julie at a tea party along with her father, mother and sisters Sophie and Antoinette. She saw them again at a performance of Mozart's *Magic Flute* and noted how 'handsome' the Saxe-Coburg princesses were.[29]

Any hopes Julie might have had of continuing her summer idyll and remaining in Europe indefinitely were sadly dashed when her major-domo, Tutolmin, received instructions of the most threatening kind from Rostopchin in St Petersburg. Tsar Paul had grown suspicious of Julie's continuing absence from Russia and was demanding she be brought back in time for the weddings in October of her two sisters-in-law, Alexandra and Elena. An emissary, Count Panin, was even sent from Berlin to see Julie and impress upon her the crisis that her permanent separation from Konstantin would precipitate and to pass on the emperor's insistence that she return.[30]

Julie must by now have confided the truth of her unhappy marriage to her parents and her intention never to return, only to receive an entirely unsympathetic response from them. Such decisive action would be disastrous for Prince Franz and Princess Auguste and would, they were convinced, bring shame and dishonour on the family.[31] The advantages that Saxe-Coburg had to gain by Julie's continuing union were far too great to be jeopardised. In mid-September, having spun out her stay to the last possible day,* Julie once more despondently embarked on the long tedious carriage ride back to Russia.

Julie arrived back at Gatchina on 11 October (22 October NS), just in time for fifteen-year-old Grand Duchess Elena's wedding to Prince Friedrich Ludwig of Mecklenburg-Schwerin. Tsar Paul himself conducted Julie to Elise's apartments: 'Here she is,' he announced triumphantly, 'she has come back to us after all, and looking splendid.'[32] Elise was greatly surprised; she had not been expecting to see her friend in Russia again. Julie explained that she had returned under duress, fearing that Tutolmin and Renne would be punished for not bringing her back. But she was delighted to see Elise's baby daughter, Maria, who had been born on 18 May (29 May NS), though the joy of her arrival had been tempered by rumour that she had been fathered by Adam Czartoryski and not Alexander. The signs were there: both Alexander and Elise were fair and blue-eyed; the baby, as the spiteful empress was quick to point out, had dark hair and brown eyes. Once sown, the seeds of suspicion could not be suppressed and soon afterwards Tsar Paul dispatched Czartoryski to a low-status diplomatic post in Sardinia. This act of effective banishment greatly distressed Elise, who was aghast at the insinuations about her child's paternity, but the rumours persisted.

Only a week after the marriage of Elena, sixteen-year-old Grand Duchess Alexandra Pavlovna – who had been jilted by Gustav of Sweden in 1796 – was married, also at Gatchina, to Archduke Josef of Austria, palatine of Hungary. This union with the brother of the Austrian emperor had been engineered to consolidate the new coalition between Russia and Austria against Napoleon. But there was one significant difference in the marriage contract this time: Alexandra was allowed to retain her Russian Orthodox faith. The

---

*   It is unclear how much time Julie actually spent back in Coburg – it would seem she was there at the beginning and end of her six-month sojourn and the rest of the time at Carlsbad and Töplitz.

wedding on 30 October 1799 (19 October OS) would be the first and only marital alliance between the Hapsburgs and the Romanovs, a distinguished union indeed, but one that left Alexandra distraught at having to leave Russia and her family on 21 November (10 November OS) for Vienna, much like her sister Elena had been carted off shortly before her to the Mecklenburg palace at Ludwigslust. Even Tsar Paul had been in tears at Alexandra's departure, recognising that his daughter (much like the German brides brought to Russia for his sons) 'was being sacrificed' for political expediency. He feared that he would never see her again (he didn't).[33]

Much to Julie's dismay, her protector and ally Madame de Renne was enlisted by the empress to accompany the young bride Alexandra on her journey and Julie would not see her again until April 1800; was this a form of oblique punishment perhaps?[34] Alexandra seemed doomed to experience similar tribulations to Julie. In Vienna she gained an implacable sister-in-law in Empress Maria Theresa – second wife of the Holy Roman Emperor, Francis II – and was the butt of considerable hostility towards her Russian Orthodox faith from the Catholic Austrian court.

That month of October back in Russia had not been as terrible as Julie might have anticipated; there had been several joyous celebrations and numerous palace balls in the wake of the two weddings, and she now seems to have recovered her health thanks to her cure at Carlsbad – and was enjoying riding out with Elise in the last days of autumn before the onset of snow.[35] In addition, there was heartening news of Russian successes in the campaign against the French. On 27 December Julie 'welcomed' her conquering hero husband Konstantin back from the Italian campaign, he having demonstrated considerable courage at several engagements including the battle of Pont du Diable at Mont St Gotthard in September. However, the campaign in Italy had, although audacious, been suicidal and was followed by a Russian retreat and the return of Suvorov to St Petersburg in disgrace. He died soon afterwards.[36] Tsar Paul was nevertheless proud of his son's exploits and after a Te Deum of thanks bestowed on Konstantin the Order of St George, 2nd class, and the formal title Tsesarevich, even though the fundamental law of Russia designated that title, as opposed to Tsarevich, for the heir to the throne only. Konstantin's imperial elevation was an undisguised mark of Paul's favour and of his continuing distrust of Alexander.

The reunion with Julie also was a considerable surprise. The months away fighting in Italy – including a gruelling fighting march of 186 miles across the Alps in twenty-one days – had matured, and even mellowed, Konstantin. Elise noticed it too: the campaign had been 'to his advantage. He had grown – literally.' He was now unexpectedly attentive, gentle and even loving towards his wife.[37] In response, Julie's behaviour towards him softened. Knowing that she had no other option, she tried hard to adapt to this new, improved version of the man she had married and encouraged him to continue on this gratifying path of self-improvement. During the winter of 1799–1800 she accompanied Konstantin to Tsarskoe Selo, where he was sent by the tsar to rigorously drill the Horse Guards as punishment for some perceived failure or other on their part. Konstantin did so with his usual brutal alacrity, but it was a miserable, humiliating time for him and for Julie. They lived in a house at Tsarskoe Selo that Catherine the Great had bought for Konstantin some time before, but their life there, recalled Countess Golovina, was 'absolutely devoid of the dignity befitting their rank'.[38]

Bored and restless, Konstantin had soon slid back into his old, ingrained ways. In the evenings he took to bringing officers of his regiment back home to carouse and drink and 'dance to the harpsichord' in Julie's presence in ways that 'would not have been seemly in a household of a much lower rank'.[39] Caroline Bauer in her memoir was more explicit: 'In the presence of his rough officers [Konstantin] made demands on [Julie], as his property, which will hardly bear being hinted at.'[40] Drunkenness brought out the very worst of his erratic and licentious behaviour: Konstantin raved at and insulted his men, and soon turned violent towards Julie again. On one occasion, in the company of a group of officers, the topic of female beauty came up. Konstantin began to praise Julie's charms. 'She blushed and was embarrassed; the Grand Duke insisted and then finally demanded that she provide material evidence of his words'. When Julie flatly refused, he 'furiously tore at her dress.'[41]

Embarrassed and frightened of the rowdy company Konstantin kept, Julie was constantly ill at ease. Inevitably the intense cold at Tsarskoe Selo that winter took its toll on her, for she was forced to endure life in a freezing, unheated house, without the support even of Elise. She caught a chill – possibly the influenza that was then rampant – and nearly died of fever. In anticipation of her death Tsar Paul had even given instructions for a Prussian-style funeral.[42] But she recovered and returned to St Petersburg to convalesce. Throughout this time Julie had continued to be plagued by letters from her father demanding money, no doubt partly to recompense him for the expenses he had incurred maintaining her entourage during her stay in Coburg. No sooner had she returned to Gatchina in October 1799 than she had sent him 10,000 rubles. By December she was protesting that she could not afford more as she only had 3,000 left in her own treasury until the next instalment of her allowance in January 1800. Tsar Paul had promised to send another 10,000 on her behalf, she reassured him, but by the following April the money had still not arrived.[43]

In February 1800, Konstantin and Alexander were commanded to join Paul and his court in his newly constructed and forbidding red-painted Mikhailovsky Castle in St Petersburg. The design and construction, achieved at colossal expense, was medieval and martial, 'with moats, swing bridges, secret staircases and a labyrinth of corridors'; the paintwork was still wet, their rooms were damp and the atmosphere heavy with moisture that created a ghostly mist throughout. Elise and Julie remained at the nearby Anichkov Palace until their accommodation was finished.[44] On finally being installed Julie seemed quite taken with the Mikhailovsky: it was like a 'fairy castle', she told her father. Konstantin took her on a guided tour and showed her their new apartment with its magnificent view over the frozen River Neva.[45]

A German visitor, the dramatist August von Kotzebue, who was granted a private view of the palace, was shown Julie's room on the 'piano nobile' where his attention was drawn to a clock, which bore the inscription *'L'amour reduit à la raison'* ('Love reduced to reason'). This must be an allusion to an engraving of the same name by Pierre Prud'hon in which Cupid is seen chained to a bust of Minerva, the Roman goddess of wisdom, turning his head to gaze at a beautiful, voluptuous seated woman nearby. Kotzebue remarked that 'here, under the eyes of such a beautiful and amiable princess, that is, however, no punishment for love.' In contrast to Julie's more spiritual and esoteric instincts, in Konstantin's room nearby he noted the grand duke's preference for the more physical, fleshly aspects of love: 'a copy of the hermaphrodite from the Villa Borghese and one of Venus leaving the bath from the Florentine Gallery'.[46]

Julie seemed to be in good spirits once more and had recovered her health sufficiently to go out into the snow and enjoy the specially constructed ice slides – a popular but hazardous pastime during the Russian winter. A precursor of fairground roller coasters, these huge slides, known as 'flying mountains', were built on a wooden framework to a height of 80 feet and covered in ice which was watered every day to keep the surface slippery.[47] It was a welcome diversion from the heightened tensions at the Mikhailovsky, where Paul's obsession with his own personal security had grown in tandem with his increasing paranoia about attack and assassination. Pious and religiously observant the tsar might be, capable even of occasional acts of benevolence, but Paul's inherent despotism and lack of human compassion was now propelling him into a reign of terror as he sought to undo all the liberal vestiges of his mother Catherine's reign. He now inaugurated the imposition of draconian search and arrest orders by the St Petersburg police, a stringent clampdown on freedom of speech and a ban on the importation of foreign books and journals; all letters leaving Russia were censored.

Paul had reason to fear for his crown; dissent and opposition to his rule was growing and with plotters closing in, he retreated more and more to the self-imposed prison of the Mikhailovsky. He became convinced that his own sons were plotting against him. Even Paul's

Scottish physician, Dr John Rogerson, was alarmed at how 'the incoherence of his movements increases and becomes more manifest from day to day.'[48] Everyone at court, from the lowliest servants to members of his immediate family, lived in terror of the tsar's next unpredictable outburst, for he seemed to be on an inexorable descent into madness.[49]

It was a terrible time in particular for Elise, who absolutely doted on her baby Maria, affectionately known as Mäuschen – 'little mouse'. But she had been sickly from birth, fell ill with fever and diarrhoea in June 1800 and died on the 27th (8 July NS). After the baby's burial at the Alexander Nevsky monastery, she and Julie had gone to Gatchina to commiserate. Alexander felt the baby's loss as deeply as his wife, but their relationship had suffered a fatal cooling and his attentions wandered in the direction of a succession of ladies at court.

He was also now distracted by having become privy to a plot by a camarilla of political opponents, led by Count Nikita Panin, to remove Paul from power and place him, Alexander, on the throne. According to Panin, the country was threatened with 'revolution and massacres' and 'nothing but the abdication of Paul could save it'.[50] Together with St Petersburg's military governor, Count Peter von der Pahlen (the husband of one of Elise's ladies in waiting, Countess Pahlen), Panin urged Alexander that Paul must be removed from power. Alexander was afraid of his father and took some persuading. The conspirators misled him into naively believing that a temporary regency would prevail until Paul – who would be packed away to some country estate with his mistress – had recovered his mental faculties (much as the Prince Regent was appointed in Britain during the 'madness' of King George III). Alexander reluctantly agreed; he had tried hard to fulfil the military roles thrust on him by his father but had found them increasingly burdensome and resented Paul's tyrannical control. But he insisted that he did not wish any physical harm done to him.[51]

On the night of 11 March (23 March NS) 1801, Alexander and Konstantin, now placed under house arrest with their wives by

Paul, sat down with him at the Mikhailovsky for an extremely uncomfortable supper party, Paul convinced that Alexander was plotting against him and Alexander anxious that his father was going to have him imprisoned.[52] Meanwhile, a group of officers from the Preobrazhensky Guards and Alexander's own regiment, the Semyonovsky Guards, were getting increasingly drunk as they plotted Paul's demise. It was a bitter winter night, with the wind coming off the frozen River Neva, when, approaching midnight, Pahlen and his soldiers surrounded the palace while others made their way inside through a back entrance and, overpowering the guards patrolling the hallway, found their way into the tsar's apartments. Here they found Paul in his nightshirt hiding behind a screen; he had ordered the door into his new mistress Princess Gagarina's room to be locked and there was no way out. Accounts of what happened next are contradictory but it would appear that the terrified Paul was then cornered by the out-of-control conspirators, heady with Count Pahlen's champagne, who, thinking he was resisting arrest, piled into him, knocking out the only lamp in the room as they did so. In the ensuing struggle in pitch darkness, Paul was hit on the cheek with a heavy gold snuffbox, he fell and was set upon, his skull smashed against the floor, and was finally throttled with his own sash that had been hanging on the bedpost, after which he was kicked and trampled on.[53]

No amount of mortician's cosmetics could disguise the state of the corpse, with its mangled face, which was black and blue, and its head half stoved in. Julie and Elise tried as best they could to restrain and comfort Maria Feodorovna, who was in a most hysterical state. They implored the empress not to go and see Paul's body, but she could not be persuaded and insisted on all her children accompanying her. Entering the room she 'uttered fearful shrieks'. The embalmed corpse, like that of Catherine before him, lay there on display, 'painted and varnished like a doll and wearing a hat to hide the injuries to his head'.[54] The following day, after considerable persuasion, Alexander had to go out on the balcony overlooking Palace Square and tell the gathered crowds that his father had died of an 'apoplectic stroke'. Konstantin, who appears to have slept through most of what had happened that night, made no overt expression of regret.[55]

Alexander was crushed and incredulous at the way things had played out. He had never wanted to be tsar, and most certainly not in such horrifying circumstances, and declared himself incapable of taking the throne. 'How should I have strength to reign with the remembrance that my father was assassinated constantly before my eyes?' he asked. It was Elise who rose to the occasion and gave him the strength to get through this crisis. The imperious dowager empress, Maria Feodorovna, stepped in as the controlling force while the timid Alexander vacillated, this despite the fact that only two weeks previously, she had suffered the devastating loss of her seventeen-year-old daughter Alexandra, wife of Archduke Joseph, who had developed septicaemia after the birth of a daughter.

For the Russian people at large, Paul's death was an act of deliverance; for Julie it meant release from imprisonment in the feudal fortress of the Mikhailovsky, which Alexander promptly closed down. The period of uncertainty and turmoil that followed the funeral obsequies for Tsar Paul was punctuated by the fasting of Lent and a series of doleful Easter services, after which Julie begged the new tsar to allow her to leave Russia. She did so on the pretext that her mother was ill and she needed to go to her but in reality she was desperate to escape her faithless husband, who even now was dreaming of being set free to marry Helena Lubomirska, a Polish princess he had met in the summer of 1800 when on manoeuvres at Rovno.[56] However, rumours were filtering out that Julie too had taken a lover. It would be no surprise if she had strayed, given her romantic nature and her longing to be loved, not to mention Konstantin's constant and blatant pursuit of other women.

There had already been talk about Julie's close friendship with Konstanty Czartoryski, but in the summer of 1801 allegations began circulating that she had been caught up with a handsome thirty-year-old cavalry captain named Ivan Linev. The relationship appears to have developed at Gatchina the previous autumn, where Linev – who was in the elite cavalry squadron that formed Tsar Paul's personal

guard – was often on duty, and that it was orchestrated by an intermediary, Alexander Ushakov, one of Linev's fellow officers. For his
own idle amusement, Ushakov had written secret amorous letters
and poems to Julie supposedly from Linev and planted them under
a cushion on the sofa on which she used to sit. By all accounts Linev
did not realise he was being played when Julie found them and began
giving him longing looks and eventually suggested an assignation in
one of the pavilions in the park at Gatchina. Other clandestine meet-
ings followed there, with Julie supposedly even leaving a mannequin
propped up by a window in her room 'reading a book' by candlelight
to disguise her absence.[57]

Julie and Linev, it would seem, were willing dupes. Ushakov later
openly boasted of how he had played a trick on his comrade.[58] The
memoirist Alexander Turgenev was convinced the letters were a
ploy to discredit Julie, connived at by Konstantin to provide him
with ammunition in obtaining the divorce that he earnestly wished
for in order to marry his latest mistress. Turgenev believed that the
handsome but gullible Linev (to whom he was distantly related) had
'assumed the title of lover of the Grand Duchess – without a doubt
for money, and with the assurance of impunity' in what he described
as an unjust 'slander' of Julie and her reputation. In return for Linev's
deceiving her into believing he was in love with her, Konstantin
would pay off his old drinking companion's debts.[59]

This was the best, and only, 'defence' that Julie was ever given;
for, whatever the initial circumstances, a romance clearly developed
between her and Linev. Court intrigue grew when rumours of the
affair were circulated by Prince Pavel Lopukhin, half-brother of Tsar
Paul's last mistress, Princess Anna Lopukhina. She had replaced
Ekaterina Nelidova as Paul's favourite in 1798 and Julie and Elise
had both taken a strong dislike to her, tolerating her 'merely with
the consideration that politeness demanded', and only after they
had been commanded to do so by Paul. Had there been an element
of spite therefore in Lopukhina's brother spreading the gossip?[60] To
further compound the truth or falsity of the rumours, it was noticed
at the end of 1800 that Julie had been putting on weight. Tsar Paul

was delighted to see this as he longed for a grandson, but no pregnancy was officially announced.

There is very little evidence to go on; however, Maria Feodorovna's
lady in waiting Alexandra Smirnova comments in her memoirs that
eight days before Tsar Paul's murder Julie suffered either a stillbirth
or a miscarriage. (Smirnova is unclear whether the child had been
carried to term.) The birth appears to have been brought on by a
fright after Paul went on a deranged rampage claiming the palace
was on fire. Furious at the loss of a longed-for grandson, and para-
noid about conspiracy, he placed his sons, their wives and the
empress all under house arrest.[61]

Court gossips at the time inevitably insinuated that the child
was the product of Julie's supposed affair with Ivan Linev.[62] Maria
Feodorovna was enraged and confronted her daughter-in-law.
Although Julie protested her innocence, it was enough to persuade
the dowager that the scandal was too damaging and that Julie was
better out of Russia than in. She therefore did not oppose Alexander
agreeing to her speedy departure, even though the failure of the marriage reflected badly on Konstantin, who had also been humiliated
as a cuckold.

Driven out of Russia by her unhappy marriage but also the dowager's unremitting hostility, the last mention of Grand Duchess
Anna Feodorovna Romanova was published in the *Kamer-fur'erskii
zhurnal* on 30 July (11 August NS) 1801. On 13 August she left St
Petersburg.* The *Corriere Milanese* and other European papers
reported the official line that she had set off for Coburg to visit
her mother, 'who was dangerously ill'.[63] Linev left Russia shortly
afterwards, under a false name (Count Benievsky), having been
dismissed from military service because of the gossip. He followed
Julie to Germany, though at a distance.[64] The affair appears to have
been hushed up in Russia at the time, but over the years insinuations
emerged of how Konstantin's 'ill usage ... drove [Julie] to form an

---

* With Julie's departure from Russia we move into the Gregorian calendar in
use in western Europe. Henceforth all dates will be according to that system with
Old Style dates referred to in brackets only where necessary for clarity.

intrigue with a young Russian officer' and that 'the justice, no less than the clemency of the Emperor Alexander, protected her from the vengeance of Constantine', when she left Russia with the said officer in tow. Elsewhere it was suggested that, as an act of revenge, Konstantin had wilfully encouraged the rumours of Julie's infidelity with Linev in order to plague her happiness in her new life. Some attempted to discredit her with hints of indiscreet behaviour; veiled comments were made about Julie's spontaneous manner, that she was 'free and bold' and that her 'imprudent levity' had been in part the cause of the embitterment that had led to the breakdown of her marriage with Konstantin.[65]

Julie's sudden departure prompted considerable consternation among her entourage, no more so than with her former lady in waiting Sophie de Campenhausen. She had been tasked to accompany Grand Duchess Elena – now a princess of Mecklenburg-Schwerin – from Ludwigslust to visit her mother, the dowager empress, at Pavlovsk in the summer of 1801 and could not resist confiding to Renette in St Petersburg that she had seen Julie there, adding somewhat cryptically that she had 'made her conquest and was quite mad about it'. Indeed, Julie had 'never looked more beautiful' – so beautiful on the evening Sophie saw her that 'it had set my head spinning. It is one of the most beautiful faces I have ever seen.' Julie was in her element, which is why Sophie could not understand her rush to leave Russia. It 'was the worst thing [Julie] could have done', she told Renette at the end of July; Sophie was 'very angry with her' for not at the least delaying her departure until after Alexander's coronation, due to be held in Moscow on 15 September.[66]

At the time, candid comments about Julie's impetuous behaviour were studiously avoided in family letters, but her position at court had clearly become untenable. Sophie de Campenhausen had not even dared put the details in a letter to Renette about the suspicions surrounding Julie's 'precipitous departure' from Russia and the 'scandalous rumours that have been circulating on this subject'. They had 'caused me a lot of pain', for 'so much has been said and talked about it, especially in Russia and so publicly.'[67] Writing later, Renette's son thought Julie's precipitate action had been a mark of 'that trait of independence and youthful petulance in her character which yielded with difficulty to the eccentric moods of her husband and to the authoritarian interference of her mother-in-law'.[68]

Was the Linev saga all a frivolous intrigue in which Julie had rapidly found herself out of her depth? Alexander Turgenev wrote that Linev was nothing but a scoundrel who had preyed on Julie's vulnerability. He claimed that he left Russia because Julie had demanded it as she was in love with him, but, declared Turgenev, 'there is nothing more unfair in the world than such a slander.'[69] But the rumours cannot be explained away: Julie seems to have been basking in the euphoria of a romantic conquest after years of being the butt of an abusive husband. Madame Lieven, who was totally devoted to the dowager empress, placed all the blame on Julie in a letter written to Madame de Renne in 1802. The grand duchess had misjudged Maria Feodorovna, she said; she had been like a mother to her and had even taken her side against her own son. The recalcitrant Julie had not shown her the obedience she owed her; had she done so, everything would have been different.[70] Certainly, Maria Feodorovna later reprimanded Konstantin for never trying to deal with the 'incompatibility' between himself and his wife, brought on by his 'instability'; he had made no attempt to listen to his wife and 'to live in conjugal peace'.[71]

Public awareness of the unhappy German princess's situation seems to have percolated beyond the walls of the Winter Palace. Haunting echoes of Julie's presence in Russia for those few painful years lingered on after her departure in the words of a popular Russian song then in circulation. In 'The Sound of a Sad Piano', a thinly disguised Julie bitterly mourns her misfortune, her unfaithful husband and the abuse by him of the sacred oaths she took as an innocent bride. She begs for her anguish to be eased: 'Everything is contemptible: loyalty, honesty, duty, love ...' The sheet music for the song was reprinted twenty-seven times over the following years and mentioned in popular Russian literature, where it was seen as 'an expressive vignette' epitomising the romantic sentiment of the 1800s. It is almost the only trace of Julie that remained in Russia.[72]

CHAPTER 8

'THE CATASTROPHE
FROM THE NORTH'

Julie's journey out of Russia and back to Coburg during August–
September 1801, under the nom de plume 'Comtesse de Romanov',
could not have gone unnoticed for she travelled homeward across
Europe in a grand cavalcade of eight carriages. Konstantin,
Alexander and Elise had wanted to escort her to the border, but had
had to travel to Moscow instead to prepare for Alexander's coronation. So Julie travelled only with her key staff of Madame de Renne,
her daughter Renette and a new major-domo replacing Tutolmin,
Jules-Gabriel de Seigneux, who had been recommended by his cousin
Pierre-Samuel, the governor of Julie's brothers in Saxe-Coburg. She
had been very anxious to get back home, for Auguste truly was once
again sick: 'I am coming, my best good [mama],' she wrote to her,
'if I could fly I would be there already. I will look after you so well,
that everything must get better again. I expect both weal and woe,
I will see you again, so soon, so suddenly – but to have to find you
ill is terrible!'[1]

She must have been under great strain at this time, for there was
not just the worry about her demanding mother, who seemed to
be forever ill, but worse, the unrelenting financial pressures that
hung over both Julie and her cash-strapped parents. As an imperial
Russian grand duchess, even outside Russia, her position demanded

a certain level of accommodation and service appropriate to her station, which inevitably brought great expense. She did not wish to be a burden on her parents, but her ladies were, Julie said, 'such terrible *grandes dames*' and had high expectations too, but she had assured her parents that she would bring as small an entourage as possible.[2]

In early September 1801, the *Corriere Milanese* reported that Julie's cavalcade, after nearly a month on the road, had been met at the major crossing point of the Oder River at Küstrin by the Russian envoy to Courland, Baron Burkhard de Krudener. From there it was escorted to Berlin by a court official, Count von Voss, so that Julie could pay a brief visit to Queen Luise, whose husband, Friedrich Wilhelm, had acceded to the throne in 1797. The Prussian court had, at that time, been celebrating the centenary of the accession of Frederick the Great and the creation of the Kingdom of Prussia and had been welcoming numerous royal guests. Luise, of the house of Mecklenburg-Strelitz, was very taken with Julie and the visit marked the beginning of a close friendship. Julie thereafter became a popular visitor to the palace at Charlottenburg, which was Luise's preferred residence to that at Potsdam (the Neues Palais in Berlin being rarely used in this period).

After leaving Berlin, Julie was not able to travel directly to Coburg, for the ducal family were still living in the house on Steingasse while the refurbishment of the Ehrenburg Palace was being completed, overseen by her uncle Friedrich Josias. Instead, she was met by Franz, who escorted her to the family's secondary residence at Saalfeld, which accommodated them until the Ehrenburg was ready to stage a formal homecoming reception. Auguste was away in Bayreuth at that time, nursing her sister Princess Sophie Henriette of Leiningen on her deathbed. It was not until 12 September that the family were reunited in Saalfeld, where they spent the next month socialising, riding, walking, playing card games and marking Julie's twentieth birthday on the 23rd.

On the afternoon of 22 October, the family finally proceeded to Oeslau in the northeast suburbs of Coburg, where they were greeted by large crowds and proudly escorted to the Ehrenburg Palace by

Friedrich Josias in the company of 'dragoons ... postillions, the local and the Neustadter rifles, the jaegers, the equerries and scholars, the princes', and the rest of the huge retinue.[3] A laudatory poem written for Auguste's birthday in January that year by Moritz von Thümmel, a courtier and sentimental poet, had spoken of how the duchess's 'eyes long for Anna', whom she still saw as 'a child – as Jülchen / Creeping through our fir trees after a butterfly'. Another verse appeared in Coburg on the very day of her arrival back in her homeland: 'She comes! ... Ruthenia's princess comes ... Ah, our Jülchen is here!'[4]

Despite the family celebrations, Julie's parents were highly ambivalent about her return and justifiably anxious about the prospect of maintaining not just her – in a specially furnished fifteen-room apartment at the Ehrenburg – but her entourage too. Duchess Auguste bewailed the problems to the new Coburg finance minister, a Prussian martinet named Theodor Kretschmann, recently appointed by Duke Franz to sort out their perilous finances. Referring to Julie's flight from Russia and the concomitant shame of her failed marriage as 'the catastrophe from the North', she contemplated Julie's impending return with nothing short of horror. It 'stands like a storm cloud before me; my heart bleeds that I cannot look forward to this with pleasure,' she told Kretschmann.[5]

Julie's father had, on 8 September 1800, inherited the dukedom upon the death of his father, Ernst Friedrich, and with this new burden he had even more reason to worry about the sorry state of the public purse. These concerns no doubt prompted the forthright Auguste to seek financial assurances from Tsar Alexander, who responded in a conciliatory and supportive letter on 11 September that 'I have the very best wishes for you as well as my sister-in-law whom I cherish from the bottom of my heart ... I have no doubt that Your Highness is also firmly persuaded that my only desire is to contribute to your happiness in any way that is within my power to give.' Shortly afterwards Alexander's 'contribution' was clarified: it was reported in the German press that Julie's 'illustrious brother-in-law' 'has given her the considerable sum of 80,000 rubles in annual maintenance'.*[6]

Alexander wrote again to Auguste in April the following year, emphasising that 'my sister-in-law will receive exactly the same rights and privileges as she has received in Russia, and my Mother and I are both absolutely of the same opinion as Your Highness that it will be preferable that my sister-in-law should make her home henceforth at Coburg with all the financial support as befits her station.'[7] Is there the suggestion here of a joint decision to keep Julie out of harm's and scandal's way in the obscurity of Coburg? For some time to come her name would appear in the official almanacs of the Russian court but no public announcement was made of her separation from Konstantin, or that her absence from Russia was permanent.

In the Russian State Archives (GARF) there is a cache of thirteen hastily scribbled letters that Julie sent to Maria Feodorovna from Coburg during those first months out of Russia, which maintain the pretence that she had left on another extended visit to her sick mother. It is clear from their evasive content that she was trying to spin things out for as long as she could without arousing suspicion – both with the Russians and maybe with her parents too. Even at a distance Maria Feodorovna exerted her power over Julie, as a stickler for the correct observation of family duty. Time and again Julie begged the dowager's forbearance, that she needed to '*prolonger mon séjour*' to Coburg all the time her poor mother was so unwell and a source of so much *inquiétude*. She played the dutiful daughter-in-law to the hilt – sending greetings for birthdays and her thanks for presents received, kissing Maria Feodorovna's hands in gratitude, enquiring about her health and perpetually apologising for not writing very much, or very often. If enquiries about her return to Russia were made, the response from Julie seems to have been that *maman* was *très souffrante* but that she herself was now suffering from *des maux de tête insupportables*, which were the reason for

---

*   It is extremely hard to compute a modern equivalent, but 80,000 rubles in 1801 were certainly worth in excess of £1.4 million today.

the *barbouillage* and *griffonage* of her letters. All she could do was grovel and prevaricate frantically, piling on the faux humility and her *attachement le plus respectueux et le plus sincère* to her *chère Maman*. But there is not a word about her intention of returning to Russia and within about six months the letters ceased.[8]

None of this obfuscation by Julie could mollify the disdain and despair of her sister Antoinette.[9] She had good reason to be concerned, for she was now married to Maria Feodorovna's brother, Duke Alexander of Württemberg, after having been given a modest wedding at the Hofkirche in Coburg – a far cry from the lavish ceremony for Julie in the Winter Palace. Fortunately for the Coburg family, the debacle of the Julie–Konstantin marriage had not deterred the Romanovs from establishing another marital link with them, or the Coburg family from continuing to look to Russia for support. The Duke of Württemberg was, however, hardly a catch. A 'shockingly ugly', uncouth and gluttonous man, he was renowned for his avarice.[10] The beautiful Antoinette had no love for him, but his prospects were on the up and up now that he had transferred from the Austrian to the Russian imperial army. Although the couple initially lived at the Württemberg summer residence at Schloss Fantaisie near Bayreuth, Duke Alexander was appointed governor general of Livonia, Courland and Estonia in 1800 and was for most of the time thereafter based in Mitau (now Jelgava, Latvia). Antoinette disliked living there and in 1803 the couple moved to St Petersburg. In the Russian capital she imperiously rode out the gossip about her sister's departure to become close friends with her sister-in-law Maria Feodorovna. From this favoured position Antoinette worked assiduously on advancing the cause of her Coburg brothers, Ernst and Leopold, while remaining highly judgemental of Julie.[11]

Julie's life back in Coburg, separated from all the attendant luxuries of the Romanov court, must have rapidly palled with its parochial limitations. But in the spring of 1802, it would appear that she had other, serious preoccupations. A story persists, based on comments made in a letter by Queen Luise of Prussia of 18 May 1802, that

Julie had recently given birth. Writing to her brother Georg, who was living in Italy at the time, Luise told him that 'Anna was happily delivered, and the child was brought to a village in Franconia.'* Then she added, somewhat cryptically, 'What a fate for an imperial and grand ducal child. He should have something – along with the others – out of it.'[12] To be born some time in early May 1802 – depending on how quickly the news reached Queen Luise – the child would presumably have been conceived shortly before or just after Julie's departure from Russia in mid-August 1801. He could not, surely, have been Konstantin's, for the couple were entirely alienated from each other and if he had been he would have been third in line to the Russian throne, so hardly likely to be concealed. But what opportunity would there have been, in the turbulent days after the murder of Tsar Paul, for Julie to have been able to resume her supposed affair with Ivan Linev, who seems the only other obvious candidate?

The allusion to the child having royal status has prompted a researcher in Hungary to claim that he was fathered by Julie's brother-in-law, Alexander, and that the absence of all further evidence of the boy in Germany is explained by the fact that he was brought up in Hungary under the name Sandor Vajda, Sandor being the affectionate form of Alexander and Vajda being the surname of his adoptive parents.[13] There certainly is tenuous evidence that Julie and Alexander's affectionate friendship, and his deep admiration of her, had brought them perhaps too close during her years in Russia. Add to that Alexander and Elise's undisguised and growing indifference to each other and the close proximity in which the two couples were living at the Winter Palace in the spring and summer of 1801 after abandoning the Mikhailovsky, and there is opportunity enough for Julie and Alexander to perhaps have had a brief sexual encounter. But it is also apparent that by the spring of 1801 Alexander was

---

*   The location is vague, for Franconia is a geographical region of Germany that was once a duchy of the Holy Roman Empire and extended across Hesse, Thuringia, Bavaria and Baden-Württemberg. Coburg was located just inside the border of Upper Franconia.

deeply smitten by one of Elise's ladies, Princess Maria Naryshkina. Although their affair did not become sexual until 1803, Naryshkina was known to be Alexander's abiding passionate preoccupation for many years, and he later had several illegitimate children by her.

There is only one tantalising clue that offers support to the idea of a secret pregnancy. It comes in December 1802 from Julie's fifteen-year-old sister Victoire, who, writing to Renette, now back in St Petersburg with her mother, made a telling comment. Julie, she told her, was 'so much healthier and happier this winter than the last one', adding that during that winter of 1801–2 'she had had to be shut up in her room all the time', the implication being that she had been suffering one of her regular bouts of ill health and was unable to see people. But could this have been to conceal an advancing pregnancy? Julie's apartments at the Ehrenburg were certainly extensive enough for her to have been well separated from the family.[14]

There is a gap in any letters to, from, or about Julie in the period November 1801 to April 1802, except for the cursory letters that she wrote to Maria Feodorovna which are devoid of personal detail bar her headaches, though the prevarication over a return to Russia in itself might suggest she was staying away for a very good reason. Nor is there any comment by anyone in Julie's immediate orbit other than Victoire to suggest what might have happened: where exactly the child was born and when, and what became of him, beyond Queen Luise saying he had been taken to a village in the vicinity. But the feint of illness is something that was applied by Auguste to conceal a later pregnancy of Julie's and she must have been privy to the arrival of this child, as too would Julie's close companion, Madame de Renne.

The suggestion by Laszlo Vajda that Julie could have disappeared, entirely on her own, to an obscure castle in Bohemia to have her baby there in secret simply does not hold water. First, as a Russian grand duchess the protocols attached to her status would never have allowed her to do so unaccompanied – Julie always travelled with a considerable retinue; and second, Alexander had allowed her to leave Russia on the strict understanding that she would live quietly at Coburg. What evidence there is in Victoire's and other letters, as well as the diary of Friedrich Josias at that time, make it clear that Julie was most definitely back in Coburg during the period September 1801 to July 1802 bar one or two brief trips; her presence at Saalfeld prior to that is also confirmed in letters written by Sophie de Campenhausen to Madame de Renne when she was there with Julie; by newspaper reports, such as the *Journal de Francfort*, which confirmed she was 'still in residence in Coburg' in March 1802; and by Kostgelder accounts in the Coburg Archives attesting to the maintenance costs of Julie's household from December.[15]

So the puzzle remains – did Julie give birth to a child in the spring of 1802 in secret at Coburg and is it remotely possible that this child was indeed the son of Alexander I? If so, as a prince of the blood, why would he have been spirited off to Hungary to be adopted and brought up there, living out his life as a teacher named Sandor Vajda, who died in 1879 at Rimaszecs (now Rimavská Seč, Slovakia)? Julie never made any allusion to him in any surviving letters, nor did Alexander, nor did her sister-in-law and confidante Elise; and even Queen Luise, who first noted the story, made no further reference to the child. In later years Alexander categorically declared that his sister-in-law's reason for quitting Russia was 'because her health had been entirely destroyed'.[16] Might this have been part of the cover for Julie's pregnancy and her hasty departure?

That first year back in Coburg must have been very difficult for Julie: soon after the supposed birth of the child, she lost her close ally Madame de Renne – who returned to St Petersburg in August 1802 with Renette – and was left with no one to confide in. She had little social life beyond trips with her mother and Victoire to Karlsruhe and the baths at Bad Homburg near Frankfurt, or visits to the Württembergs at Schloss Fantaisie. Julie's primary concern was to stay in touch with Elise, Renne and Renette in Russia for they were her lifeline and had 'a special place in my heart'. She spent days on end 'killing' herself – so she told Renne – feverishly writing long and often distracted stream-of-consciousness letters to them and to

Elise.[17] The letters are full of often petty distractions, such as worry about missing the courier, forgetting to put letters in envelopes, the late arrival of money from Russia, problems with a footman sent from Russia by Antoinette, or the inadequacies of local Coburg dressmakers and drapers. Julie sent to St Petersburg for gowns, hats and parasols; and needed a new Russian uniform for Jules-Gabriel de Seigneux, who could not be expected to carry on wearing his old Coburg court uniform. Even the black tea served in Coburg was bitter and she ordered green tea from Russia. But her inner life at the time remains a total mystery to us.[18]

Julie's hunger for letters, for news, was insatiable. Elise in Russia speaks of having a batch of letters delivered to Julie in Coburg via an intermediary, Countess Anna Protasova, in August 1802. But even as Julie's closest friend, she seems to have been mindful of the stigma of her ambivalent social status – as neither widow nor divorcee, and a runaway to boot. She admitted in a letter to her mother that 'everyone thinks that to go and see her would be to risk being thought badly of at court.' 'Poor Anne,' she added ruefully, 'her existence is sad indeed.'[19]

Shortly after Madame de Renne's departure, Julie hired a replacement lady in waiting, Charlotte von Schlammersdorf, known as Lotte. Although she was from an old noble German family, Lotte incurred the disapproval of both Elise and Antoinette, who had wanted Julie to hire a Russian and who rued the loss of the trustworthy – and perhaps watchful? – Renne. 'I cannot help regretting that the Grand Duchess has lost such a reasonable and sympathetic advisor in you,' Elise told Renne, when she was leaving Coburg. The two women had been discussing the fact that Julie was already begging Elise to help her obtain a divorce from Konstantin, presumably because she wished to marry Ivan Linev, who had left Russia for her sake. According to one of Julie's friends, he had 'loved her with a passion', but she was prevented from seeing him all the time she was living with her family and was intensely secretive about her relationship with him. As for being free to marry him, 'the formal divorce cannot take place so soon,' Elise had insisted to Renne. In

Russia there were an 'indescribable number of obstacles that oppose it' – not just political and moral, but also religious ones.[20]

After celebrating the birthdays of Sophie and Victoire on 16 and 17 August with a party and fireworks at the Ehrenburg, Julie, Lotte and Sophie, accompanied by Seigneux, went on an eight-day visit to Antoinette at Schloss Fantaisie, 54 miles southeast of Coburg, not far from Bayreuth. The castle, nicknamed 'Fantaisie' in 1763, had been inherited by Duchess Friederike von Württemberg in 1793. She had restored the palace and its park, creating a beautiful baroque garden with a pavilion, cascade and Fountain of Neptune. It had become a favourite of the Coburg family since Antoinette's marriage, and they were regular visitors, often using it as a staging point en route to the spa at Carlsbad.

Nearby Bayreuth was at the time very popular with Bavarian families as well as French emigrants. It was at Fantaisie, where the sisters loved to dance on the gleaming parquet floors of the White Hall, that Sophie had met her future husband, a French refugee named Emmanuel Mensdorff-Pouilly, in May 1800 when he was paying a visit to the Württembergs.[21] He had neither wealth nor noble status but was renowned for his courage. Since fleeing the French Revolution he had been serving as a cavalry captain in the Austrian army against Napoleon. As a man without family (his brother and parents were all dead) or a homeland, and a Catholic to boot, he was far from the ideal candidate. But Emmanuel was romantically good-looking, as paintings of him testify, and the family did not oppose the obvious and growing love between the two.[22]

The chance of some welcome cultural stimulus for Julie came at the end of October 1802 when Jean Paul, one of the notable writers of the German Romantic period and much admired by Julie's mother, took up residence in Coburg where he would remain for the next couple of years before moving to Bayreuth. The ducal family entertained him to dinner and it was all most congenial. Auguste was 'my most ardent reader', claimed Paul; he found them all charming and cultured and the 'Grand Duchess' (Julie) 'so beautiful'.[23] She no doubt enjoyed Paul's novels as much as her mother, for like those of Rousseau, they featured well-observed, high-minded female characters such as Clotilda, the poetic heroine of *Hesperus* (1795), with whom she could identify.[24] Long and complicated they may have been but these novels helped Julie to while away the tedious evenings in Coburg, along with her other great passion – music. In a letter to Renette in November 1802, Victoire excitedly told her how the family had all thrilled to the visit to the Ehrenburg of 'a great virtuoso', the fifteen-year-old prodigy Carl Maria von Weber. He had been on a concert tour and had stopped off in Coburg on his way home to Augsburg to play some of his piano pieces for them.

Victoire and Julie sang a lot together, she told Renette; they often made music all evening and held small concerts for the family on Sundays.[25] Recently, they had sung the trio from *Iphigénie en Tauride* by Gluck with a male member of the entourage, and had cajoled Sophie, Ernst and others into taking part in a new one-act comic opera, *Maison à vendre*.[26] They were planning an ambitious project for the winter: Cherubini's *Le Porteur d'eau*, another comic opera premiered in 1800, and were recruiting members of the family and household to sing the various roles. 'You can just imagine', Victoire wrote, that at first Julie was 'quite afraid of singing in front of many people', but they found her voice 'very pretty'. Indeed, singing made Julie seem even prettier, for when performing, 'her lovely face somehow obtains a charm all its own.'[27]

All these musical plans were interrupted when most of the family went down with measles early in 1803. Shortly before Auguste's birthday on 19 January, seventeen-year-old Ferdinand had fallen sick and was covered in nasty pustules. His siblings were not allowed to go near him but nevertheless they succumbed, Duke Franz too, who remained sick for the whole winter and whose hypochondria made him constantly fearful of imminent death. Julie had sat with Victoire to keep her company and read to her and soon fell very ill herself, with a severe fever, all of which she later described in great detail in a long letter to Madame de Renne in St Petersburg. She was afraid that she had lost her looks, but as Victoire noted, 'her mirror told her to the contrary.'[28]

Being laid so low by illness had perhaps been a catalyst for Julie to express her frustration at not being able to practise her religion. She had been back in Coburg for more than a year now and had not once been able to take Orthodox communion – a fact that members of her entourage had noticed. She remained obliged, as a Romanov grand duchess, to maintain an observance of the Russian court protocols into which she had married or her already difficult social position would be further compromised (hence the disapproval from Russia when she did not hire a Russian replacement for Madame de Renne). But there was no Russian Orthodox priest in the city to administer it to her. Could she not obtain permission for the priest who resided in Berlin to be sent to her? she asked Renne. Otherwise, she could perhaps go to Leipzig, which had a Russian Orthodox church and was nearer, to take holy communion at Easter. Would it be too much for word to be sent by the dowager empress in St Petersburg that the priest in Leipzig attend her at Coburg, and how much would she have to pay him?[29]

In June of 1803, Queen Luise of Prussia made a visit to Coburg and wrote to her brother that Julie was 'a delicious woman'. The sight of her 'is the biggest reproach for Constantine', she averred, and she was right: the grand duke's estranged wife was beautiful, clever and desirable – and still very young. Elise in Russia expressed precisely the same thoughts when she heard that Julie was in Strasbourg that September. She was still very pretty, so they said, and although Julie was now at an age when Elise felt she should not exploit her beauty, she admitted that 'with many ifs and buts, I wouldn't swear that the Grand Duke [Konstantin], on seeing her again, would not fall in love with her once more.'[30]

Konstantin, however, was pressing hard for a divorce, in order to facilitate a morganatic remarriage to his latest mistress, a Polish courtier named Zhanetta Grudzinskaya, the sister of Alexander's favourite, Princess Naryshkina. But the process would be a long and difficult one: there had been no divorces in the Russian imperial family since Peter the Great had banished his first wife Evdokiya and the subject was weighed down with a host of legal and constitutional difficulties. Maria Feodorovna, in upholding the strict ethical values of the Prussian royals, had always been a stickler for respect of conjugal duty and was implacably against the idea, even though her son Alexander had no great objection. When it came to protecting the dignity of the imperial Russian throne and the respect due to the late tsar Paul, the dowager was intransigent. Divorce would bring 'ruinous consequences for public morals as well as the lamentable and dangerous temptation for the entire nation'. It would undermine popular respect for the sanctity of marriage and for the Russian Orthodox faith itself. All the time that Konstantin was still married to Julie, her name would still be proclaimed in prayers for the imperial family in church. Konstantin should be 'a model of virtue for his subjects'; divorce would only undermine public confidence 'in our superiority, which together with the feeling of reverent respect, secures the tranquillity of the empire'.[31] Maria Feodorovna would only concede if he found himself a suitable royal candidate. 'Go to foreign lands and stay at the courts of different sovereign princes of Germany,' she exhorted him, 'and choose a bride who is in all respects worthy of you.'[32] Konstantin rejected the suggestion; he disliked German princesses, he insisted.

With divorce matters at a stalemate, during 1803 and 1804 Julie's life became even narrower when she lost the close companionship of her remaining two sisters. Jean Paul had visited again on 22 October and rhapsodised to a friend: 'Here you would not lack nourishment for the spirit, for there is hardly anything more beautiful than our three princesses.'[33] But that happy triumvirate of Sophie, Julie and Victoire was broken up on 21 December 1803, when the plump and pretty Victoire was ruthlessly married off aged sixteen to Emich Karl, Prince of Leiningen, who was thirty-nine years old and the widower of her late aunt Sophie – Auguste's sister, who had died only two years previously. Emich Karl, who had sided with the Austrian–German alliance against Napoleon, had recently taken refuge with his relatives in Coburg after the advancing French armies had attacked and burned down his palace at Durkheim and seized all his territories.[34]

The match was a disappointment to Auguste and Franz, who had nursed much greater ambitions for Victoire. The previous year Franz had nominated her as one of eighteen mainly German princesses on a list of possible replacements for the barren Josephine, when First Consul Napoleon began plotting to divorce her. But with only a slim dowry to offer, they were obliged to settle for 'an unextravagant and sensible compromise' in Émich Karl. Victoire's subsequent role at her home at Amorbach, where the couple were granted residence after the reconstitution of their territories in 1806,* was only too predictable – as a young and healthy brood mare to provide an heir for her childless husband.[35] She did not disappoint, producing a son almost precisely nine months after their wedding, but her marriage to an ill-tempered and bitter man who was frequently sick was a matter of endurance rather than joy.

Sophie, Franz and Auguste's eldest child, born in 1788, was still unmarried at the age of twenty-six, which was very late indeed for a woman of noble birth. Prince Albert's biographer later suggested that she had refused 'many eligible proposals of marriage of her own rank', holding out for a love match, which she appears to have found with Emmanuel Mensdorff-Pouilly. Less generous versions of the story suggest that she had accepted him as a last resort. Be that as it may, in choosing a Frenchman, Sophie adopted Catholicism upon her marriage on 23 February 1804 and despite its lower status and her sister Antoinette's disapproval (what would the dowager empress think? she said to Madame de Renne), it would prove successful and happy, marred only by Sophie's persistent ill health.[36]

In early May 1804 Julie travelled to the Charlottenburg Palace at Potsdam with her twenty-year-old brother Ernst to visit Queen Luise, 'trying to forget about her troubles' and, as Luise told her husband Friedrich, because she 'hopes for your support in her miserable

---

* Emich Karl was awarded the property as compensation for the loss of his ancestral palace during the French invasion. The Benedictine abbey was secularised and a Lutheran royal court established there. But the principality of Leiningen went through many upheavals and changes over the next few years and was eventually incorporated into the kingdom of Bavaria.

affairs'.[37] Even the British press took note of her august presence there: the London *Star* of 24 May reported that on 8 May 'The Russian Grand Duchess, consort of the Grand Duke Constantine is arrived in Potsdam' and that apartments were being prepared for her in the palace.

By the time Julie left with Ernst on 20 June, returning to Coburg via Dresden, Luise had become deeply attached to her and was, like Elise in Russia, left with a 'dreadful emptiness' after she had gone. 'I don't think you need to be reminded of how much I love you and that I will always adore you,' she wrote to Julie. 'I am deeply grateful to know you so completely and love you so dearly; do always stay in touch with me ... God knows all I would have given just to keep you here longer,' she wrote on 21 June, adding, 'We were so intimately close that separating us was a cruel act of fate.' Indeed, Julie's popularity at the Prussian court, despite her jokingly being referred to as 'the Greek pagan' for her Russian Orthodox faith, had been such that her departure had left 'universal desolation ... in its wake'.* 'My ladies are mourning your charming presence,' Luise told her. The Prussian court must have been a most dull and sober place, for according to Luise the 'soulfulness, gaiety, pleasing talents [and] lovability' of Julie and her engaging entourage had transformed it during her and Ernst's visit.[38] The story goes that during this visit to Berlin, Konstantin attended a ball at the Prussian court where he caught sight of a 'beautiful Being', but when he drew closer to investigate, 'to the astonishment of the whole assembly, he instantaneously quitted the room in evident perturbation of mind – It was his wife, the much-injured Grand Duchess Anne. All the ignominy fell back upon him, & her situation excited the utmost sympathy wherever she went.'[39]

---

* Luise and Julie seem to have shared a natural vivacity that made them ideal friends. Sophie, queen of the Netherlands (the daughter of Julie's sister-in-law Ekaterina Pavlovna), later wrote of Luise that she was 'one of the greatest flirts that ever lived on the throne ... She was passionately fond of dress, dancing, every sort of amusement and dissipation ... She belonged to those few privileged persons who posterity has turned into a sort of poetic perdition' (Jackman and Haase, *Stranger in The Hague*, 351–2).

Undoubtedly the friendship and approval of Queen Luise herself were important in smoothing any objections to Julie's presence as a separated wife of dubious social status at the German court. They are a mark of Julie's very warm and vibrant personality and the depth of her close female attachments, at a time when she so badly needed them. In many ways Luise seems to have taken the place of the now more geographically distant Elise. Over in St Petersburg the increasingly sad and lonely empress clung to her cherished memories of her lost sister-in-law, telling her mother that the small study in which she wrote was 'consecrated to memories of cherished people' – her mother's bust; a portrait of Julie; and views of Kamenny Ostrov, where she had spent most of the summer of 1801 with her family visiting her from Baden. This small private space was her retreat and her refuge. It 'would always hold happy memories all my life, as well as regrets'.[40]

CHAPTER 9

'She Lives in the Most Perfect Oblivion'

Julie's visit to Queen Luise in Berlin had been a much-needed morale booster, which she had followed with a visit to Amorbach in September with her mother, to stand as godmother at the christening of Victoire's newborn son, Karl. But by the autumn of 1804 she was encountering serious financial problems; she had already borrowed from her father to cover the salaries of her staff – Lotte, Seigneux and her chambermaid – and was deeply embarrassed that she could not yet repay him. The profligate duke was very much under the thumb of his finance minister, Kretschmann, who had introduced a necessarily draconian overhaul of the Coburg finances in order to right the duchy's teetering economy, and Franz was badgering her to repay him.[1]

Julie's fourteen-year-old brother Leopold worried that her entourage, particularly the penniless Lotte, who proved also to be sickly, was a huge drain on her resources and that Tsar Alexander, who was footing the bill, might not approve.[2] But there was an additional problem: the monies he had awarded, generous though they might have sounded, had rarely arrived from Russia on time or in their entirety. Julie was 'greatly embarrassed' about all this, she told her father in a letter on 8 September 1804: the expensive social trip to Berlin had thrown her into a desperate situation. She was 'very short of money' and she begged him to wait a little longer. She was already trying to sell some of her diamonds in Frankfurt, a matter she had initiated with the help of Elise via her mother in Baden. All she could do 'to satisfy you as soon as possible' was to try to borrow money against their eventual sale. Auguste, too, was complaining to Antoinette in Russia, who sensed that Mama was 'not entirely pleased with [Julie]'. The stress was making Julie ill; the scribbly handwriting of her letter to Franz reflects her growing state of panic.[3]

In addition to all her pressing money worries, Julie was distressed by another ongoing and still unresolved issue – Ivan Linev. He had remained on the periphery of her life these last three years, but we don't know where he was or how often Julie met with him, if at all, or at what point their relationship ceased to be a sexual one. Julie's Swiss biographer Alville suggests Linev may have been residing in Strasbourg, in Alsace, 230 miles from Coburg, which would explain Julie's visit there the previous year. But by 1805 he appears to have had enough of being a long-distance lover, and with all hope gone of Julie obtaining a divorce any time soon to marry him – as seems to have been her original wish – he wanted to go home to Russia. Elise in Petersburg seems to have been privy to what was going on, having been there at the relationship's inception in Russia; she certainly is the only one to mention Linev by name in connection with Julie. She told her mother on 18 June 1804 that Linev had written to Alexander specifically asking to be allowed to return and resume his military career, 'with Anne's consent', Elise feeling 'that a young man cannot live in idleness, as he has been doing for the past three years'. But she feared that his return to Russia would cause trouble for the imperial family: 'I tremble for the moment when he appears again on the horizon; it will reawaken all the dormant gossip on this subject.'[4]

In fact, the pot was already being stirred in Russia by Antoinette, who could not resist taking swipes at Julie, despite conceding to Madame de Renne in a letter of 8 July 1805 that when her sister had been in Berlin the previous June she had been considered to be 'amazingly pretty and loveable' and had been extremely popular at court. But Julie, she thought, was 'not really happy but pretending she is; you know what a kind creature she is but also how heedless'. That heedlessness perhaps had been her downfall, for Antoinette could not resist an oblique reference to Linev and how because of him Julie's life had turned sour: 'When I think back over so many things I feel downright frightened by all that was sacrificed.' Julie's 'certain male friend', she noted, had now 'been as good as struck out of the list of the living; when I consider what the wretched plaything cost, the tranquillity of her life, the splendour and the agreeable nature of her situation'. Far worse in Antoinette's eyes, however, was 'the disgrace of her family' that this affair had caused; the Saxe-Coburgs had managed to survive the scandal but 'if only there were a way of contriving that all of that had never happened.'⁵

It is understandable therefore that for most of that year – from April to October 1805 – Julie hid herself away at Schloss Fantaisie to avoid the wagging tongues. Jean Paul, who was now residing in Bayreuth, saw her there and spoke with affection of her 'beautiful, childlike, but strong' presence.⁶ However, by November Julie's health had once more collapsed, her mother noting in her journal that 'for three days Jülchen has had the cramps again that two years ago brought her close to death, they were so violent that night. She lay there like a departing angel, the paragon of pain in every move of her beautiful face.' Her daughter's suffering tormented Auguste: 'Poor Jülchen! Your unfortunate life has, since childhood, been plagued by hardships.' She knew that it was her fault: 'It was I who led you toward your despair,' she admitted and she was mortified at the thought of all Julie had had to endure in the ten years since she had left her in that distant foreign land. Her daughter was 'lovely and clever', but she feared that her vulnerable nature would always lead her 'good heart' astray and it would be a long time before she found peace.*⁷

Julie's innate kind-heartedness can be seen in the letter she made

---

* It is important to note that these highly self-recriminatory comments by Auguste in her journal were redacted from the only published edition, translated by Queen Victoria's daughter Beatrice and published in 1941. Beatrice took it upon herself to heavily censor many of the entries that refer to Julie, but an original full transcript can be consulted at the Royal Archives at Windsor.

the effort to write to Alexander in Russia on Linev's behalf. She told him how unwell she had been again and was a 'poor invalid' who was grateful to receive word from her 'dear Alex': 'permit me to continue to still call you this,' she asked in excessively reverential tones, for she could not bring herself to address him formally. A letter she had recently received from Alexander had proved to her 'that I have not been entirely erased from your memory'. She was sorry that her illness had prevented them from meeting when he was in Berlin and Dresden, for she longed to see him as soon as she was recovered: 'Please send me two words to agree a place where we can meet where I could rejoice with happiness at seeing you again.'[8]

But that was not why she was writing: 'It is for a Friend that I address my prayers to you. It has been a year since I've seen Lin[ev], and he has constantly written to me about his desire to re-enter your service – other events prevented it – and he has joined the staff of General Mickelsonn instead.'* The general had told Linev that he needed Alexander's approval to return to Russia and Julie begged 'dear Alex' now to 'show your goodness and not abandon him! I know that he has no recourse to your protection other than as one to whom you are sincerely and inviolably attached.' The letter confirms that Julie's relationship with Linev was over: 'It is a brother whom I recommend to you who has for a long time ceased to press his advantage to me,' she told Alexander. 'Believe that you have a true friend in me.'

Considering Julie's warmth and demonstrable love and loyalty

---

* General Ivan Michelson – a Baltic German also known as Johann von Michelsohnen – had played a major role in the suppression of the Pugachev Rebellion of 1773–5. He was commander of Russian forces on the western borders holding back encroaching Turkish forces on the Danube. So Linev was a long way from Julie before he even returned to Russia to join the military campaign against Napoleon. For his combat with the Sumsky Hussars during the battles of 1807 he was awarded the Gold Sword for bravery. In 1813, he left the army with the rank of colonel and retired to the family estate of Dubrovo-Linevo in Ustyuzhensky district, which he had inherited from his father, where he later married and had children. He died there on 3 February 1840.

to Alexander it is disappointing to discover that his sister in Weimar was exchanging less than charitable remarks about Julie in her correspondence with her mother Maria Feodorovna in St Petersburg at this time. Their comments, made in barely concealed code by switching into Russian from their usual mix of French and German, talked disparagingly of 'V.K.' (*velikaya knyagina*, grand duchess) – with Maria Pavlovna observing pityingly in March 1806 that Julie now lived 'in the most perfect oblivion'.[9] Perhaps this was why Julie seemed so anxious for their approval and had written to her sister-in-law in Weimar asking to meet. But Maria Pavlovna told her mother she found Julie 'supremely unpleasant' and wished to have nothing to do with her. One can only infer that the reason for this is linked to Maria Pavlovna's revelation to her mother that 'the King was very in love with V.K.' – the allusion being to King Friedrich Wilhelm of Prussia – and that for this reason Julie's relationship with Queen Luise had cooled.[10] Maria Feodorovna in Russia had pumped her daughter for more on the subject, to be told that when Queen Luise had become aware that her husband was infatuated, she had been 'deeply embarrassed' and had also been upset that people in Berlin had found Julie more beautiful than her. And yet she had not broken with her; they were still writing to each other.[11]

The uncertainties of her life and her anomalous social position were about to get much worse for Julie with dramatic political changes taking place in 1806 as the European monarchies found themselves sucked into a rapidly developing conflict with Napoleon Bonaparte. In 1799, having overthrown the Directory, the French revolutionary government that had seized power in 1795, and still only a young general in the French army, Napoleon had proclaimed himself first consul of France. There was no limit to his hubris: in December 1804 he crowned himself emperor at Notre Dame Cathedral and the following year embarked on a mission to put an end to revolutionary anarchy and re-establish law and order in France under his authoritarian rule. As emperor he now considered himself on a par with the heads of two other great military powers: the soon to be defunct Holy Roman Empire and Russia.[*]

Britain was alerted to Napoleon's territorial ambitions in 1803 and in defence of its trade in the colonies had declared war on France, in 1805 launching a devastating naval campaign against the French under Lord Nelson, which culminated at Trafalgar in October. Napoleon thereafter switched strategy, having already decided two months earlier to concentrate his campaign on land with the creation of a vast new conscript *Grande Armée*. But to confront his enemies he had to march this army east, crossing the Rhine and invading the German territories. En route he achieved a major victory against the allied forces of Russia and Austria in a closely fought battle at Austerlitz (now Slavkov u Brna in Czechia) on 2 December 1805.

It was a difficult time politically for beleaguered Saxe-Coburg-Saalfeld. The family was very reliant on Russian patronage, as was Prussia, but since 1781 Russia had turned away from the old Russo-Prussian alliance that had prevailed earlier in the eighteenth century and had now aligned with Austria, leaving Prussia increasingly out in the cold. For the Coburgers, loyalties were divided between fellow German states which supported the Austrian–Prussian alliance and Russia under Tsar Alexander I. Julie's brother Ferdinand had followed his uncle Friedrich Josias into the Austrian army and service with the Hussars, but Ernst and Leopold had been earmarked since childhood for careers in the Russian army and had already received considerable preferment from the tsar. In 1805 these two brothers – with Leopold now elevated to the rank of general – had set off for Moravia to take up their military posts, only to arrive at Russian army HQ just after the battle of Austerlitz.

In the spring of 1806 Duchess Auguste contemplated the family's fears: 'Poor Germany, what will thy fate yet be, given over to the caprices of a despot, who recognises no limit to his own lust for power, and to whom all means are justifiable to gratify his passion . . .

---

[*]   In response to Napoleon's declaration, the Hapsburg king of Austria, Francis II, declared his collective lands to be the Austrian Empire.

what future can my poor devastated country expect, she who once in olden days defied the Roman Eagle!'[12] She knew that the storm was now 'creeping over Saxony' and Germany's future lay in the hands of a 'successful adventurer, who founds his greatness on destruction'.[13] In July 1806 sixteen of the German states were forcibly united under Napoleonic 'protection' with the creation of the Confederation of the Rhine, and the following month thousands of French troops began pouring into Germany. By September they were approaching Coburg, prompting Julie's parents, after much agonising, to hastily pack and flee north to their residence in Saalfeld. They were installed there with Leopold by 2 October where they were joined on the 7th by Sophie and Emmanuel Mensdorff-Pouilly with their baby Hugo.

But Julie did not go with them; nor did Ernst, who had chosen to fight with the Prussians, for a reluctant King Friedrich Wilhelm had finally been persuaded by his more politically astute wife Luise that Prussia could no longer afford to remain neutral and had joined the coalition forces of Russia, Austria and Britain. Meanwhile, the Coburg family, who had assumed they would be safe from the encroaching hostilities in the Thuringian Forest, realised that they had in fact fled straight into the war zone.[14] At Saalfeld, they watched the Prussian regiments march by in the valley, heading for confrontation with the French, who had now occupied Coburg, 50 miles away. Soon they could see great fires burning in the French encampment beyond Saalfeld. The following morning, 10 October 1806, the family awoke to the sound of a barrage of muskets. They crowded at the windows to watch as, against the noise of booming cannons and volleys of infantry, they saw the French advancing out of the Thuringian Forest and down the hillside.[15]

It must have been a terrifying sight for there were 12,800 Napoleonic forces moving in three columns across the forest and heading for the River Saale, to be taken on by the much smaller Prussian–Saxon contingent of 8,300 – consisting of a mounted battery and two Saxon infantry regiments – led by Prince Louis Ferdinand of Prussia. These men valiantly attempted to block the French march on the city from six in the morning until two in the afternoon. Auguste later wrote of the 'terrible blood-curdling din that was kept up by drums and bugles' as cannon balls 'whistled past quite close to the Schloss, and yet no-one would come away from the window to which we were as if glued'.[16]

The Prussian troops could not hold the line against such superior forces and were viciously routed, the French losing only 200 men. Prince Louis was mortally wounded but refused to surrender. His naked corpse, wrapped in a cloth, was eventually brought into the castle courtyard with the wounded. Emmanuel Mensdorff-Pouilly was distraught, having been a close friend of the prince, and ensured that the body was taken away and reverentially laid out in the church with a crown of laurels placed on his head. Not long after, residents of the local town arrived, 'begging for aid against the excesses of the troops', for the French were now running riot, robbing and pillaging.[17]

The family set off back to Coburg soon after – passing the battlefield strewn with bodies not yet buried and seeing the depredations visited on local villagers by the invaders. 'Terror still stood in the faces of the poor peasants,' recalled a member of the entourage. 'Duke Franz shared out all the money he had among them' as they passed through village after village that had been sacked, their 'inconsolable inhabitants weeping in front of their devastated homes'.[18] As the group passed through Gräfenthal they heard news of a further engagement at nearby Jena-Auerstadt, on 14 October, in which Ernst had taken part and which had ended in catastrophe for the Prussians. Auguste was distraught: they had been 'beaten at every point, pushed back and entirely split up'.[19] It was a terrible time for the Prussian royal family; Queen Luise's health had been bad during the winter of 1805–6, after the loss of her baby son Ferdinand, but nevertheless she had joined Friedrich Wilhelm on campaign in Thuringia. But with the defeat at Jena-Auerstadt the couple had fled into East Prussia and across the River Oder, eventually heading north to Memel, from where they sought the protection of Alexander I.

Auguste recorded with dramatic finality in her journal on

7 November that 'Germany's ancient Princely Houses must now bend their proud necks under [Napoleon's] iron sceptre.' On 15 December 1806, Saxe-Coburg-Saalfeld – along with Saxe-Weimar, Saxe-Gotha, Saxe-Meiningen and Saxe-Hilburghausen – was incorporated by Napoleon into the Confederation of the Rhine. Prince Leopold noted in a letter to his brother-in-law Mensdorff-Pouilly how grave the situation was for his parents; unlike his own cautious self, they were not frugal. His father, in a spate of irresponsible spending, had, to Leopold's horror, recently bought a monkey and two birds 'and this at a time when we don't know whether we ourselves will have enough to live on if Kretschmann does not show good will'.[20]

French occupation forces would remain in Coburg for another eight months, during which time the duchy was greatly impoverished; all its revenues were sequestrated in November and the financial indemnities were colossal, with Saxe-Coburg forced to pay 981,000 francs to Napoleon. The ducal family became heavily reliant on their servants to obtain the supplies they needed and Auguste was right to dread how her husband's frail health would withstand the stress. In early December he collapsed with a high fever and on the 9th Duke Franz died in Coburg, broken-hearted at the depredations that war had wreaked on his homeland. In view of the absence of his heir, Ernst, who had fallen seriously ill with typhus in December while with the Prussian army in Königsberg, the French installed an administrator known as an *intendant* as military governor.[21]

But where had Julie been all this time? In September 1806, shortly before the French invasion, and loath to be stranded in the backwater of Coburg now that her two sisters had left home, she had left on an extended visit to Prague, where Sophie was living. She was joined there by Auguste at the end of February the following year, who noted that Julie was living in 'cheerful quarters on the Promenade in the new part of town'.[22] Auguste had been attempting to get to Warsaw to beg Napoleon's intercession over the continuing French occupation of Coburg but had only got as far as Berlin before being told that he had left the city. So she had turned back and headed to

Prague instead to join Julie. She stayed for a fortnight, grateful for the 'peace and order which reigned in my dear Julie's house', a most congenial residence that she found so soothing after the turmoil and grief of the previous months in Coburg.[23] Auguste declared she had 'not been this happy for a long time, so joyfully free of concerns . . . God's blessing be upon you dear Jülchen who so loves creating joy!'

Soon after, Ferdinand arrived on leave from his Hungarian garrison, and by early March they received news that Ernst had recovered and was on his way home. But Schloss Ehrenburg, when Auguste returned, seemed a lonely and forbidding place in the absence of all her children except Leopold. The 'old paternal home' was 'empty and lifeless' until Victoire arrived with her baby son on a visit in April and they spent some happy days together at her little country retreat at Ketschendorf just south of Coburg.[24]

In August of 1807, Julie travelled to the spa town of Liebenwerda, 120 or so miles north of Prague, to take the waters for yet another bout of illness. It is from here that she wrote an extremely impassioned and heartfelt letter to her 'very dear cousin' Friedrich Wilhelm – a rare surviving piece of evidence, long hidden in the Russian State Archives, of the depth of feeling that Julie for the most part had to keep hidden from view. Her opening words were an expression of the 'profound sorrow' she felt at 'the picture of [Friedrich Wilhelm's] nation's misfortunes', in reference to the recent treaty concluded at Tilsit at which Napoleon and Alexander had carved up much of Europe between them, leaving Austria and Prussia humiliated.[25] Friedrich Wilhelm and a pregnant Queen Luise had both attended and been forced to witness Prussia – despite Luise's desperate pleas to Napoleon – being hit with savage war indemnities. The king was also forced to cede vast swathes of Prussian territory in the Polish provinces for the creation of a new Grand Duchy of Warsaw, to be controlled by Napoleon through his ally the king of Saxony.

For Julie, and despite her strong attachment to Tsar Alexander, Friedrich Wilhelm's defeat was a tragedy; she was sorry she was a mere woman, she told him, and only had her tears to offer him. He was 'a martyr to the good cause', but she was sure that 'this crown of thorns will yet change into one of laurels, into a crown of flow-ers'.[26] For now, however, 'Germany is lost,' she admitted; she was in mourning for the 'ravages' that the French administration had wrought on her Coburg home. Her preoccupation with Friedrich Wilhelm's situation ran very deep, and, as she emphasised in heavy underlining, her feelings remained <u>unalterable</u>: 'I would be able to contain them, if necessary, but never deny them and I repeat it to you again here. Your friendship is my happiness and my glory; take it away from me? Never! You would wound my heart beyond repair, but I will continue to cherish You in silence.'

Julie poured out her feelings here in ways that suggest their rela-tionship had been, and still was – for her at least – a very precious one. There were 'emotions in the soul', she explained, that were 'dif-ficult to express', but which hinted of love. Julie clearly felt unable to go into the details in a letter that might be read by unwelcome eyes, but at some point between her first visit to Berlin in 1804 and 1807 it would seem that she and the Prussian king might well have had an affair or at the least had forged a deep romantic attachment.[27] Her sister-in-law Maria Pavlovna was certainly convinced of it.

At the end of July 1807 news had come that Coburg was to be restored to the family, 'owing to Russia's kindly intervention', as Auguste noted.[28] Mercifully the duchy had retained its sovereignty and had avoided being forcibly absorbed into one of the bigger German states such as nearby Bavaria. It has been suggested that Julie had privately addressed an appeal to Alexander to argue Coburg's case with Napoleon; she may well have done so, given her mother's failed attempt.[29] On 28 July, Ernst returned to the city in a triumphant processional, to a barrage of church bells and cannons, to take up his dukedom.

In mid-September, just as he and Leopold set off to Paris to pay dutiful homage to Napoleon, Julie returned to Coburg from Prague after a year's absence. In the event, Napoleon was not in Paris when the brothers arrived. Neither of them hurried back but spent their time while waiting to attend the emperor enjoying the city's carnal pleasures – to Ernst's eventual cost.* Back home, their incorrigible matchmaker mother, despite the disaster of Julie's Russian marriage, was busily fostering another Romanov alliance – this time between Ernst and the tsar's fourteen-year-old sister Anna Pavlovna. Alexander approved of the match but his mother, who had absolute power in the final decision, was implacably opposed to it, having a pathological dislike of the Saxe-Coburgs. Undaunted, Ernst set off for St Petersburg in August to claim Anna's hand, 'which was promised to him when he was still too young', according to Leopold. 'Ah, the journey could be so important for him,' Auguste wrote in her journal, 'the foundation of his life's happiness or it could shatter it forever.' Was Julie's fate in her mind as she wrote it? If so she was, nevertheless, willing to take the risk.[30]

---

* In Paris Ernst became embroiled in an affair with a woman named Pauline Panam, who followed him back to Coburg where she subsequently fell pregnant. He tried to fob her off with promises of getting Julie to take her on as a lady in waiting. Julie very quickly 'dispelled his illusions' and did nothing to help Ernst in advancing his sexual adventures, which reminded her too much of Konstantin's behaviour. Panam sought revenge for being brutally discarded and in Paris in 1823 published her *Mémoires d'une jeune grecque*, which caused a sensation, not to mention considerable grief and enduring embarrassment for Ernst and his family. In the end, the wily Auguste finally saw Panam off, warning: 'I am indulgent but vengeance is in my power' (Nisbet, *Caroline Bauer and the Coburgs*, 33). Panam's son Ernst August was allowed to use the surname von Saxe-Coburg-Saalfeld but died at the age of only twenty-three.

CHAPTER 10

'SOME THINGS OF WHICH I
DO NOT WISH TO SPEAK'

Not long before the fortunes of Saxe-Coburg were recovered and
the family began rebuilding their lives, Julie found herself once
more in a state of crisis. Sometime around the end of January or
beginning of February 1808, she fell pregnant. With her life so
socially circumscribed, and – aside from her small entourage – only
her mother and brother Ferdinand for company at home in Coburg,
there is only one possible candidate as father of the child. Julie's
40-year-old chamberlain, the domineering Jules-Gabriel-Emile de
Seigneux, about whom sources tell us virtually nothing until now,
appears to have gained ascendancy over her at a time when she was
lonely, depressed and extremely vulnerable. Linev had returned
to Russia; her object of adoration, Friedrich Wilhelm, was out of
reach. At twenty-seven she had no hope of divorcing and remarrying, of having a genuine relationship free of scandal, or of having
children born of a legitimate union.

How galling it must have been for her, now that her sisters were
all married and happily producing babies and showing them off
to their grandmother, that she had to conceal her own expected
child's existence, in the certain knowledge that she would not
be able to keep it. But was she seduced or willingly complicit?

The Polish socialite Countess Rosalie Rszewska, who later met Seigneux, spoke of him as having developed a passion for Julie 'as intense as it was tyrannical'. Without close friends to warn or advise, Julie had initially been flattered by his devotion only to be quickly swallowed up by the oppressiveness of his controlling personality. This resulted in Seigneux dominating over all her personal and financial affairs, and, as Rszewska put it, led to 'a long subjugation with very little happiness'.[1]

The Seigneux family were from the Vaud aristocracy of Lausanne in Switzerland, though they had originally emigrated there from Savoy. Jules-Gabriel – or 'Seigneux the Younger' as he was referred to by Julie initially – had been appointed to her household through the recommendation of his distant cousin Emile Seigneux, who also appears to have been employed by Julie until his retirement in 1802. When she visited home, Antoinette, a sharp judge of character, had taken a strong dislike to both men, finding them 'repellent' and not fitting for their situation in Julie's entourage.[2]

Prior to joining Julie's household as its head, or major-domo, Seigneux the Younger had seen service in the Prussian army and was married with three children. But while on a visit home to Lausanne in October 1803 he had mortally wounded a friend named de Crouzaz in a pistol duel and had been forced to flee back to Coburg under cover of night and implore Julie's protection. In his absence, he was condemned to five years in jail by a tribunal in Lausanne. His wife separated from him soon afterwards and they were divorced in 1805; Seigneux now invested his energies in his new mistress in a manner that Julie seems to have been unable to control.[3]

In the spring of 1808, all the welcome respite that Julie had enjoyed during her quiet year of recovery in Prague was overturned by the anxiety of her pregnancy and the pressure not only to conceal it, but – as a grand duchess still married to a husband who was in Russia – to find somewhere safe and out of sight where she could give birth. In the meantime, as her pregnancy advanced, she chose to spend time in quiet seclusion in the small private garden, with its own little house once owned by the Wangenheims that she had purchased from her father in November 1803, where she could indulge her love of flowers. It was created from a section of the Coburg Hofgarten located between the Schlossplatz and the Veste.[4] Otherwise her life at home with Auguste was an uneventful round of walks, dinners, card games and family chitchat, and avoidance of any overt discussion of the truth of her desperate situation. But her mother clearly knew and was weighed down with worry, as she confided to her journal on 28 June: 'Oh Julie, your picture merges so painfully in the confused images of the future!' Her precious daughter seemed to her 'more forlorn, more ill today, and my tears flow uncontrollably'. But even here in her private journal, Auguste admitted that there were 'some things of which I do not wish to speak or to write' that 'press on my poor heart'.[5] But not for long: worries about the war and the continuing march of Napoleon soon distracted her, for her dear son Ferdinand, now promoted to colonel, was going off to fight with Count Blankenstein's Hussars.

On 6 July 1808 Auguste recorded Julie's early morning departure for Switzerland, the family having been told she was going to spend the summer and autumn there 'for her health'. It was Seigneux who apparently found the residence where Julie would live in absolute privacy for the next three to four months. He had been told of an elegant but unpretentious and secluded property that had come up for rental near Lake Geneva.[6] Known as the Villa Belle Rive, it had been built in 1710 and was tucked away below the main carriage road, just up from the south bank of the lake. Directly on the water nearby lay the small but bustling town of Cologny; Geneva was 2 miles further south along the lakeside. It was 'a plain, quadrangular, three-storied mansion of moderate dimensions' with green shuttered windows, fronted by a colonnade and with a balcony that ran round three sides of the first floor. Its front façade offered a fine view across the lake with the Jura Mountains beyond and was surrounded by pleasant vineyards sloping down to the water's edge.*[7] Inside, the rooms were 'light, with enormous windows, and studiously decorated in a style, which, if not quite over-ambitious in taste, was, at least, unobtrusive: polite Louis XV décor in the salon, sculpted panels in the bedrooms (woodland motifs, squirrels and oak leaves), and an ante-chamber hung with dark paintings of fallen stags and forgotten battles'.[8]

In Romanov terms Belle Rive would never have passed muster as good enough for a grand duchess, but the house was an ideal hideaway. Or so Julie hoped. Alas, word soon got out about the mysterious 'Russian princess' who was resident there, about whom nothing was known and who 'doesn't see anyone'. When Julie did once venture forth in town for a theatre performance it was noticed that she had a 'very sad' air about her. The French writer Benjamin Constant, who was staying in Cologny at the time, eventually discovered that the lady was apparently waiting for instructions from St Petersburg on the correct protocols that she should observe in Swiss society as a Russian grand duchess and until a response arrived from Russia she could not receive visitors. This was of course a ploy to protect Julie's by now obvious pregnancy from prying eyes.[9] But curiosity did not abate, and it soon became clear that she could not give birth in secret here. Alternative plans would have to be made.

During the time Julie was in retreat a major congress between Napoleon and Alexander took place from 27 September to 14 October 1808 at Erfurt in Thuringia. Alexander had chosen the location for its closeness to Weimar, 24 miles away, where he wanted

---

*   The villa had been owned by a Jean Diodati who had died in 1807 and was descended from the notable Calvinist theologian, preacher and translator of the Bible Dr Giovanni Diodati, who had been a friend of the poet John Milton. Lord Byron famously took refuge at Belle Rive during a summer of intense writing in 1816 and thought it 'the most beautiful house of all around the lake'. It was he who renamed it Villa Diodati after the family who had owned it, and it has since become a tourist attraction for being the location where Mary Shelley wrote *Frankenstein* when she and Percy Shelley stayed there with Byron that summer. (Edwards and Edwards, *His Master's Reflection*). The French writer Honoré de Balzac rented the house briefly too, in 1833–4.

to visit his sister Maria Pavlovna, Duchess of Mecklenburg, who was sick. He was joined there by his brother Konstantin and by Auguste, who went to pay her respects to him. She was disappointed to find the once handsome Alexander already ageing and his otherwise fine character spoiled by 'a certain weakness and vanity'. But she happily chatted with her son-in-law Konstantin and was left with an overwhelming feeling of regret: 'What might have been made of this young man, had he had a different upbringing, and grown up in other surroundings!' she mused.[10]

Over the eighteen days of the congress the two emperors wined and dined each other, enjoyed French plays, rode out daily and hunted hares on the field of the recent battle of Jena, in between reaffirming their alliance agreed at Tilsit, in preparation for a looming war with Austria. During their many tête-à-têtes Napoleon confided to Alexander his intention of divorcing Josephine and finding another wife from among the gene pool of young and fertile European princesses. He had his eye on one of Alexander's remaining unmarried sisters – perhaps Ekaterina? Alexander prevaricated; his mother and Ekaterina were horrified and rejected the idea. Soon after Alexander returned to Russia Ekaterina was married off to the Prince of Oldenburg. Well then, maybe Anna, suggested Napoleon the following spring. But she was technically spoken for, Alexander having long since promised her to Prince Ernst of Saxe-Coburg. Anxious not to offend the French emperor, the Romanovs launched a succession of delaying tactics. Ultimately, Napoleon's pursuit of Anna Pavlovna was as much of a failure as Ernst's. The French emperor quickly lost patience and, in any event, would never have tolerated his bride keeping her Russian Orthodox faith; he opted instead for Marie-Louise, Archduchess of Austria, whom he married in March 1810 (no matter that his poor sacrificial bride had found the idea abhorrent but had had no power to refuse). By 1812 Ernst's hopes of a Romanov alliance had also died on the vine, 'the Empress-mother not being sincere in it', as Leopold later admitted.[11]

If, in October 1808, Alexander had thought to drop in on his sister-in-law Julie while in Erfurt – which was only 75 miles from

Coburg – he would have been disappointed to find she was not there. It is doubtful whether any family members were informed of Julie's precise location other than 'Switzerland' during these lost months and she is not mentioned beyond Auguste's journal, and only then in veiled terms. For this reason, we do not know exactly when a heavily pregnant Julie left Belle Rive to give birth to her baby. But she headed north from Cologny to the pretty little tucked-away town of Kaiserstuhl in the Swiss canton of Aargau, high on the mountainside above the River Rhine on the border with Baden.

Julie confirmed Kaiserstuhl as the name of the place where her son was born in a letter to Ernst in 1815 – but why so far away? Perhaps it was simply because it was so isolated; nevertheless, it was quite a journey across Switzerland for a woman close to term. Kaiserstuhl was in a Catholic part of Switzerland and so within a day or two of his birth Julie's son was taken back south, to Trub in the canton of Bern, where he was baptised by a Lutheran pastor on 20 October 1808 as Eduard-Edgar Schmidt-Löwe. His 'parents' were named in the register as Carl Schmidt-Löwe, a 'travelling artist from Hamburg', and his wife Sophie Müller, but they appear to have played no further part in his life.* Julie's 1962 biographer Alville (Alix de Watteville) had great difficulty unravelling the few available facts surrounding Eduard's birth, even based in Switzerland as she was, with access to families who knew Julie's story. Eduard's arrival in the world remains a mystery, further obscured by a bogus claim made in a German genealogy published in Marburg in 1983, and repeated in Jacques Ferrand's *Descendances naturelles des*

---

* Genealogy websites give the date of birth as 28 October but the baptismal record, no. 82 in the register at Kaiserstuhl, confirms that the baby was baptised on 20 October although it does not give his date of birth (see *Cours*, 106, note 25, 258). But the fact that this much is known about Eduard, whose existence was acknowledged (though not overtly) as Julie's son, and who later had a comfortable life at Duke Ernst's court, makes the likelihood of her supposed first son, Sandor Vajda, born in 1802, being totally excluded from her life hard to accept. Surely if he had been Julie's son he would not have been sent so far away and without some attempt to provide a life befitting his station, like Eduard, as the son of a grand duchess?

souverains et grands-ducs de Russie in 1995, that his father was none other than Alexander I.[12]

All this subterfuge must have been arranged well in advance, presumably by Seigneux, but what connections or influence could he have had in this? It is more likely that a central figure in Julie's later life, Dr Rodolphe Abraham de Schiferli – who in 1805 had been appointed professor of surgery and gynaecology at Bern University – had been consulted for advice, or possibly had even delivered Eduard himself at Kaiserstuhl.

For the first year, however, little Eduard was taken into the care of the pastors of the Swiss Reformed church at Trub before being sent to be educated for five years at the Pestalozzi Educational Institution located in the castle at Yverdon, 73 miles west of Trub in French-speaking Switzerland. The choice is an intriguing one, for Julie clearly had an interest in the work of Johann Heinrich Pestalozzi which may have come from the Romanovs, or even Schiferli, who were all admirers of his educational methods, based on the precepts of Jean-Jacques Rousseau. Alexander I had been introduced to Pestalozzi's work by his mother Maria Feodorovna and met him in Basel in 1814, where Pestalozzi travelled to petition him – armed with a personal letter from Julie – to persuade the Austrians not to take over his institution at Yverdon for use as a military hospital.[13]

Despite the terrible wrench of having to leave him, the arrangements made for her son seem to have cheered Julie, for on 22 December when she arrived back in Coburg, Auguste noted with pleasure that her daughter was 'looking so well and so blooming' though she reported a few days later that she was suffering from agonising toothache (sensitive teeth being something often suffered by women post-partum).[14] In the wider family it was reported by Auguste that Julie had now recovered from the 'illness' that had taken her to Switzerland and they remained none the wiser. That same month Victoire arrived from Amorbach with her two children and was joined by Sophie from Prague and Antoinette from St Petersburg with theirs. For the first time in several years all four sisters were together again and enjoyed the summer months *en famille* before, in July 1809, Antoinette and Julie set off for Prague to see Ferdinand, who had been wounded at the battle of Wagram and was recuperating there.

The year that followed began with yet more physical problems for Julie – in February she was suffering from severe inflammation of the eyes, a problem that seemed to have regularly recurred the older she got and which may well have been a continuing side effect of the venereal disease with which Konstantin had infected her.[15] She was also greatly saddened by news of the deaths of her much-missed lady in waiting Madame de Renne in St Petersburg in June – just as she had been talking of returning to Julie's service – and her beloved friend Queen Luise of Prussia, who died unexpectedly at the age of thirty-four barely a month later, possibly from pneumonia.*

In May 1810 Duchess Auguste announced her intention of making her first visit to Switzerland, which at the time was becoming a popular tourist venue, 'Helvetism' being very much the growing trend in early nineteenth-century literature. No doubt Auguste was familiar with Albrecht von Haller's poem 'Die Alpen', a popular celebration of the Swiss mountains.[16] She set off from Coburg, accompanied by Leopold and Ferdinand, taking the coach road south via Nuremberg and Ulm to Lake Constance on the Swiss border and then southwest to Zurich. As they crossed the German border, they entered an unspoilt fairyland of breath-taking beauty: Switzerland! 'the bosom of romantic nature ... the land of innocence and happiness', as the Russian historian Nikolai Karamzin rhapsodised at the time. 'The air here appears to have something animating. I breathe with more ease and freedom ... Every breeze seems to excite in my heart sensations of delight. What a country! ... what scenery!' Switzerland was indeed a paradise of beauty, rustic charm, cleanliness and simplicity

---

* In 1808 Queen Luise had made her first and only visit to St Petersburg at Tsar Alexander's invitation, where the Romanovs accommodated her and Friedrich Wilhelm in Julie's former apartments at the Winter Palace, which were specially furnished for their use. The Romanovs entertained them lavishly, including a masked ball for 16,000 and showered them with extravagant gifts. For Luise Russian opulence had been like something out of the *Arabian Nights*.

of manners, and Auguste was enchanted by it.[17] Travellers were, however, warned that they should prepare themselves for the dramatic heights and precipices and be mindful of the 'depths of the abyss, and the aspect of danger' that might trigger attacks of vertigo.[18]

On 10 June, Julie joined her mother in Bern, accompanied by her lady in waiting Lotte, Seigneux and also Rodolphe Schiferli, who seems to have been travelling with her as a *cavalier d'honneur* and may also have attended as her personal physician.[19] The good citizens of Bern were, inevitably, extremely curious to inspect Duchess Auguste and her distinguished daughter, for Russian imperial highnesses did not often come their way. On the 12th, Auguste and Julie were invited to a ball given in a splendid pavilion by an influential local magistrate, Christophe-Frédéric Freudenreich, and his family at which they were introduced to the leading lights of Bernese society. One of the guests that evening gushed about Julie's charm and beauty and the impact of her beguiling presence and how 'everyone had eyes for nobody but her'. A few days later she appeared at a ball given by the French ambassador at which she wore 'a diamond headband, a gift from Empress Catherine', which she herself said was of 'inestimable value', together with 'a matching hair comb, collar and sleeve trim' – all of which made her 'still prettier than ever'.[20]

Julie clearly enjoyed being the centre of attention after having had to hide herself away during her pregnancy. Even Auguste noted during those social occasions together in Bern that 'Julie enjoys herself very much here and becomes amazingly flirtatious.'[21] It is, retrospectively, a significant observation, for it echoes remarks made in an English magazine regarding Julie's flight from Russia in 1801, where the author wondered whether her behaviour at the Russian court might perhaps have been less than virtuous – frivolous even. Having been 'driven to despair and revenge' by Konstantin's degeneracy and cruelty, she may 'in her turn have in some degree retaliated her spouse's conduct, by delighting in affairs of coquetry.'[22] There are certainly undercurrents that occasionally surface in Julie's story that suggest she was actively seductive.

Before Auguste continued her Swiss travels south to Geneva, she took the tourist coach ride through the alpine valleys and picturesque waterfalls around Interlaken, Lauterbrunnen and Grindelwald in the Jungfrau region of the Bernese Oberland, which were all on the essential tourist trail, while Julie headed to Neuchâtel for a couple of days. Auguste was sorry to leave Bern on 22 June, knowing that Julie was very unwell again – suffering this time from abdominal pains. The 'Bernese doctor' (which might be a reference here to Schiferli) thought she was suffering from 'hardening of the liver' – jaundice perhaps? Auguste thought this likely since Julie's skin often had a yellowish tinge.[23] She was advised to take the cure at the sulphur baths at Bad Schinznach in Aargau, 56 miles northeast of Bern, where a society lady visiting the spa took note, with a mix of envy and admiration, of Julie's arresting presence: her elegant turnout, her beautiful 'celestial' figure and her 'eyes of a very particular charm'.[24]

Julie returned to Bern at the end of June, where her gracious and honoured presence was noted – as 'Sa Altesse Imperiale madame la grande duchesse Constantin de Russie' – at an agricultural fete at the Hofwyl estate of Bernese educationalist and agronomist Philipp Emanuel von Fellenberg. At Hofwyl, Fellenberg ran an experimental boarding school similar to Pestalozzi's at Yverdon which took in pupils from all over Europe, including Russian Orthodox ones, and was a valuable point of contact with her faith for Julie.[25] Local dignitaries were by now eager to make her acquaintance; she conquered hearts again when she was invited by the mayor of Bern, Count Nicolas-Frédéric de Mulinen, to visit him and his family at Hofstetten near Lake Thun. One of her fellow guests, Suzanne Eynard-Chatelain, remarked that she was 'one of the most attractive women I have seen.' There was something so natural and unaffected about Julie, she wrote to a friend, yet it did not detract from 'the dignity of her rank'– she had 'a kindness that you cannot resist' and her spoken French 'couldn't be better'.[26]

By September she was staying at the Hôtel du Lion d'Or in Lausanne on Lake Geneva, when the recently divorced former French empress Josephine arrived in the area from Chamonix, having been in Switzerland on and off since June adjusting to her new

Julie's father Duke Franz inherited the Saxe-Coburg-Saalfeld title in 1800 when the Duchy was already saddled with huge debts.

Duchess Auguste, Julie's domineering mother, had enormous ambitions for the dynastic futures of her seven children.

The Veste Coburg, the ancestral home, dominated the landscape but was cold, rat-infested and not conducive to family life.

Julie aged six, with her brother Ernst at the Ehrenburg Palace.

Julie, her mother and sisters endured the arduous forty-day journey to St Petersburg in a Berline de Voyage such as this.

The approach to Riga, capital of Livonia on the Baltic Sea, which was the last major stop on the post road to St Petersburg.

The three Saxe-Coburg sisters who travelled to St Petersburg to be vetted by Catherine the Great. **Top:** Antoinette, who married the Duke of Württemberg; **Centre:** Sophie, who became Countess von Mensdorff-Pouilly; **Bottom:** Julie, who achieved the distinction of marrying into the Russian imperial family.

The family's first stop on entering Russia was Grand Duke Konstantin's palace at Strelna, 21 miles outside St Petersburg.

The opulent court of Catherine the Great at the Winter Palace must have been an overwhelming first sight for Julie.

Julie's three brothers were renowned across Europe for their good looks and military prowess. **Top:** Ferdinand married into the fabulously wealthy Koháry family; **Centre:** Leopold charmed his way into the arms of the Princess of Wales; **Bottom:** Ernst inherited the Dukedom and became the father of Prince Albert.

Grand Duke Konstantin, a difficult, pugnacious personality, prevaricated for two weeks before choosing Julie as his bride.

Julie's portrait, specially commissioned by her father at the time of her marriage in February 1796.

The Marble Palace on the Neva embankment was a wedding present from Catherine the Great to Julie and Konstantin.

The Grand Church of the Winter Palace in St Petersburg where Julie and Konstantin were married.

The ageing empress in 1794. Julie lost a major protector in her when Catherine died two years later.

Swiss tutor Frédéric-César de La Harpe had a formative influence over Catherine's grandsons Alexander and Konstantin.

Emperor Alexander I, Catherine's favoured grandson and a loyal ally to Julie after she left Russia.

Empress Elizaveta Alexeevna, a German princess like Julie, was her closest confidante during Julie's difficult years in Russia.

Catherine the Great's eccentric son Paul I was feared by his family and had many enemies who plotted against him.

Paul's scheming German wife Maria Feodorovna disliked her daughter-in-law Julie and created much unhappiness for her in Russia.

Emperor Paul set up a Prussian-style court at Gatchina, where he mercilessly drilled his soldiers in daily parades.

The Ehrenburg Palace at Coburg as it looked when Julie arrived from Russia in 1801.

Grand Duke Konstantin as viceroy of Poland in 1830 not long before his death.

Duchess Auguste of Saxe-Coburg spent much of her old age at Ketschendorf (in the background), where Julie often visited her.

Julie's beloved Swiss home, Elfenau, outside Bern, where she settled in 1814.

This portrait of Julie at Elfenau was sent to her sister Victoire and for many years hung at Frogmore House, Windsor.

Rodolphe Schiferli took charge of Julie's affairs in 1812 and became an indispensable member of her household. She never got over his death.

Julie's youngest sister Victoire, Duchess of Kent, with her little daughter Victoria, born in 1819.

Queen Victoria married her cousin Prince Albert, son of Julie and Victoire's brother Duke Ernst of Saxe-Coburg. They both adored their 'Aunt Julia'.

A member of Albert's entourage for his 1840 wedding to Victoria was Julie's illegitimate son, Baron von Löwenfels.

In 1848, Queen Victoria sent Franz Xaver Winterhalter to paint Julie's portrait as a gift for her mother Victoire. It is the last image of Julie.

life as a divorced woman and travelling incognito as the 'Comtesse d'Arberg' in the company of her daughter, Hortense.[27] Josephine was staying in some comfort at Dejean's Hôtel d'Angleterre, the premier venue located on the outskirts of Geneva in the fashionable garden suburb of Sécheron, and some time in early October Julie paid her a visit. 'I have seen the Grand Duchess Constantine,' Josephine wrote to Hortense, who had now left for Paris; 'she came to see me twice, and I have been once to see her. She is charming, elegant, graceful, and amiable. She has the most beautiful figure possible and unites with that charming features.' But, Josephine added most tellingly, 'she has the air of not being happy.'[28]

Seigneux was with Julie on this trip and according to Josephine's lady in waiting, Madame Avrillon, appeared to be passing himself off as a 'Russian gentleman' (in order presumably to evade the ban on him re-entering Switzerland after the duel in 1803). Madame Avrillon reiterated what Josephine had said: although the grand duchess's conversation was 'animated' it was nevertheless 'stamped with a kind of melancholy' and she was told that Julie 'lived a very retired life', for she was 'separated from her husband, as everyone knew'. Avrillon could not help noticing the overweening presence of Seigneux; she had heard, she added in the most delicately oblique way, that 'there was more than zeal in the devotion he showed to the princess.'[29]

Was Seigneux the cause of Julie's unhappiness and was she by now desperate to extricate herself from his unsettling presence? On doctor's orders, she was soon off on her travels again, to spend the winter in Italy for the sake of her health. On 17 October 1810 Julie, accompanied by her entourage* in four carriages, left Switzerland, travelling through Martigny, Sion and down to Gliss on the northern slope of the Simplon Pass, from where the road rolled past spectacular views over the southern chain of the Alps to Domo d'Ossola

---

* This included Lotte von Schlammersdorf who according to Auguste had arrived with Julie in Bern but was ill again and 'looked nauseous' – perhaps from travelling the mountainous Swiss roads. She appears to have died in 1812 in Coburg (*Jahrbuch*, 59; *AP*, 31).

(Domodossola) in Piedmont.[30] This once extremely perilous carriage journey had only recently been made viable for ordinary travellers, after Napoleon had ordered the construction of a remarkable new road in 1801 that could take three carriages abreast. It had been constructed at phenomenal speed by 1805, thanks to the non-stop labour of a workforce of some 30,000 men.

By the end of the month Julie was in Milan. A delightful account of her can be found in the memoirs of the Italian artist Giuseppe Bossi, whose studio in Milan she visited on the 25th in the company of Seigneux. Bossi was very taken with *la granduchessa*, whom he found to be 'a beautiful woman with fine features, very graceful, elegant'. The following day he met her at her hotel, the Albergo i Tre Re, and took her on a tour of Milan's famous sights – the Roman amphitheatre, the school of mosaics, the Basilica of San Lorenzo, the Arch of Peace by Luigi Cagnola, the Church of San Celso, the painting of Sant'Anna by Andrea Salaino, and the Palazzo Reale. He recalled with great pleasure how at dinner afterwards they had talked of art and politics and he was deeply impressed: 'This woman has lovely speech and infinite grace.' The following day Seigneux came to Bossi's studio early with a gift: 'a golden snuff box decorated with [Julie's] insignia in rubies' that she wished him to have as a memento of her. In gratitude Bossi presented her with a drawing of 'The Triumph of Love' (possibly a reference to Petrarch's poetry) and was very sad to see her leave.[31]

By January 1811 Julie was once again stunning high society – this time in Rome. On the 30th, the *Courrier de Turin* reported that several German newspapers had commented 'with admiration on the magnificence that Grand Duchess Constantin had shown during her stay in this town'. 'All the diamonds which this princess wore around her neck and in her hair were of the size of the biggest solitaires.' Her gown was 'sprinkled with little diamonds' too. Julie stayed in Rome until mid-April then travelled on to Naples before returning to Bern in May, and finally, after almost a year and a half's absence, made a visit back home to Coburg in October. Auguste was overjoyed to see her and threw a great family dinner and concert to celebrate. Julie stayed until the end of January 1812 in time to mark her mother's birthday, when they lunched together and 'drove out to the Rosenau [her mother's summer residence outside Coburg] in the afternoon in sledges, remaining for dinner'.[32]

By now the overbearing Seigneux had been removed – somewhat suddenly and mysteriously – from Julie's household. Surviving documents regarding Julie's household in February 1812 already refer to Rodolphe Schiferli as being in charge of her affairs. It has been suggested that either Prince Leopold or his brother Duke Ernst, both of whom had grown increasingly concerned about Seigneux's hold over their sister, had engineered his removal and his replacement by Schiferli.*[33]

Rodolphe Abraham de Schiferli was born in Thun in 1775, and after studying medicine in Jena and Paris in the late 1790s, had during 1802–5 served as senior medical officer (*Oberfeldarzt*) of the federal Swiss troops and vaccinator of the canton of Bern (1805), before being appointed to his professorship at the Academy of Bern. In recent years he had suffered poor health after a serious bout of typhus and had been forced to give up his official posts for a less taxing appointment as physician to Duke Friedrich of Mecklenburg-Schwerin (widower of Julie's sister-in-law Elena Pavlovna, who had died aged eighteen in 1803) when he had fallen sick while visiting Bern. It was a grateful Friedrich who, on his recovery, had recommended Schiferli to Julie as a *cavalier d'honneur*, and by June 1810, according to Auguste's journal, he was travelling with Julie's entourage in Switzerland.[34]

But Schiferli had a wife, Marguérite, whom he had married in 1803, and two sons, Fritz (born 1806) and Maurice (born 1809). He seemed a paragon of kindness, loyalty and virtue in comparison

---

* Mary Lavater-Sloman sees Ernst as being the instigator, quoting him as saying that Seigneux kept his sister in 'pathetic slavery', but the source for this has not been found (Lavater-Sloman, 'Schweizerjahre', 694). Schiferli and Leopold had struck up a close friendship, for in 1813 Schiferli sponsored Leopold's induction to his masonic lodge, L'Espérance in Bern. As for Seigneux, nothing more is known of him beyond his death in Geneva in 1834.

with Seigneux. But barely a year after he joined her household – and sources give no prior warning of this – Julie gave birth to a daughter, whose father was acknowledged as being Schiferli. It is hard to imagine that Schiferli's wife would not have known, but even if she did, a divorce would have been out of the question for she was the daughter of a well-known Swiss theologian and statesman, Johann Samuel Ith. Schiferli's devotion to Julie – and hers to him – necessitated a discreet tolerance, to suit all parties. Schiferli had no desire to desert his wife, nor did Julie wish for it either and, it seems, by all accounts, that their sexual relationship had been brief and that very soon it had mutated into one of deep and abiding trust and friendship. But it left Julie bereft, still, of a fulfilling romantic life with a man who was free to love and perhaps marry her.

We know very little of the circumstances of this second birth, for Julie did another, most necessary, disappearing act in early April to a little place called Unter-Siemau, only 5 miles south of Coburg. It was impossible to keep the pretence from the family for long: in a letter to his sister Sophie in March 1812, Leopold told her that Julie had been 'very ill' and had been experiencing 'violent cramps'.[35] But Sophie was not fooled. She was angry that Julie had not taken her into her confidence and concluded that it was 'preferable that mama should know nothing', to spare Auguste from the anguish she had suffered the first time, with Eduard. But Sophie admitted that she was 'tormented by curiosity' as to who the father was, and prayed it was not a married man (perhaps thinking of Schiferli).[36] Auguste, however, clearly knew, for she alluded to the pregnancy in veiled terms in her journal: how Julie's poor health had really suffered that previous winter (she would have fallen pregnant around September 1811), and how, in early April, she was leaving for the countryside where the air would do her good. She insisted on visiting her there every few days, even during the frequently bad weather and 'despite the wind and snowdrifts' that persisted into spring. She of course makes no overt mention of the daughter Julie gave birth to on 20 May but euphemistically talks of being there a week after the birth and finding Julie 'suffering and fatigued'. Auguste remained a constant visitor until June while Julie continued to recover from the delivery, keeping up the subterfuge of illness in her journal.[37]

On 30 May 1812, Julie's baby was baptised Luise Hilda Aglae d'Aubert – perhaps in tribute to her dead friend Queen Luise – at Trub, where her half-brother Eduard had also been baptised and was probably still living in the care of the pastors. She seems always to have been referred to as Hilda, and after being fostered was officially adopted at the age of nine by French Protestant refugees Jean-François Joseph d'Aubert and his wife Louise-Julianne Besler, who brought her up in Geneva with Julie hovering at a distance as a very discreet godmother.[38]

On 19 June Julie reappeared at Ketschendorf, 'like a dear and rare apparition', and remained in Coburg that summer to recuperate. She was well enough to dress up for the reception there for the French emissary on 26 June and with her mother received a visit from Rodolphe Schiferli and his wife in July. Auguste was happy to report on Julie's recovery: 'I had not seen her prettier or more cheerful in a long time.'[39] She enjoyed the remainder of the summer, made up of family meals and visits to the theatre and rounded off by a considerable birthday party thrown in her honour on 23 September, the first she had enjoyed with the family for six years. Auguste indulged in a long and colourful description of these celebrations in her journal, although the actual birthday procession planned by Ernst had to be postponed for a couple of days due to torrential rain.

On 28 September, in the Seidmannsdorf valley beyond Ketschendorf, Julie was received by a gathering of friends and family dressed in old German costume, as a 'long festive procession' of trumpeters, heralds in armour and knights 'just like a picture from the old days' paraded past her, 'manly and splendid like the . . . noble princes of Saxony'. Then came her sister Sophie 'in black velvet, with ermine and pearls' and Leopold 'black and white like a Knight of St John'. It was, Auguste recorded with delight, 'a really most beautiful sight and the most vivid presentation of the high age of chivalry that could be imagined'. But the celebrations also prompted admissions of deep regret in Auguste about what Julie had lost of her 'springtime':

'She could never purely enjoy the beautiful days of first youth, the May of life which only blooms once! Ah! Storms of all kinds have assailed her, early tempests which destroyed her happiness and our hopes. It is lost, this beautiful glittering time, and scarcely a happy memory remains for the poor thing, so often has she been cheated and nearly continually made ill by it.'[40]

There is a clear suggestion here of how Julie's two illegitimate pregnancies had brought unwanted complications to an already difficult life and perhaps Julie had begun to find her mother's enduring angst too much. By Christmas of 1812 she had moved out of her apartments at the Ehrenburg, in what seems to be a concerted effort to be independent of Auguste's overbearing presence, and had taken up the rental of an apartment in the old ducal residence on Steingasse where she had grown up.[41] Here, at New Year 1813, Julie entertained her family to lunch in her abode, which was 'decorated with little orange trees and flowers and lit up with lanterns', followed in the evening by *tableaux vivants* of scenes from *Romeo and Juliet*. Shortly afterwards she re-emerged into society, appearing at a ball 'uniquely beautiful in old-Swiss costume, dressed like a painting by Holbein' and attending family gatherings at the Rosenau.[42] With Leopold soon to depart for Vienna, Julie then threw a large family tea party on 15 February, as always proving to be the perfect hostess.[43] But the family was subdued at the thought of Leopold once more departing for the Russian army, which, after the disastrous French occupation of Moscow, had routed the invaders from their homeland during the savage Russian winter of 1812–13 and was now intent on nothing less than driving Napoleon all the way back to Paris.

By March the French had retreated to Dresden and Auguste was overwhelmed by 'the same oppressive feeling of dread as in the year 1806' when northern Germany had been overrun by them. By the end of the month the Russians were in Leipzig – and Auguste welcomed them as liberators. She and Julie commiserated together in the lovely springtime surroundings of the Rosenau in April, but Auguste was alarmed, for not far from their home the remnants of Napoleon's exhausted and desperate *Grande Armée* were 'swarming ... like a plague of locusts and devastating everything that comes their way'.[44] Then came news of a major and 'furious' battle at Lützen on 2 May at which the Russians and Prussians had incurred catastrophic losses of 40,000, closely followed by another, equally devastating, three-day engagement at Bautzen on 19–21 May, after which the Russians were forced back into Silesia. There was still no news of Leopold and Auguste was not aware that he had been in the thick of both battles leading his Russian cavalry.[45]

It was while Tsar Alexander was in Silesia, during the lull of a two-month armistice declared in June, that Julie seized the opportunity of trying to meet with him on a personal matter and she begged Ernst to pass on a request when he next saw the tsar at HQ. Her objective was simple: she needed Alexander's permission to settle permanently in Switzerland for she was anxious to regularise her long-anomalous position. For the last twelve years, as a member of the Russian imperial family, she had – officially – been only temporarily domiciled abroad. Privately, her sister Antoinette had given up on seeing her in St Petersburg again: 'I no longer believe in the possibility that she can ever come back. How lucky I would have been to have a sister here in the country,' she wrote in July 1805 to Madame de Renne.[46]

Julie became increasingly anxious as she waited for a response from Alexander. 'Maybe the pretext of a cure for my health would extort a quick decision from him,' she wrote to Ernst in June, and she repeated her request to him even more urgently when she still had not received a reply by the end of July. Her chronic health problems were not a front: in this second letter to Ernst she spoke of her desperate need to seek treatment for the 'constant gouty headaches which torment me day and night' (perhaps an allusion to migraines?).[47] She could not afford to keep on travelling to the spas in Bohemia and elsewhere in search of treatment because of the expense it incurred for herself and her entourage; she needed to live somewhere where treatment was available on the doorstep. But she was also tired of her peripatetic life of perpetual subterfuge and needed to recover her spirits and sense of self. And Switzerland was the best place to

achieve that: her trusted advisor Schiferli was resident with his family
in Bern, Eduard was in Trub and Hilda not far away in Lausanne,
and she wanted to be near to all three of them.

Finally in early August a letter came from Alexander inviting Julie
to meet him on the border with Bohemia. At his request Leopold
arranged the location – 'in a pretty chateau' at Blasdorff (Błażkowa
in southwest Poland). 'The emperor had gone there quite alone,
and it was interesting to see him so. He was extremely amiable,'
recalled Leopold. Antoinette heard later that during this encounter
Julie and the tsar 'had been very satisfied with each other' and he
had agreed to her settling in Switzerland. This was just as well, in
Antoinette's view, as 'this unfortunate Germany will soon offer
refuge only to crows, everything is devastated, the happiness of so
many thousands of inhabitants is crushed at the feet of the victors
and the vanquished.'[48]

After the meeting with Alexander Julie travelled back to
Switzerland via Prague and Augsburg and by 16 August was at the
spa at Pfeffers in Walenstadt, where she stayed until 11 September.
Le Moniteur universel noted her arrival in Zug south of Zurich soon
after 'with quite a large suite' – which could hardly detract from
her wish for supposed anonymity – travelling as 'La Comtesse de
Rosenau'![49] She arrived in Bern at the end of September, at a small
house just outside town that she had rented in May 1811. It was
in this locale that she found the most perfect home – a large and
spacious two-storey house with a high mansard roof that had been
built in 1780 on an estate known as Brunnadern, originally the site
of a thirteenth-century Dominican convent. Here, after thirteen
years of wandering, Julie would finally put down roots at a place
she named Elfenau.

CHAPTER 11

'That Haven of Peace
She So Longed For'

Switzerland might have seemed a paradise of peace and beauty to
visitors at this point of the Romantic era, when the natural world
was being celebrated in literature and art, but Julie had chosen to
settle in the western canton of Vaud at a time of political tension and
uncertainty. Since its occupation (when a barony of Savoy) in 1536
by Bernese troops, Vaud had avoided the conflict between German-
speaking Protestants and French-speaking Catholics elsewhere in
Switzerland by following the Calvinist influence of Geneva and
becoming a French-speaking area. French nationalism in Vaud had
remained strong into the nineteenth century, one of its major cham-
pions being Frédéric-César de La Harpe, former tutor to grand dukes
Alexander and Konstantin. As a supporter of the 1798 Revolution,
he had welcomed the French Directory's invasion of Switzerland that
year and Vaud's elevation – as the Canton of Léman – to become
a major player in the new Helvetic Republic, which he served as a
member of its Directory.

But the creation of the Helvetic Republic with a centralised government in Aarau had stripped local autonomy from the federated
cantons and unrest and opposition had grown, especially with the
French sequestering funds from the cantonal treasuries and increasing the burden on the civil population. The Helvetic Republic was on

the brink of civil war when in 1803 Napoleon Bonaparte imposed an Act of Mediation under which Switzerland reverted to a confederacy of nineteen cantons, among them Vaud, Thurgau and Aargau, that still exists to this day. With the withdrawal of French troops from the canton of Bern, the old patrician government there reasserted itself; La Harpe in the meantime was forced to flee to Paris.

It was only now, in 1813, with Napoleon's European territorial gains being wrested back, that hopes of full Swiss independence were reviving; Tsar Alexander in particular wished to assist in Switzerland's recovery after the Russian military campaign in the Alps. He had after all been educated by a Swiss tutor and since childhood had felt a strong affinity for the Swiss landscape and work ethic. 'Everything that I know, and perhaps all that I am worth, I owe to M. Laharpe,' he had declared.[1] Alexander therefore had good reason to support the revival of Swiss republican statehood, favouring the creation of a politically neutral union of cantons as a buffer state in central Europe to protect the strategically important Alpine passes in and out of neighbouring countries. With the Congress of Vienna due to begin in September 1814, La Harpe petitioned Alexander I from Paris to defend Vaud's sovereign status. At the congress, Switzerland was subsequently confirmed as an independent and neutral state with a new constitution.

The union of twenty-two cantons into the Swiss Confederation took place in September 1814, just as Julie settled permanently in Switzerland. Alexander clearly wanted to see his unhappy sister-in-law finally settled and secure, but political considerations may well have also come into his agreement to her choice. As a senior member of the Russian imperial family, she could act as his unofficial representative in Switzerland and exert a gentle and encouraging influence over those she entertained at her home. By the same token, the Bernese government would court her support in their federal cause and even invited her to attend the ceremonial opening of the new Diet in 1817 at Bern's Eglise du Saint Esprit.[2]

With all this in mind, in November 1813 Alexander ensured that his own representative had Julie's ear by sending the Greek-born

Ioannis Kapodistrias, who had been serving as his foreign minister since 1809, on a special, unofficial diplomatic mission to establish Russian influence over Bern in the drafting of the new constitution and laws. Kapodistrias was backed in his endeavours by the arrival of La Harpe in January 1814 and in March he was officially appointed 'Extraordinary Envoy and Minister Plenipotentiary at the All-Swiss Council'. In this capacity he attended the Vienna Congress, where Switzerland's status of 'eternal neutrality' was confirmed, with Russia as its major guarantor.[3]

In October 1814 a contract was drawn up for the purchase of Brunnadern, on Julie's behalf, from a local Bernese patrician, Gottlieb Abraham von Jenner. His family were the latest of several noble Bernese families that had once owned the estate and the sale was completed by the following May.[4] In her letters, Julie referred rather too modestly to her new home as a *cabane rustique* – a 'rustic cottage' – but by St Petersburg standards it certainly would have been dwarfed alongside any of the Romanov palaces.[5] Nevertheless, Julie rapidly established a reputation here for her gracious receptions for local bigwigs from Bern as well as eminent foreign visitors passing through Switzerland.

She did little to change the house's exterior, beyond adding an Empire-style portal at the front and a drive and courtyard with a central fountain, to which visitors could arrive in suitable style. It was in the interiors that she made the most changes, indulging her love of the classically inspired Greco-Roman elegance in motifs such as caryatid heads, arches and pilasters. Everything was refurbished in this popular style: walls were embellished with marble pink stucco and covered with silk and no doubt one of the first portraits to grace them was one of Julie painted in 1813 by the Genevese artist Jeanne Henriette Rath when she had been in Bern. Tasteful prints and English copper engravings were hung alongside lyrical images of Elfenau and its surroundings by the Swiss watercolourist Gabriel Lory and his son, commissioned by Prince Leopold.

The rooms were further decorated with gilded oak panelling,

marble chimney pieces, Louis XV and XVI chairs and sofas from Paris, Empire-style soft furnishings and *objets d'art* in bronze. Indeed, bronze decoration could be seen everywhere – on tables, chimney pieces and sideboards, in six-branched chandeliers and candle holders, and in Russian incense burners. Choice pieces of Wedgwood, Russian china, tea services imported from Paris, the finest decorative vases from the Royal Porcelain Manufactory in Berlin and Baccarat glass from Bohemia all added to the elegant detail of Julie's reception rooms, as well as fine pieces by the Bernese master cabinet maker Christoph Hopfengärtner.[6] In creating these interiors she spent much time poring over copies of magazines featuring the work of French designers Percier et Fontaine in Paris.[*] She also subscribed to French magazines such as the highly fashionable *Journal des dames et des modes* with its exquisite hand-coloured fashion plates and society gossip, and its rival the *Petit courrier des dames*, as well as Swiss almanacs and yearbooks, and, no doubt more discreetly, copies of the latest romantic bodice-rippers by Friedrich Gustav Schilling such as *Little Clara's Confessions* and his semi-erotic bestseller *The Memoirs of Herr von H*.[7]

A large dining room on the southwest side of the house was created to cater for Julie's many guests and an Italian artist hired to paint the ceiling of the reception salon.[8] But the maintenance of the house and Julie's lifestyle required an army of servants: a cook and assistant, three chambermaids, a housekeeper, a butler, five lackeys, two gardeners, a huntsman and four coachmen, as well as grooms, a caretaker and a nightwatchman. And there were also of course Julie's ladies in waiting as well as Schiferli and his family, who were separately housed in an apartment above the greenhouses known as the Pavilion.[9]

The basement of the house was converted into a garden-saloon that looked out over the river but the views all around Julie's home

---

[*]   An exquisite ormolu-mounted and brass-inlaid mahogany table by the German master craftsman David Roentgen owned by Julie and probably gifted to her on her marriage by Catherine the Great was auctioned by Christie's for £193,875 in 2013.

were spectacular, for it was located in the valley of the fast-flowing River Aare, with the glories of the Bernese Oberland, the Eiger and the Jungfrau as backdrop. She gave her new home the romantic-sounding German name of Elfenau – 'the elves' meadow' – because, she said, one morning as she stepped out of her front door she was entranced by the sight of the meadow beyond sparkling with drops of dew in the sunlight. It was as though the elves had been dancing there during the night.[10] The lyrical choice of name appealed perfectly to her deeply romantic nature and harked back to a party for Auguste's birthday in January 1802 when the family had staged a magnificent 'Oberon' procession, inspired by Christoph Martin Wieland's romantic epic poem 'Oberon' of 1780 (which in turn had taken its inspiration from Shakespeare's *A Midsummer Night's Dream*). On that happy day, the family, accompanied in mock-medieval style by twelve trumpeters, had dressed up in costume: Victoire in Turkish trousers, Ernst in full armour, Emmanuel Mensdorff-Pouilly as a knight; 'then me as Titania (a clumsy Elf Queen)', as Julie had written in a letter to Madame de Renne. A poem by court poet Moritz von Thümmel had been composed soon after to commemorate Julie's appearance that day, describing her as 'Die Elfenkönigin' and it fed perfectly into Julie's sentimental view of herself.[11]

The gardens of Elfenau perfectly echoed this idyllic rural dream and were redesigned as an English-style park of winding paths, grottos and hidden groves, with a dovecote and orangery. At Julie's request, and after his marriage in 1816, Leopold sent flowers from his home at Claremont in England; Schiferli ordered tulip bulbs from Haarlem; she discussed planting *Sophora japonica* at the front of the house with her gardener – would it tolerate the cold winters in Switzerland? she wondered. Summerhouses, stables and greenhouses were incorporated into the estate design by landscape gardener Joseph Baumann, who had been recommended by Ernst. Baumann was responsive to Julie's desire for something natural, not grandiose, that reflected the tranquillity of its surroundings. He imported exotic trees from Kew Gardens, including a Japanese cord tree which is still standing 200 years later. During the 1820s a local Bernese architect,

Rudolf Samuel von Luternau, supervised many additional changes when Julie acquired some nearby land in order to extend the park. He placed gazebos and benches at particularly fine vantage points over the river and in sight of the favourite scenic attraction of Mount Gurten. By 1840, so celebrated was the beautiful park at Elfenau that it began appearing in tourist travel guides such as Samuel Walcher's *Livre de poche du voyageur en Suisse*.[12] In everything that she did at Elfenau, Julie regularly thanked and rewarded the farm workers and their families and gave them carefully chosen and generous presents at Christmas, as well as all her household staff.

There was, however, one essential missing when Julie arrived, and that was a place of worship. Her severance from Russia and all things Russian had not extended to a change in her religious practice. Julie clung determinedly to her Russian Orthodox faith in Coburg and for the remainder of her life in Switzerland, even when places of worship were hard to find. While the sentiment in some of her letters refers often to religious writings from her Moravian background, Orthodoxy had become fundamental to her daily life. As a Russian grand duchess – still – she was probably also obliged to keep up appearances and maintain the religious observance that her title had brought with it. She had initially made enquiries about building a Russian Orthodox chapel at the educational institute at Hofwyl, which took in pupils from Russia. Tsar Alexander had taken an interest in it in 1816, for he had been keen to establish a Russian Orthodox church in Switzerland, but the project at Hofwyl did not go ahead. It was suggested Julie might have a priest based at Elfenau but Julie insisted that there was nowhere in the house where she could put the iconostasis and icons and hold services. Schiferli, rattled by the need for yet more unnecessary expense, nevertheless searched for a suitable design, from which a small *'hermitage'* was constructed in the park in 1816 by Luternau, with a thatched roof surmounted by a bell tower and cross. Until then an Orthodox chapel was consecrated at the Russian legation at Bern where Julie could go and worship.[13]

Julie's spending on Elfenau was clearly considerable in these first years and at times was extravagantly beyond her means. Despite her wish for privacy, she rather enjoyed displaying the outer grand trappings of her title: her carriage bore the Russian imperial coat of arms and her servants wore court livery. Schiferli, who had now been appointed an imperial councillor by Tsar Alexander, felt obliged to ensure that her home presented an ambiance that reflected her imperial Russian status, but privately he agonised about the expense of it all. He was backed up by endless exhortations from Leopold in the years that followed that his sister's situation was highly precarious, 'because of the disorder of her finances'.[14]

Leopold had had to exert his influence from a distance for most of this time, as he had spent the last eight years fighting in Europe in the entourages of his Russian brothers-in-law Alexander and Konstantin during the military campaign against Napoleon. Now that Napoleon was in retreat, and during a lull in the fighting, Leopold had turned his attention to more prosaic matters such as his sister's perilous finances. Being instinctively frugal, he knew the extent to which Julie was still dependent on the tsar for her income and found himself constantly having to write to Russia on her behalf to chivvy up the desultory way in which her appanage was paid. He was aware that financial worries caused considerable friction whenever Schiferli tried to caution prudence in her lavish spending; indeed, from the moment of his appointment in 1812 replacing Seigneux, Schiferli had been grappling with Julie's debts, which dated back to 1809 and had been made worse by the depreciation in currency due to the war. He had wanted her to reduce her staff, but Julie had not been able to bring herself to do this.[15] Managing her haphazard affairs created moments of conflict in their relationship but there is no doubt that Julie placed great trust and confidence in Schiferli: 'It is true that he possesses a rare intelligence,' she told Ernst – 'and what is even rarer – that it is allied to a noble heart.'[16]

Leopold knew full well that Julie could be difficult. 'A certain contradictory spirit has always been one of my dear sister's traits of character,' he admitted; 'she has always had a tendency to do the opposite of what I have said.' His sister's life in Switzerland was 'elegant but without pomp', as Leopold later observed, but 'money was one of the black spots of her existence.' Indeed, her financial difficulties were so serious that Julie became volatile when confronted with them, and at one point in 1817 she even told Schiferli that as it was all proving too stressful for him she would dispense with his services.[17] Her financial problems had already necessitated the sale, facilitated by Schiferli, of several of her jewels to Monsieur Binet Mare, a jeweller in Geneva, including her diamond-encrusted Order of St Catherine.[18]

On 14 January 1814 Julie had a surprise visitor: Leopold arrived, announcing that Tsar Alexander would shortly follow, for he had recently entered Basel as part of the Allied advance on France. Instead, and to Julie's horror, her estranged husband Konstantin appeared on her doorstep two days later with Leopold. The reason for this very quickly became apparent: Alexander had instructed his brother to attempt a reconciliation with Julie – after thirteen years of separation. It was by no means an altruistic gesture, but one of dynastic expediency: Alexander and Elise had been long estranged and had had no more children since Elizaveta in 1806, who had died two years later. After thirteen years on the throne, Alexander still had no legitimate male heir, for the only son born to him, Emanuel in 1814, was the product of his long-standing affair with Maria Naryshkina. He had to prepare for the growing possibility that Konstantin might well succeed him. Securing the line of succession was paramount, as Alexander's brother Konstantin well knew, and he was insistent about his desire to live with Julie again, for he of course wanted his own offspring to inherit the throne. He announced that he would wait in Bern for her decision, but Julie was adamant: there was no going back.

She later confided to a friend how painful she had found that meeting, to which Leopold was also a witness. He had initially hoped for a successful outcome, for Konstantin was not only his brother-in-law but also his superior in the Russian army. He knew that the couple's long separation had damaged the prestige of the

Saxe-Coburg house and he tried to convince Julie that Konstantin had changed and become 'wiser and more reasonable'. But after seeing them together over two days of intense discussions, he could see that the only way in which a reconciliation could be possible would be if Julie were to meekly submit to her duties as a wife and 'close her eyes to certain things' about Konstantin. Julie would have none of it and repeated her request for a divorce.[19]

Nothing in the world would make her return to Konstantin, and to Russia, for Julie knew it would destroy her sanity and wellbeing. And if proof were needed of her husband's still latent savagery, on 19 January (6 January OS) just before he left Bern, Konstantin celebrated the Russian Blessing of the Waters ceremony to mark Epiphany by ordering his suite down to the River Aare and commanding them to dive into the freezing cold and fast-flowing waters fully clothed. Could Julie have needed any more telling confirmation that she had done the right thing?[20]

Auguste was not surprised when she received a 'disquieting letter' from her daughter about the encounter with Konstantin: 'I cannot blame her for refusing to resume a life of brilliant misery ... a reunion could never be a happy one.' Many years later, after Julie's death, Leopold gave a tepid explanation to his niece Queen Victoria of how her aunt had turned down 'the possibility of regaining a great position', and how she had been unable to 'bring herself to consent' despite Konstantin's avowed admiration for her.[21]

With Julie having seen off Konstantin's cynical attempt to rekindle their marriage and Leopold now elevated to the rank of lieutenant-general by Tsar Alexander, Duchess Auguste had diverted her attention to the marital situation of her other children. In July of 1814 her daughter Victoire, who had married Prince Karl of Leiningen had suddenly been left a widow at twenty-eight with two young children and very little money. Auguste, who was not that troubled by Prince Karl's death ('his many good qualities were somewhat spoilt by his hasty temper and obstinacy'), would need to be on the lookout for a replacement, for her 'poor child' was, she knew, 'going to be severely tried by the difficult circumstances which face her'.[22]

Far more concerning, however, was seeing her three very good-looking sons – who had all mercifully survived numerous battles during the recent wars – suitably married off. She made the most of having all three of them at home with her in Coburg in August–September 1814; not long afterwards Ferdinand was the first to announce to his mother his 'brilliant matrimonial prospects'.[23] Having served with distinction throughout the Napoleonic Wars as a cavalry officer in the Austrian army and now aged thirty, he had captured an enviable bride in Princess Maria Antonia Koháry de Csábrág et Szitnya. She was not just beautiful, but the only daughter of the prodigiously wealthy Hungarian nobleman Ferenc József Koháry, whom the Austrian emperor raised to prince ahead of their marriage on 2 January 1816. Ernst attended the ceremony in the chapel of the Archbishop's Palace in Vienna (the bride 'covered with jewels like a rosebud') after which prodigious amounts of money were spent on nine days of wedding celebrations, like something out of the *1001 Nights*, involving hundreds of gypsy musicians entertaining guests dining on thousands of sheep, pigs and chickens slaughtered for the occasion.[*][24]

Five months later, Ferdinand's marital success was trumped by his brother Leopold in London, when he captured the heart and hand of Princess Charlotte of Wales. Leopold's triumph would rapidly propel him to the forefront of European royalty, not to mention bring money pouring into his until then empty coffers, though his self-interested mother mourned his 'complete severance from his former existence and from us all' and agonised over how she would come to terms with it.[25] The marriage, as she well knew, provided an important opportunity for the Saxe-Coburg family to recover ground and respect after the debacle of Julie's flight from Russia and the gossip about her still ambiguous marital status. But the removal of all her

---

* In 1818 Ferdinand converted from Lutheranism, creating a Roman Catholic branch of the Saxe-Coburg family, whose descendants would go on to produce kings of Portugal (1836) and Bulgaria (1909) as well relatives in the royal houses of Romania, Yugoslavia and Brazil.

children from her immediate orbit left a lonely Auguste to retreat to her home at Ketschendorf, where she now spent most of her time.

The wheel of fortune continued to turn in Saxe-Coburg's favour when, a year after Leopold's marriage and having failed to land a bigger catch in Russia, 33-year-old Ernst settled for a 16-year-old German bride: Luise, sole heiress of Saxe-Gotha-Altenburg, a far wealthier duchy than Saxe-Coburg-Saalfeld. In a most loving and generous gesture, Julie sent Luise a magnificent diamond necklace as a wedding gift. Luise was beautiful and clever and vivacious – a romantic ingénue, a sweet and trusting creature who genuinely believed her marriage to Ernst was a love match. But like Julie, the man the innocent Luise married turned out to be an incorrigible reprobate with no care or concern for her physical or mental welfare. Ernst already had courted scandal with Pauline Panam (see footnote page 146) and since then had had a string of mistresses. In January 1816 he had fathered an illegitimate daughter, Berta, by a woman he had had an affair with in Paris. The girl had been taken to live with his sister Sophie, who was then residing at Julie's old house on Steingasse (Julie having given it up when she settled permanently in Switzerland). Ernst and Luise's marriage on 31 July 1817 produced a son, Ernst, eleven months later, for whom Julie was nominated as a godparent, though absent from the christening. By November that same year Luise was pregnant again.

Julie, who had always been reticent about attending large family gatherings, did not travel from Switzerland for any of these weddings, although she arrived in Coburg on a visit not long after Ernst's. She must have felt greatly demoralised, shackled as she still was to Konstantin. Indeed, Auguste was perennially consumed by a sense of guilt regarding Julie's unhappy marriage and her Russian-based sister Antoinette was becoming anxious that the situation be resolved. She wanted to see Julie safely married off again, she confided to Renette; in her eyes, Julie was a coquette who could easily captivate some chivalrous new husband, so long as she did not forget the 'modesty of our sex' in the process. Behind the scenes,

Leopold too was busy lobbying both Alexander and Konstantin for the divorce to finally go ahead.[26]

During that long period of waiting, Julie had made a habit of commiserating with fellow spurned wives: first ex-empress Josephine in 1810 and in the autumn of 1814 with Princess Caroline, estranged wife of George, the English prince regent, when she passed through Switzerland en route to Italy. Ostracised from the royal family and sick with stomach cancer, Caroline had stopped off in Bern, where she heard that Napoleon's wife, ex-empress Maria Louisa (whose husband was now exiled to Elba), was also in residence. She invited both Maria Louisa and Julie to visit her and the three women subsequently met several times. As Caroline's biographer, Robert Huish, wrote after her death in 1821: 'No two individuals of illustrious rank ever met in a foreign country, who independently of consanguinity, had greater cause to sympathise with each other than the Princess of Wales, and the Grand-duchess of Russia.' He noted that the meeting of the two mistreated wives had taken place 'to the manifest annoyance and discomfiture of many long-headed politicians in this country [England].' It is interesting to note that despite all Julie's efforts to say nothing publicly about the circumstances that had led to her leaving Russia, Huish was aware that 'the actual cause which led to the separation . . . is known to everyone who is in the slightest degree acquainted with the history of the Russian court.' Grand Duke Konstantin, it would appear, was neither liked nor respected in Europe: comparing him to the present prince regent (a man also much hated) 'would be comparing the most polished gentleman to an orangutan', he concluded.[27]

Not long afterwards, Julie travelled to Coburg for the winter. In January she laid on a great party for Auguste's fifty-eighth birthday, as she always did whenever she was with her mother. She extended her stay through that summer of 1815, the year when peace was finally achieved in Europe with Napoleon's defeat at Waterloo. Mother and daughter spent a restful time together at Ketschendorf and at the Rosenau, which was now undergoing extensive renovations in the Gothic style. Julie finally left for Switzerland with her entourage on 31 October. So much for her supposed desire for anonymity: en route, several national newspapers noted the progress of the 'Countess of Rosenau' and her 'numerous and brilliant' suite, which by the time of her return had regained a familiar face – Countess Ekaterina Vorontsova, a favourite lady in waiting of Julie's, who had accompanied her out of Russia in 1801 but had then gone back to St Petersburg.[28]

In August the following year, Julie's mother finally made a longed-for trip to see Elfenau. Her enthusiastic account, much like her journey to Russia, is full of detailed and lyrical descriptions of the scenery that convey her intense love of nature and the landscape. 'My favourite pleasure is wandering around in God's beautiful world,' as she says, and she shares also a valuable account of several people making a regular appearance in Julie's growing social circle.[29]

After a five-day journey Auguste arrived at Elfenau on 2 September 1816 and was immediately entranced not just by the ambiance of Julie's 'welcoming home' but by the warmth of her entourage. Her own rooms were 'like the whole house, very comfortable' and outside was an absolute delight: 'When you come into the courtyard, [there are] many flowers and orange trees, white benches under the windows; it could come straight out of any novel, this pretty, unshowy estate, with everything so clean and spotless right down to the outbuildings of the work people.'[30]

That first morning, when they went for a walk in the gardens, Auguste was overwhelmed by the beauty of the snow-capped mountain peaks 'gleaming like apparitions from another world above the nearer wooded hills'. She and Julie spent a great deal of time outdoors when the weather was fine, walking in the wooded glades of Elfenau and taking in the Alps 'in their full glory in the morning sunlight'. They often dined together outside or sat in the sunshine, Auguste sketching and Julie reading to her.[31]

Auguste was greatly impressed by the people in Julie's social circle whom she met, local Bern dignitaries from leading patrician families: Nicolas-Rodolphe de Watteville (a member of the Bern cantonal

government, who served in the Federal Diet in 1817), Nicolas-
Frédéric de Mülinen (a major figure in the Bernese government) and
Emanuel-Frédéric de Fischer (a district judge and future mayor of
Bern).* Julie became close friends with these men and their wives.
The social scene in Bern at the time was small and somewhat limited,
with 'the only public amusement' being 'a very indifferent German
theatre'. Julie made up for it by entertaining a great deal at Elfenau
and visiting the homes of her acquaintances, where she was a sought-
after guest for receptions and musical soirées and much admired
not just for her lovely singing voice but also for her beauty and
vivacity.[32] The French ambassador to Bern, Count Louis Talleyrand
(cousin of the famous politician), and his wife paid regular calls at
Elfenau. Julie also met the secretary to the British legation, Henry
Addington, and on 17 September the British Envoy Extraordinary
and Minister-Plenipotentiary to Switzerland, the 'learned, shrewd
and serious' Stratford Canning, when he was en route to Lausanne
from the Congress of Vienna. He was accompanied by 'his incredibly
beautiful wife', Harriet, whom he had recently married, a woman
'with the loveliest black eyes and who looks as blooming as a rose'.
Auguste was particularly taken with her 'elegant toilette' in comparison to the 'tasteless' style now favoured by English ladies.[33] In
his memoirs, Canning later recalled the 'liberal hospitality' at Julie's
home which was gratefully received, he and his wife having found
the social scene in Bern extremely limited and dull after London.[34]

There was, however, one lady in Julie's circle who particularly
struck Auguste. That was 'Generalin Demborska', by whom she
meant Metilde Viscontini Dembowski, an Italian from the Milanese
gentry who, according to Auguste, had 'married a Polish general on
Napoleon's orders'. Here was another fellow sufferer with whom
to share her experiences, for like Julie, Dembowski had suffered

---

* Both the French and German versions of these names occur in sources for this
period relating to Julie, hence Niklaus-Rudolf von Wattenwyl, Niklaus-Friedrich
von Mülinen and Emmanuel-Friedrich von Fischer. Bern residents tended to use
the French form of their names, and although both occur in sources, the German
forms were not used extensively until the twentieth century.

violence and abuse at her husband's hands and had recently fled to Bern with her four-year-old son, Ercole. As a separated woman she was, by necessity, 'living a very secluded life' in a huntsman's house that Julie had rented to her on the Brunnadern estate. Auguste found her 'one of the most likeable ladies I know, very refined, clever, modest and with a silent sorrow in her beautiful face which makes her even more interesting'.[35] There is no doubt that Dembowski's 'silent sorrow' was symptomatic of her bitter battle for a legal separation and custody of her other son, Carlo, in Italy, in which she had solicited Julie's and Schiferli's help. They had both been highly sympathetic to her troubles and had written letters in support of her cause to the highest authorities, including the Austrian chancellor Metternich in Vienna (Milan having recently been returned to Austrian control at the Congress of Vienna). Metilde Dembowski later gratefully acknowledged the 'adorable princess' Julie's 'compassionate heart' and her 'touching goodness' in letters to Schiferli after she left Brunnadern that October.*[36]

As autumn drew in, Elfenau became even more enchanting; Auguste and Julie drove out to the lake at Thun through the 'still verdant, fruit- and flower-filled Thun valley which is the most fertile imaginable'.[37] On 23 September they celebrated Julie's thirty-fifth birthday together; Auguste was fulsome in her hopes for the future: 'May this splendid day be the model for the new year which begins today for my good, good Jülchen! May health and a joyful contented heart embellish her every day; she has at last found that haven of peace she so longed for; Father in Heaven! Maintain and safeguard her uncomplicated, harmless good fortune so that no new storm in her life might destroy it.'

A visit to the Fischer residence once more inspired a long description in her journal – of the old French-style castle, with its 'beautiful

---

*   In 1817 Dembowski obtained a legal separation and access to her sons. She later met the French writer Stendhal, who fell passionately in love with her but she rejected his advances. She later became caught up in political conspiracies in Piedmont, but died prematurely of tuberculosis in 1822.

avenue of chestnut trees and in the courtyard a huge fountain', and a lovely garden 'where very rare flowers are still in bloom'. 'It is a long time since I have seen anything as strikingly beautiful as the location of Oberried and could spend days looking around this richly various area without ever tiring!' Auguste wrote. 'Oh who can ever get enough of looking at the beauty of this unique country!'[38]

Just before Auguste's departure, Julie arranged a ball for her and her entourage; Julie's own people all came in Swiss costume 'and I could barely hold back my tears at their warm farewell'. It was a terrible wrench to have to say goodbye: 'I cannot express how reluctant I am to leave here where I have been so endlessly joyous and fortunate, as completely free and relaxed as I could wish in this beauty. It feels so thoroughly good to be in Julie's loving vicinity, she is so kind, so highly pleasant, so concerned to bring me joy, without appearing to be so.'[39] She was particularly touched to leave the 'lovable Demborska' and the 'kindly Wattevilles'. That evening, 30 September, she poured out her heart to her journal: 'I loved my little bedroom so much, whose white painted walls make it so clean and cheerful; I write *for the last time* in my beloved Cabinet, smelling of flowers, where on so many a bright morning I looked with delight at the shining glaciers peeping in all their splendour over the nearby mountains in the high blue sky, and where now the moon shines in sad and dull. God's best blessing on this welcoming and graceful home!'[40]

The next day, Julie and Rodolphe Schiferli accompanied Auguste as far as Basel. Something 'gripped my heart', Auguste wrote, as she left beautiful Elfenau. It had worked its magic on her, as it did everyone who visited, and she knew that the memory of it would stay with her for ever.[41]

In November 1817, the Saxe-Coburg family once more found themselves caught up in momentous events that would impact on their status when, after only eighteen months of marriage to Leopold, Princess Charlotte died after suffering greatly giving birth to a stillborn son. 'It was like lightning out of a blue sky,' records Auguste, 'for who could ever have thought that this healthy young woman would only survive her confinement by a few hours ... And now my poor son stands alone in a foreign country amid the ruins of his shattered happiness.' She also worried 'what this death and the annihilation of all our hopes would be for Julie'. The news might be too much for her and she wrote to Schiferli that she was 'afraid that she might fall seriously ill from the painful shock'.[42]

In England Princess Charlotte's death had plunged the entire country into a state of profound national mourning, but behind the scenes it had also triggered an unseemly, covert race when 'the royal brothers rushed in patriotic matrimonial Quixoticism to the continent, in search of Protestant consorts, who might give an heir to the British throne'.[43] This unexpectedly brought the Saxe-Coburgs straight back into the frame, even as Leopold saw his own British dynastic hopes crushed. For the still unmarried Edward, Duke of Kent, now found himself urgently in need of a bride, his eldest brother George having no other legitimate heir than the deceased Charlotte. The next brother in line, William, Duke of Clarence, was also still without a wife (though he had fathered a vast brood of ten illegitimate FitzClarences with the actress Mrs Jordan).

With the marriageable princesses of Europe throwing their caps at them and hiring the services of the fashionable portrait painters on the Continent, the English bachelor dukes pensioned off their mistresses and set off on the hunt for brides, with 'the widowed Leopold, the modern *Ulysses*, soothing his own griefs, by acting as *Mercury* in the courtships of his uncles-in-law'.[44]

The Duke of Kent had long lived in contented but childless unmarried bliss with his acquiescent French mistress, Madame de St Laurent. But he was now portly, bald and fast approaching fifty, so decided it would be expeditious to secure for himself a nice fertile Baden princess to produce some legitimate offspring now that Princess Charlotte's death had elevated him to third in line to the throne. Borrowing money from Tsar Alexander he set off for Europe, hoping to secure Princess Amalie of Baden. But thanks to the wily 'diplomatic manoeuvres' of his brother-in-law Prince Leopold, the duke's attention was drawn to Leopold's sister, the now widowed and languishing Victoire of Leiningen.[45] Victoire was reluctant to marry again but, as regent for her son, had been under considerable strain trying to manage his affairs and Leopold persuaded her to accept a perfunctory offer from the duke. After meeting Edward only once, Victoire accepted. He meanwhile, had quietly divested himself of Madame St Laurent (who went without protest, unlike his brother-in-law Ernst's mistress, Pauline Panam). Any currency the Kents had in terms of royal status (for in the duke's eyes, the Leiningen princess was very much second best and had little to offer) would be down to whether or not they could produce a child. But even then, if either of the duke's older brothers, George, Prince Regent, and William, Duke of Clarence, produced a legitimate child, any Kent progeny would be subordinate to it in the succession; and if all three failed to conceive an heir, their younger, still unmarried brother, Adolphus, Duke of Cambridge might yet triumph.

The Kents were married in a Lutheran ceremony held in the overpowering setting of the Riesensaal – a hall decorated with giant caryatids – at the Ehrenburg Palace on the evening of 29 May 1818. When they went through a second, Anglican ceremony at Kew Palace on 11 July, it was alongside Edward's brother William and his bride, Adelaide of Saxe-Meiningen, the couple having met only a week before. A month previously Adolphus joined the race, by marrying his second cousin, Augusta of Hesse-Kassel, but as the seventh son he was very low in the pecking order should he produce a child. By November, when she and the Duke of Kent went on a visit to Julie at Elfenau, Victoire was pregnant. The couple stayed for ten days to take a tour of local beauty spots, after which Julie left to spend another winter in Coburg with Auguste. It was while she was back home that, in the company of Leopold, she met up again with Tsar Alexander at Münnerstadt, 44 miles west of Coburg, when he was en route to the Congress of the Holy Alliance in Aachen, to discuss the thorny subject of her divorce from Konstantin. Julie seemed happy at the outcome but insisted on no public reference being made to it.[46]

That winter of 1818–19 at Coburg, despite four of the seven Coburg siblings (Julie, Ernst, Leopold and Sophie) being reunited, was very subdued. Sophie was frail and suffering from depression; since her marriage in 1804 she had produced six sons in very quick succession and had recently lost one of them.[47] She now was a cause for concern for Auguste: 'Her sufferings and melancholy frame of mind overcloud the evening of my life,' she wrote. And Leopold was still in deep mourning for Charlotte and remained in a detached state of solemn silence for the most part, so much so that, as Auguste recalled, 'all felt depressed by his sorrow.' She fervently wished that in the year to come she would not 'have to weep over any fresh graves'.[48]

Far from it; the year 1819 brought two new members into her family and with their arrival a revival of the Duchess of Saxe-Coburg's ambitions for the dynasty, even as her much-troubled daughter Julie approached final release from the shackles of her Russian marriage. Julie's misery had not gone unnoticed by the traveller Marianne Baillie, who, writing of a visit to Bern in 1818, had noted her presence in the neighbourhood and how she had been married off 'in pursuance of one of those horrible schemes of state policy, where every better feeling of the heart is cruelly sacrificed and overborne'.[49] Another English visitor that autumn, Miss Harriet Pigott, also wrote from Bern of the presence of the 'Grand Duchess Constantine of Russia', who lived in 'perfect seclusion at her lovely villa' and who was 'separated from her barbarian ducal husband'. While she seemed highly sympathetic to Julie's difficult position and the 'mental suffering' she had endured, as did all visitors who mentioned her presence in Switzerland, Miss Piggott did not like the sound of the 'Swiss physician' Schiferli, who – so she had heard – 'reigns supreme over [Julie's] mind and over her household', and who, even with the 'constant residence of his wife', had not been able to 'evade the breezes of defamation'.[50]

Both Miss Baillie and Miss Piggott also noted Leopold's mournful presence in Bern and his being 'almost continually alone', gripped by lingering despair at the loss of his wife and no doubt also his chance to be consort to a queen. But consolation came elsewhere when his sister Victoire emerged triumphant from her second marriage and laid the foundation of Leopold's future unique position of influence over the British monarchy. She and the duke had been living at Amorbach to avoid his English creditors, but when Victoire was close to term he drove her home to Kensington Palace in a hair-raising 427-mile carriage ride, so that she could give birth on English soil. At 4.15 on the morning of 24 May, Victoire gave birth to 'a pretty little princess, as plump as a partridge', according to her proud father.[51]

An ecstatic Auguste received the news in Coburg on the 31st and hurried off a note of congratulation to Victoire: 'My God, how glad I am to hear of you ... I cannot find words to express my delight that everything went so smoothly ... I cannot write much ... dear mouse ... for I am much too happy.' She had every confidence that this little girl, although at present only fifth in line (after the Prince Regent and the Duke of York – who were both childless – the Duke of Clarence and her father), was headed for the throne, for 'the English like Queens'.[52] The child would be given the first name of Alexandrina – a grateful and deliberate nod to the tsar – though Grandmama Coburg called her Mai-blühme ('May Blossom') and to her mother she was Vickelchen, from her second name, Victoria.[*53]

Three months later, on 26 August, Auguste's cup overflowed yet more. At the family's summer home, Schloss Rosenau, Duchess Luise gave birth to her second son, for whom his father Ernst chose the old Saxon name of Albert. Nothing could stop the cogs of Grandmama Coburg's brain from going into overdrive. Even while

---

* William, Duke of Clarence's wife, Adelaide, had also quickly fallen pregnant after their marriage, but gave birth to a baby daughter prematurely, two months before Victoire, on 27 March 1819. Technically, the Duke of Cambridge had beaten his brothers to the line when his wife Augusta gave birth to the first legitimate grandchild – a son – the day before Adelaide. But his triumph was cut short by the arrival of Victoria. The long-suffering Adelaide conceived again soon after March 1819, but miscarried later that year. Another daughter born in December 1820 survived for only three months and the couple suffered further tragedy with the stillbirth of twin boys born in 1822, all these tragic losses thus consolidating Victoria's direct line to the throne.

those two sweet grandchildren were being rocked in their cradles, she began plotting a great future alliance of the Saxe-Coburgs and the British Hanoverian monarchs. Luise's beautiful little Albert, would, Auguste said, be 'the pendant to the pretty cousin' – her darling English Mai-blühme.[54]

But then, only six months later, poor ill-fated Victoire was once more crushed. At a modest cottage near the seafront at Sidmouth on the Devon coast, where the family had decamped to save money, the Duke of Kent fell ill with pneumonia. He died on 23 January 1820, leaving Victoire a widow again, just as Julie received the news she had so long been waiting for. Tsar Alexander had issued an imperial edict announcing that the Holy Synod of the Russian Orthodox Church had finally granted her a divorce – after twenty-four years of marriage.

CHAPTER 12

'DIE ELFENKÖNIGIN'

By 1819 the dowager empress Maria Feodorovna had finally retreated from her position of bitter intransigence over the Konstantin–Julie divorce. This was prompted in part by the birth of a son to her favourite younger son, Nikolai, who in 1817 had, to her satisfaction, found himself a German princess, Charlotte of Prussia. She, like Julie, had converted to Russian Orthodoxy and had taken the name Alexandra Feodorovna on their marriage and produced a son – the future Alexander II – within a year. Failing any legitimate sons being born to his two older brothers, Nikolai would be next in line to the throne, and his son after him.[1] The pressure was therefore lifted from Alexander and Konstantin; in any event, by this time, Konstantin had received final and irrevocable confirmation that Julie would never return to him. In a brief and rather recriminatory exchange of letters, she had reminded him that 'I have already told you that I left you because we did not share the same moral values.' The veiled intimations of his sexual profligacy are clear. This, Julie insisted, was the fundamental cause of her fleeing the marriage and she repeated emphatically that 'having no other reasons than this, I cannot return to you.' Her letter must serve, she insisted 'as satisfactory proof of my determination in this case to leave you for ever'.[2]

At that same time, Tsar Alexander had set their divorce in motion, writing to Julie from St Petersburg in early January 1820 to confirm the faithful promise he had made to her that he would do so, when they had met briefly in Münnerstadt in December 1818. He apologised that the divorce negotiations had been protracted for a year by the death of his sister, Ekaterina Pavlovna, Duchess of Württemberg, and a period of court mourning for her.[3] When the Holy Synod, after much deliberation, finally gave its approval on 19 March (OS; 1 April NS), Alexander issued an imperial edict granting the divorce. In it he emphasised the fact that in 1801 Julie had 'retired to foreign lands because of her health being utterly broken' and that, after nineteen years of separation she 'cannot return to Russia'. Alexander's annulment of the marriage was accompanied by a new codicil to the Law of Succession, in which, although he permitted future unequal marriages in the Romanov family, he stipulated that any children of those unions would be deprived of their right to the succession.[*4]

Announcing the divorce, the British press considered it highly laudable that it had been effected 'without the display of any angry or vindictive feelings on either side, or the exposition of mutual errors' and reported that Julie was allowed to retain 'her appanage, titles, and other rights, appertaining to her rank' (though this did not include the Russians covering the costs of running her household or any shortfall in her expenditure). The press was puzzled to note, however, that 'the most singular part ... is that her Imperial Highness, notwithstanding her divorce, is permitted to retain her title of marriage, which very title her husband has, since her divorce, legally granted to a second consort.'[5] Konstantin had certainly wasted no time in remarrying: only two months after his divorce and ignoring his mother's demand that he seek out another suitable German princess, he contracted a morganatic marriage with his Polish mistress, Zhanetta Grudzinskaya. She, however, was only granted the title Princess of Łowicz; that of 'Grand Duchess' remained Julie's. Konstantin later confided to his mother that he

---

*   This codicil was overruled by Alexander III in 1889 when he prohibited all unequal marriages in the Romanov family. Two later Romanovs, Grand Duke Mikhail Mikhailovich and Nicholas II's own brother Grand Duke Mikhail Alexandrovich, were both banished from Russia for contracting morganatic marriages and the latter's only son, Georgy, was excluded from the line of succession.

'had contracted this marriage in part so that his descendants would not compete with Nicholas's line'. Maria Feodorovna was relieved that 'the possible regrettable implications of the union have been nullified' by his doing this, but she was already worrying about the prospects for her youngest son, 23-year-old Mikhail, 'because of the total lack of Princesses. There's really a complete dearth of suitable girls.'[6]

For Julie, this final act of severance, according to her sister-in-law Elise, provided the one thing she craved above all else: 'She longs only to be forgotten.' However, as Elise explained, Julie 'rightly feared that the fracas over the divorce will draw attention to her, and cause new conjectures to be made, perhaps new rumours to be invented, whereas, for years, her life had given no cause for it. She fears she will be met with contempt, insult perhaps.'[7] Despite yearning for so long to be free of Konstantin, Julie now realised the social consequences that divorce might bring, and it worried and depressed her. She also feared the effect that the divorce would have on her mother and the status of her whole Saxe-Coburg family. Immediately after the announcement, she left for the restorative effects of the spa waters at Baden and the degree of privacy afforded her there.

In Russia, Elise and her mother-in-law were also preoccupied with the impact this Romanov divorce might have on public opinion, for the family were seen as the upholders of Orthodoxy. To her credit, Julie had been scrupulous in requesting how the reasons for the divorce be worded: as she had been away from Russia for so long and her health prevented her return, she simply had not wished 'to be an obstacle to the happiness he [Konstantin] might find in another union'. There was never any mention of blame by Julie for his abusive treatment of her. Nor is there anything to be found in family correspondence that has survived, beyond the typically self-interested comment by Antoinette – who had dreaded the shame the divorce would bring on her personally – that the family had all come through 'an epoch that has given us a great deal of bad blood'.[8]

*

The early part of 1820 turned out to be a highly stressful time for

Julie, when, on top of the final negotiations for the divorce, the news came out of the blue of the death of her brother-in-law the Duke of Kent. For some time she had found it difficult obtaining news from England of her 'beloved mouse' Victoire. 'I would know nothing more than what is in the newspapers,' she told her in a long and effusive letter of condolence, if it were not for the help of an intermediary, Victoire's German lady in waiting, Baroness Späth. The contents of the long, rambling and distressed letter that Julie now wrote indicate a highly distracted state of mind veering from the meditative, to the philosophical, to the theological as she mourned this terrible blow in an extravagance of grief. 'If fate needed another victim from our family, why shouldn't the arrows all strike me, upon whom misfortune has already visited itself in so many ways?' she declared. She had read the sad details in the English newspapers and shared in her sister's distress, but her own life too was 'terrible' at present. Life was full of sin and pain and suffering but she trusted in God's love and in the future life in eternity with him.[9] In expounding her religious beliefs in this regard – and no doubt in deference to the religious education she and Victoire had shared, rather than her adopted Russian Orthodox one – Julie quotes heavily from a Lutheran book of weekly meditations on Bible verses by Heinrich Zschokke, who had settled in Switzerland in 1796.[10] Julie's elaborate letter of condolence was very much a reflection of the mawkish preoccupation with the rituals of mourning then prevalent, but Victoire was nevertheless devastated to be made a widow again within six years, with all the concomitant loss of income and status.

Julie's current state of 'heartrending misery' over the duke's death was, she admitted, compounded by considerable physical pain: she was still plagued by trouble with her eyes, bad headaches and the poor state of her nerves.[11] By July she had taken herself off to the spa at Baden* in yet another desperate search for treatment, where on the 13th she was reunited with Auguste. Auguste had brought with

---

* There were several spas bearing this name at the time but in all cases here the reference is to Baden-Baden in the Grand Duchy of Baden.

her Antoinette, who was on an extended visit to Coburg. The three women shared a house together in Baden for several weeks, during which they were entertained by King Maximilian of Bavaria and Princess Amelie of Baden. The king of Württemberg made available a special six-horse carriage and squire for their exclusive use and they toured the countryside and visited many historic castles in the area. Contrary to Julie's deep-seated fears that she would be socially ostracised as a divorced woman, she was received and entertained with great 'deference and politeness' by all her royal peers during her stay in Baden, as Rodolphe Schiferli wrote to his wife on 9 July. There was no question of the grand duchess not being publicly accorded the marks of their esteem, which appears to have been in part a sympathetic response prompted by Konstantin's hasty remarriage. Behind the scenes, the exhausting demands placed on Schiferli in organising the accommodation, the provisioning of Julie and her entourage and the entertaining of their many guests put a great strain on him, as he struggled to find and hire tea services, domestic servants, chefs, waiters and musicians and send out invitations.[12]

The entourage had not been back at Elfenau for long when Schiferli was commanded by his mistress to pack everything up yet again, this time for a trip to Interlaken and the Bernese Oberland. For the first time sources inform us that Julie was accompanied on this trip by twelve-year-old Eduard, who, once her new life in Switzerland had stabilised, had come to live at Elfenau under the guardianship of Schiferli, to be educated with his two sons Moritz and Fritz. It is unclear whether Eduard actually knew at this point that Julie was his birth mother, but privately in 1815 she had written to her brother Duke Ernst asking him to ennoble her son in order to secure his status and future financial security. Although she would have preferred some more remote royal family to do this in order not to draw attention to her relationship to Eduard, three years later Ernst was able to obtain a title for Eduard from the king of Saxony. He was now to be known as 'Eduard Schmidt-Löwe, Edler von Löwenfels'. To complete the new persona, Schiferli composed a bogus genealogy, describing Eduard as having had a learned and distinguished father who had died in the wars in Spain against Napoleon.[13]

On the trip to the Bernese Oberland Eduard enjoyed having the company of his friends Fritz and Moritz Schiferli, who were travelling in the entourage with their father and mother. In later years Fritz remembered the handsome and gifted Eduard as 'the liveliest, the wildest, also the most defiant of us three, but very talented and he learned easily and had a noble open nature'.[14] It is not known whether Julie openly presented Eduard to people as her son but certainly when the party travelled on to Italy, she may not have felt the need there to disguise their relationship. At the Hôtel de Londres in Genoa they were joined in November by the intrepid Auguste, who had decided once more to travel to the warm south for her health and had brought Leopold along with her, in order to have 'the joy of this winter in Italy with Jülchen'.[15] The group had chosen Genoa because the widowed Duchess Charlotte Amelia of Saxe-Gotha-Altenburg – mother of Ernst's wife Luise – was now living there at the Palazzo delle Peschiere, in the company of her major-domo, Franz Xaver von Zach, who had been court astronomer to Charlotte's late husband. As men of science, he and Schiferli gravitated to each other and struck up a close friendship. Zach was greatly taken by Julie and visited her and Schiferli in Switzerland a few years later, declaring his abiding love for its 'dear and peaceful inhabitants' and speaking of Julie as 'HH the *legitimate* Empress of all the Russias'.[16]

After Julie's party had travelled on south to Florence they returned to Switzerland, only to set off again in September 1823 when Julie went in pursuit of yet another cure – this time at Aix-les-Bains – where both she and Schiferli (who also suffered poor health) took long daily treatments at the baths.[17] But Julie was dissatisfied with their hotel and, after only a week, insisted they all decamp. She rented a house – the Maison Duvernay – with a terrace overlooking vineyards, at considerably greater cost, where Schiferli was once more stressed and burdened with arranging the entertaining of a succession of visitors including the Duke and Duchess of Beauvilliers. He was longing to get home to his family but en route back to Elfenau Julie insisted on stopping off to visit acquaintances in Geneva, in Rolle, in Morges and in Lausanne.

Whenever she was back at Elfenau from her frequent travels Julie devoted a great deal of time to building an elegant and welcoming environment for the many international visitors she was now receiving, as a notable person of rank. From kings and queens, princes and grand dukes of many reigning European houses – Sweden, Mecklenburg-Schwerin, Hesse, Liechtenstein, Prussia, Orange, Russia – to celebrated poets such as Karl Bonstetten and the revered Russian Vasily Zhukovsky; the noted philosopher Pyotr Chaadaev; military men such as Helmut von Moltke; and many other writers, musicians, ambassadors, diplomats and ministers from Russia, England, France, Austria, Germany, Belgium, Holland and Sweden. Schiferli kept a detailed visitors' book of all their names.[18]

To all intents and purposes Elfenau became a mini Russian court abroad, *the* unofficial, private meeting place for the European diplomatic corps. As a result, it was not without its cabals and spies, the most notable being the French representative of Louis XVIII in Switzerland, the Marquis de Moustier, who turned out to be sending secret reports back to the Ministry of Foreign Affairs in Paris. Moustier appears to have stirred up trouble among some of the other guests which threatened to compromise Julie's important social standing. It prompted Prince Leopold, who was scrupulous always about protecting his sister's position, to write to the government in Paris pointing out that 'in a small town where society cannot avoid each other, misunderstandings become a real scourge'.[19] Bearing in mind that members of the Bernese government and aristocracy were regular and welcome visitors at Elfenau, with Julie's social life centring around her friendship with the influential Swiss families of Fischer and Watteville – whom Auguste had enjoyed meeting in 1816 – and the mayor of Bern, Count Nicolas-Frédéric Mülinen, one can see why Leopold was so concerned. In response to Leopold's letter Moustier was promptly recalled.

Because Elfenau was quite modest in size, in order to accommodate all her many guests Julie rented two local houses at Mettlen and Muri; things must have been looking up financially for she also bought more land, at Muri, and increased the size of the woodland on her estate. Leopold, who had for years been exhorting Schiferli by letter to reduce Julie's debts, by now had ceased to interfere in her spending, out of exasperation.[20] But he told his brother Ernst that Julie's financial 'inconveniences' were 'partly her fault'. 'Her yearly income should be quite sufficient for an enterprising woman,' he declared, but she had made a mistake in choosing to settle in Switzerland, for everyone knew it was 'very expensive' now that it was a major tourist venue. Julie would have done better to buy a house in Coburg, he concluded; it would have been 'cheaper and more natural', but she had 'got a little bored' with her modest home there.[21]

Among the first visitors Julie received was the poet Karl Bonstetten, who had revered Julie since visiting Coburg after her return from Russia. He came to the 'fairy garden' of Elfenau to visit 'Titania' in August 1820, bringing with him another poetic admirer of Julie's, Friedrich von Matthisson. During their eight days in Bern the two men visited 'the loveable Grand Duchess' daily, as Bonstetten noted. He rhapsodised about her 'delightful country seat' where 'beautiful nature holds me here softly clasped and many good people greet me with a warm welcome. I love Elfenau and the Queen of the elves yet more.'[22] He and Matthisson read their verse to her and, inspired by Julie as a kind of fairy muse, Matthisson offered up a poem he had written in her honour:

> Titania commands. See, everything becomes bright like
>   stars.
> And every wave of her magic wand extends her fairy
>   kingdom.
> What magnificent valleys, hills and groves are resplendent
>   in this show of bliss.
> In truth, you are held within an enchantment, O Elfenau.
> Sorrow's night is banned from your Tempe's bounds

Where everything smiles,
And pure sun and moon and aether gleam.
When the elves weave their moonlight dance,
Through purple blossom rings out
Near and far
'Blessed be thy life, Titania'.[23]

In March 1824, the Elfenau idyll was disturbed by news of the
unexpected death of Julie's sister Antoinette, at the age of forty-four.
Most recently she had been travelling a great deal around Germany
and Austria with her daughter Marie and had spent time in Coburg
with Auguste. After seeing Julie in Baden in 1820, Antoinette had
returned to St Petersburg where she and the Duke of Württemberg
moved into a mansion in the Yusupov Garden, provided to her husband as head of the Directorate of Communications, to which he had
been appointed in 1822. But at the end of February 1824 Antoinette
fell ill with erysipelas, a serious bacterial skin infection, which led
to cellulitis and killed her two weeks later. The Saxe-Coburg and
Russian imperial families went into mourning and Antoinette's body
was brought back to Germany, to be interred in the ducal crypt of
the church at Schloss Friedenstein in Gotha.[24] Julie did not travel to
Gotha for the funeral, but in May, on her way home to Coburg from
Nice, Auguste stopped off at Elfenau to commiserate over their loss.
Not long afterwards, she also saw her five-year-old nephew, 'little
Alberinchen' as the doting Auguste referred to him, when she visited
Ernst and Luise at Rosenau. Grandmama Coburg was smitten with
his 'large blue eyes and dimpled cheeks'. With his blond hair and
angelic looks he was utterly 'bewitching'.[25]

With Sophie, who was plagued by ill health, now living closer to
home at Mainz, where her husband Emmanuel had been transferred
after five years in Prague to take command of the fortress, Julie set
off on a visit. She joined Auguste there in June 1825, arriving in
time for them both to be utterly repulsed by the aftermath of an
execution by guillotine in the market square, and seeing the 'hearse

of the decapitated being escorted by police to his lonely grave'.[26] From there, Julie travelled on to take the cure at Wiesbaden, while her mother, now sixty-seven and undeterred by her exhausting travels, finally made her first trip to England, escorted by her grandson Prince Karl of Leiningen, to visit his mother Victoire, whom the duchess had not seen for seven years.

Victoire was staying at Leopold's home, Claremont, at the time, and he had sent a carriage to collect them from the boat at Dover. During the journey Auguste, with her characteristic enthusiasm, noted the loveliness of the Kent countryside and at Chatham, 'the sight of the heavenly Thames which stretches out to the distant sea … alive with innumerable ships'. This was excelled only by the view of London from an open chaise at the top of Shooter's Hill. It was, she wrote, 'the most beautiful view in the world.'[27] At Claremont the duchess was welcomed by Victoire, her daughter by her first marriage, Feodore, and her Mai-blühme. She found little Victoria a 'lovable child' and has left us a delightful description of the six-year-old: 'Her face is just like her father's, the same artful blue eyes, the same roguish expression when she laughs. She is big and strong and as good health itself, friendly and cuddlesome[,] I would even say obliging – agile, poised, graceful in all her movements.'[28]

The two of them muddled along happily in a mix of German and Auguste's 'inadequate' English during her ten-week visit. Grandmama Coburg found her English granddaughter 'incredibly precocious for her age' and perceptively noted one particular thing about the little girl's manner: 'When she enters a room, and greets you by inclining her head, according to the English custom, there is a staggering majesty.'[29] Many years later Queen Victoria recalled that visit; her grandmother was 'a good deal bent and walked with a stick, and frequently with her hands on her back. She took long drives in an open carriage, and I was frequently sent out with her, which I am sorry to confess I did not like, as, like most children of that age, I preferred running about.' Interestingly, and confirming the authoritarian side to Auguste's deceptive 'kind granny' image, Victoria also recalled that although she was 'excessively kind to children', the Dowager Duchess Auguste 'could not bear naughty ones' and had a sharp tongue. She scolded her severely when she misbehaved at her lessons.[30]

Auguste arrived back at Coburg happy in the choice she had made of young Princess Victoria as the future match for her Alberinchen, but it was a small window of happiness for the family before news came from Russia in December of the unexpected death of Tsar Alexander, at Taganrog on the Sea of Azov in the southwest of the country, where he and Elise had travelled for the sake of her health. In recent years, the long-estranged couple had begun to grow close again and Alexander had shown great care and concern for his wife's failing health. But in Taganrog it was he who succumbed – to what was probably typhoid fever – on 1 December 1825.

The final few years of his life had worn Alexander down; recently, he had become aware of a plot by several regiments in Ukraine to overthrow what they felt was his increasingly autocratic rule and he had become weary of the burden of being tsar. He seemed increasingly withdrawn and greatly preoccupied with his religious faith and talked often of his desire to step down from the throne and live in retirement, handing over the succession not to Konstantin, but to Nikolai.

But Alexander had not made public his plans for the succession before he died and for a few short days afterwards confusion reigned. Despite his morganatic remarriage, which Alexander had allowed, Konstantin technically could have succeeded him and, assuming this to be the case, in St Petersburg his younger brother Grand Duke Nikolai declared Konstantin to be the legitimate emperor. But Konstantin was absent in Poland, having been viceroy there since 1815, and the Imperial Guard, civil service and other senior officials had sworn allegiance to him as the new tsar, not knowing that in January 1822 Konstantin had privately informed Alexander that he was voluntarily relinquishing his claim to the throne, 'not finding in myself either the genius or talents or strengths necessary to be elevated forever to the sovereign dignity in which I would have had right by my birth'. He also did so in the knowledge that his children by this second marriage would have no right to succeed him.[31]

For the next three weeks messengers rushed back and forth between St Petersburg and Warsaw, but to no avail. Konstantin refused to take the throne, during which time the ensuing state of confusion precipitated an attempted military coup on 26 December by 3,000 officers on Senate Square against the new tsar, Nicholas I. Inspired by the spirit of the French Revolution, the conspirators demanded a constitutional monarchy, but the Decembrist Revolt, as it became known, was swiftly put down. Five of its ringleaders were hanged the following year and many more were sent into Siberian exile.

According to Rodolphe Schiferli, a messenger had arrived at Elfenau from the French embassy in Bern with the terrible news of Alexander's death on the evening of 18 December. Julie suffered greatly on hearing it, Schiferli later wrote to Auguste – with loss of appetite, insomnia and terrible headaches – but he reassured her mother that she had been able to hold on, thanks to her 'religious resignation' and despite being aware of 'the immensity of the consequences for her of this terrible event'.[32] For so long, Alexander had been her protector, her advisor and also her essential financial support. 'How will the Grand Duchess bear yet more misfortune? I tremble for her,' her lady in waiting Ekaterina Vorontsova said to Schiferli, in discussing how they would prepare their mistress for this devastating news.[33] He was already extremely anxious to secure the continuing payment of Julie's Russian appanage and applied to the Russian minister Count Alexander Benckendorff for assurances on this, gently reminding him also of outstanding monies due to Julie. But he received a frosty response; the Russian government was, to put it delicately, in some financial difficulty and there would have to be changes.[34]

The household at Elfenau meanwhile had gone into full court mourning.[35] At her little Russian Orthodox chapel in the wood Julie held a memorial service for Alexander, she and her ladies draped in long robes of black with 2-yard trains, a *pleureuse* around the bonnet and black *fichus* tied around their necks.[36] Five months later, even more upsetting news came that Empress Elise was gravely ill, and on

15 May, Julie's household were all plunged back into full mourning on the news that she had collapsed and died of a heart attack at Belyov in Tula province. She was only forty-five and had been on her way back to St Petersburg from Taganrog, having been too sick to return earlier for Alexander's funeral.

Julie grieved for Alexander and Elise very deeply, but equally disturbing on an even more personal level had been the news in February 1826 – and with it a great deal of damaging and negative public opinion in Coburg – that her brother Duke Ernst had divorced his wife Luise. Two years previously, on an accusation of her infidelity, he had forced his neglected wife to sign a deed of separation and had banished her, ignoring his own many sexual peccadilloes. Despite protests from the people of Coburg, who held Luise in high regard, she had gone to live in obscurity at St Wendel in the principality of Lichtenberg near the French border. Five years later she was dead, of cancer of the womb, in Paris at the age of only thirty; though she had, in her final years, found happiness and remarried. But Ernst had never allowed her to see her two beloved boys again.

The duchy of Saxe-Coburg, in the meantime, had risen to ever greater heights by the mid-1820s, thanks in large part to the rights its male royals then had over their wives' property. With the death of the Prince of Koháry in 1826, his son-in-law Prince Ferdinand – through his wife Maria Antonia – now inherited all the wealthy estates in Hungary and with them the new title of Duke of Saxe-Coburg and Gotha-Koháry. Ernst too was triumphant, for the recent death of Luise's uncle Frederick IV, Duke of Saxe-Gotha-Altenburg, without male issue had signalled the end of the Saxe-Gotha ducal line and necessitated the reorganisation of the Ernestine duchies.

Saxe-Coburg-Saalfeld was now reconstituted as Saxe-Coburg-Gotha, Ernst having agreed to cede Saalfeld to Saxe-Meiningen in return for Gotha, even though, given he was in the process of divorcing Luise, he had no real moral right to that more prosperous and prestigious province. Luise's family rightly contested his claim – to no avail. A couple of years later, with Julie's son Eduard having completed his studies as a forester at the University of Geneva with a glowing report, Ernst took the twenty-year-old under his wing, sending him for further training as a forest junker and hunting master with his head forester at Georgenthal near Gotha. From this position Eduard was slowly introduced into Coburg society and rose to the position of court chamberlain, ensuring the status his mother had wished for him.[37]

In the constant quest for social preferment and advantageous dynastic union, the vultures of royal ambition were always and forever circling. This time, in 1828, the innocent young prey was Julie's niece – Princess Victoria's half-sister Feodore, whom their mother Victoire was eager to see settled. Two years previously when Victoire had paid a visit to the ageing, gouty King George IV (whose spurned wife Caroline had died in 1820) he had taken rather too much note of his nineteen-year-old stepniece's blossoming loveliness. Might she perhaps be a suitable brood mare for a new heir to replace his lost daughter Charlotte? Auguste and Victoire had been horrified at the suggestion and had swiftly found an alternative compliant, though impecunious, groom for the hapless Feodore. On 18 February 1828 she was married off to Prince Ernst of Hohenlohe-Langenburg, whom she had met only twice before, and forced to leave her much-loved home at Kensington Palace and her distraught nine-year-old half-sister Victoria, to whom she was devoted, and go and live in the castle at Langenburg.

Next it was Leopold's turn to rise from the ashes of his grief and the loss of the role of royal consort. With the death of George IV in 1830, the future of Princess Victoria now seemed secure as heir presumptive to the British throne. Behind the scenes, however, Victoire and her advisor Sir John Conroy had begun working carefully and covertly towards securing a regency in the event that the new king, William IV, died before Victoria reached her majority.[38] Leopold, astute statesman that he was, was only too well aware of the political advantages of having his niece on the throne of a powerful and modernising Britain and ensured that their ambitions were defused. But still he longed for a kingdom of his own.

Early in 1830 he had been offered the vacant throne of Greece, which had recently won independence from Ottoman control, and of which Julie's friend Ioannis Kapodistrias had been elected president in 1828. Leopold had entered difficult and protracted negotiations, knowing that to accept would mean letting go of all the perks of his adopted English nationality by marriage to Charlotte – specifically his comfortable home at Claremont and £50,000 a year from the British privy purse. But while he prevaricated and weighed up his options, Kapodistrias made clear his hostility to the offer, and pointed out the many difficulties that Leopold would have to face. In the end Leopold rejected the Greek throne, deeming the country too politically unstable.[39] Instead, in 1831 he accepted the throne of the newly created kingdom of Belgium, though not without some horse-trading with the French king, who wanted it for his son. As a compromise Louis Napoleon offered his eldest daughter Louise as a bride for the widowed Leopold – an advantageous match to seal this highly political choice, which had been influenced greatly by Leopold's strong diplomatic and familial connections with the royal houses of Europe – all of which had emanated from Julie's Russian marriage in 1796.

In order to accept the Belgian crown, Leopold would ruthlessly divest himself of the loyal German mistress, Caroline Bauer, whom he had had discreetly closeted away in a villa in Regent's Park for several years. He also managed to negotiate retention of Claremont and £20,000 of his British pension to cover its running costs, but this barely dented the massive debts he had run up in England. But the Saxe-Coburg family's anticipation of Leopold's accession was marred by the news at the end of June of another shocking but hugely symbolic death – for Julie at least. On 27 June 1831, in Vitebsk, Grand Duke Konstantin died of cholera during an epidemic then ravaging Poland, and at a time of growing nationalist unrest during which his position as viceroy was being severely challenged. Not long afterwards, Julie received a letter from the new Tsar Nicholas in which he said, despite Konstantin's death, he hoped 'for the continuation of your friendly feelings, which I have always been so happy to receive. I ask Your Imperial Highness, to preserve them and to believe in the constancy of those that I have always vowed to her.'[40] It was a comforting thought but one that had little or no significance to Julie now. With the deaths of Antoinette, Alexander, Elise and now Konstantin, she was finally free of any lingering emotional links to Russia.

In a touching pen portrait, written by her close Swiss friend Margaretha Wildermeth in 1830, we have a rare sighting of Julie, now fifty years old, but looking no more than thirty-five, still an 'elegant and noble figure', 'her black eyes made charming by an expression of gentleness and melancholy'. For Margaretha, Julie's conversation was 'that of a woman who has reflected a lot on herself and others'. It was always spontaneous and natural, but the still pervading air of melancholy suggested to her friend that Julie 'care[d] neither for the world nor its vanities', even though she was 'adored and respected by the people of the country'. Margaretha was sensitive to the fact that Julie's life had been blighted by 'a compromised reputation abroad', but she was sure that 'if she has anything to reproach herself for, it is only for lack of guidance, because her soul has remained pure and virtuous.'[41]

During all these years at Elfenau, while she had continued to enjoy travelling incognito to Italy or to the various spa towns, Julie had very rarely ventured outside Switzerland for any family gatherings and her brother's inauguration was no exception. For Belgium's future was precarious at the time Leopold accepted the throne: the country had barely emerged victorious from a revolution against Dutch control* and the international treaty guaranteeing its independence and neutrality had not yet been signed. Even now, the Dutch king was planning a surprise invasion when, on 21 July 1831, forty-year-old Leopold stood on the steps of the Church of

---

* In 1815, Belgium had been created at the Congress of Vienna by the union of the Southern Netherlands with Holland (the Northern Netherlands). After an uprising in September 1830 Belgium in the south had seceded from the Northern Netherlands and Leopold was invited to become monarch of this newly independent state. But this prompted the Dutch to launch a surprise invasion in August 1831 and Leopold was forced to call in French assistance to preserve Belgian neutrality.

St Jacques-sur-Coudenberg on Brussels's Place Royale to sign the
Constitution and swear to preserve the independence and integrity
of Belgium as its king. But none of his family were present to witness
this moment as it was too unsafe to travel there. He had his kingdom
at last; but for Prince Leopold 'Belgium is just prose; it is Greece that
would have satisfied the poetic needs of my soul.'[42]

CHAPTER 13

'My House Has Become a House of Mourning'

There is no doubt that her favourite son Leopold's promotion as a European monarch marked the high point of Duchess Auguste's lifelong ambitions. But the journey she made with Ernst to visit him at the Palace of Laeken on the outskirts of Brussels in late September 1831 greatly wearied the 73-year-old and on her return to Coburg she never regained her energies. Nor did she ever exorcise the sense of guilt that had perpetually clouded her conscience. To the end of her life Auguste always referred to Julie by her German pet name, Jülchen. The Slavic 'Anna Feodorovna' remained an entirely alien sobriquet; perhaps because she knew that it had brought dynastic status to the duchy at the very price of Julie's happiness and wellbeing.

Duchess Auguste of Saxe-Coburg-Saalfeld died on 16 November with Ernst and Ferdinand at her bedside. Huge crowds stood in line to pay their respects at her lying in state at the Ehrenburg before, on the 19th, her coffin was carried off 'before day-break, by the light of torches' to be interred alongside Duke Franz's in the family mausoleum in the Hofgarten nearby.[1] Julie grieved at not being there and poured out her heart in a letter to Victoire in England:

Ah dear, dear Victoire! Could I have thought it possible, when I last wrote to you, that the next time I grasped the quill in hand for you it would be *for this*! I want to and can't put anything into words about *this* blow! My pain rebels against every expression! *She can never* really be torn from us! On and on, this magnificent spirit, ah this heart, will live on among us! Oh, Victoire, *words* cannot say it, but I would like to cry myself out on your sisterly heart.[2]

There was, however, a ghoulish coda to Auguste's interment, after rumours circulated that she had been laid to rest 'adorned with her diamond rings and richest necklaces'. Among those who had processed past her coffin was a young Bavarian locksmith named Andreas Stubenrauch, who became convinced that the duchess had been buried resplendent with precious jewels. The thought ate away at his imagination until the following August, when at the dead of night he managed to climb over the sharp spikes at the top of the iron gate that barred the entrance to the mausoleum and forced open the lock on the oaken door behind it with a crowbar. Unfortunately, Stubenrauch did not know that the entrance opened onto a sheer drop into which he fell, 12 feet down between the two coffins below. With considerable difficulty he broke into the duchess's coffin and raised the lid sufficiently to see inside. But he was disappointed to discover 'nothing save the fading remains of the Duchess' dressed in black velvet, her corpse 'covered with a glimmering white mould, that seemed to him to be phosphorescent'. To his alarm, he now discovered that clambering out of the deep tomb was impossible and he ended up spending the rest of the night trying to sleep between the two coffins until later the following morning he was found by patrolling guards. Stubenrauch was hauled off to prison and sentenced to eighteen months with hard labour.[3]

With the passing of the years at Elfenau, Julie became ever more withdrawn in response to the deaths of so many family members, as well as her Swiss friends Nicolas de Mulinen and Emmanuel de Fischer. She kept well away from the febrile world of Bernese politics when disturbances in Switzerland in 1831 in the wake of revolutionary activity in France reached Vaud. Schiferli, however, had made contingency plans for Julie's safety in response to anxious enquiries from Ernst in Coburg. He reassured him that although the area around Elfenau was peaceful, he had secured Julie's valuables and the *berlines de voyage* were ready to leave at a moment's notice. Should the need arise, he could call on a hundred men of the local civil guard to protect Elfenau. But Schiferli was confident that that would not be necessary: 'Her Imperial Highness is loved and respected here by all social classes.' In the event, the remnants of the old Bernese oligarchy were ousted without violence and a new liberal government installed.[4]

During this period, there were long gaps in Julie's correspondence with the scattered members of her family, Leopold complaining to Sophie in May 1833 that he had had no news of Julie of late. In his correspondence with Sophie at this time Julie rarely figures, although Sophie conjured up a delightful cameo of her sisters in a letter to their brother Ferdinand, when she also complained of 'Lady Jülchen' not having written to her for a year. She had to admit that 'my Württemberg' (Antoinette) had been her favourite sister: 'What a pleasure her hilarious and witty letters were.' Jülchen was 'a dear being, pleasant and charming', she conceded, 'but a rose full of thorns. One gets pricked at any moment.' As for 'poor *Wuchtel*', as her siblings called Victoire, she was 'pedantic like the English Parliament. And as wilful as a coach-horse' and it worried Sophie that Victoire put so much trust in her overbearing advisor Sir John Conroy.[5] Sophie's letter hints at a difficult relationship with Julie, not helped by the distance that so often separated them and it must have made the blow all the more painful when news came of Sophie's untimely death on 9 July 1835, in Tušimice, Bohemia. Her life had been marred by bouts of neurasthenia – possibly postnatal depression. She was hit very hard by the loss of two infant children and the long periods of separation from her husband Emmanuel, who was often away on military service. But she had at least found consolation in her great love of literature and in writing romantic fairy tales, some of which were published in Prague and Mainz, and in hosting a literary salon.[6]

Sophie's death propelled Julie into a state of deep depression: 'My heart is tired of dying,' she told Schiferli on 27 July. 'I would so love to die but I must not.'[7] If literature had been Sophie's abiding love and had carried her through difficult times, then Julie's one great consolation had always been music. She was a gifted pianist and singer and over many years accumulated a considerable collection of sheet music. In Switzerland she was able to indulge this passion through her patronage of the Hôtel de Musique in Bern. Originally built during 1767–70 as a concert hall and theatre, it had become an important social venue, renowned for the pomp of its balls and receptions for foreign dignitaries where the cream of the old Bern oligarchy regularly gathered, and for holding concerts by distinguished musicians.[8] Julie's association goes back to the establishment of the Bern Musical Society there in November 1815 by its first musical director, Franz Edmund von Weber, a half-brother of Carl, whom Julie had met in Coburg many years before.[*9]

Julie attended the Society's inaugural concert on 3 December 1815 and had her own box at the theatre but she may well have had to ignore the raised eyebrows, for polite society in Bern was highly ambivalent towards her. Its narrow, bourgeois attitudes ensured an avoidance of any reference to her questionable personal life and the unconventional domestic arrangement with Schiferli. However, having a Russian imperial highness in its midst was too advantageous to ignore. Julie's 'celebrity' status raised Bernese society's profile and at the Society a serenade was dedicated to her and a 'historical play with choirs', entitled *Alexis und Feodora*, was performed in her honour.[10]

Prior to the advent of the Hôtel de Musique Julie had found the musical scene in Bern very parochial in comparison with the great musical cities of Vienna, Prague and St Petersburg with which she was acquainted, the cultural life of the city having suffered a lack of

---

*   The Hôtel de Musique was in use as a theatre until 1903 and then refurbished, although the frontage on Marktplatz and the eighteenth-century interiors of the private reception rooms have been preserved. The auditorium was entirely remodelled and is now the kitchen area of the Lorenzini restaurant.

funding during the years of French control. The Society staged five or six subscription concerts a year, many of which Julie attended; it also was the venue for theatrical productions by troupes of German and French actors and held special concerts in support of local charities. Haydn's *Creation* and choral works by Beethoven and Mozart were popular on the programme. Julie particularly enjoyed the 'grand sound' of the choruses and was seen to applaud enthusiastically at performances of Mozart's operas *The Magic Flute* and *The Abduction from the Seraglio*.[11]

Today, the Burgerbibliothek in Bern holds Julie's extensive sheet music collection, which reflects her tastes across a wide and fascinating selection of 'opera arias, romances, arrangements of German, Italian, French, Swiss and ... Russian songs for voice and clavier (cembalo, piano) or guitar'.[12] Most of these scores bear the marks of frequent use and Julie's personal annotation of fingerings and chords; she also lovingly preserved copies of the *Giornale musicale del Teatro italiano di St Pietroburgo* and many of the soprano arias she collected were from popular Italian operas by Guglielmi, Sarti, Paisiello and Cimarosa that appealed to her romantic nature. A particular favourite seems to have been the Italian composer Ferdinando Paer, who composed fifty-five operas that are obscure to today's audiences, but who in his time was a leading light at the Opéra-Italien in Paris and had taught composition to Franz Liszt. But there is little music from Russia for the reason that most of the aristocracy did not sing in that language beyond traditional folk songs.[13] Overall the collection is a valuable time capsule, representative of the popular classical music of the first half of the nineteenth century that was enjoyed in the musical salons of Julie's day.[14] Some compositions bear dedications to her, such as that with which she was presented by Antonio Rosetti on the occasion of Tsar Paul's coronation (see page 91) and 'Divertissements pour le piano-forte à quatre mains' by Andreas Späth, who had started out as a clarinettist with the Coburg Court Orchestra.[15]

When moments of happiness did arrive in a life now plagued by failing eyesight, crippling headaches and arthritic pain in her arm,

Julie clung to tenuous links with her children – such as their marriages – even though she could not openly celebrate them. We have
so little information on Hilda and know nothing of her relationship
with Julie beyond the fact that she did occasionally visit her at
Elfenau. Her wedding to a forester, Jean Samuel Edouard Dapples,
took place at Bursinel, a small village southwest of Bern near Lake
Geneva, on 15 December 1834, which Schiferli attended as a witness,
signing the certificate as her 'trustee'. On 1 January 1836, Hilda
gave birth to a son, Ernest, making Julie a grandmother at the age
of fifty-five, by which time Eduard too had married.[16]

There could hardly be a more contrived union of the dynastic lines
of Julie and her brother Ernst – and one that ignored the consanguinity of its two partners – than that between 27-year-old Eduard and
18-year-old Berta von Schauenstein. For she was Ernst's illegitimate
daughter, the product of an affair he had had in Paris in 1817 with
Sophie Fermepin de Marteaux – the very same year that he had
married his unwitting bride, Luise of Saxe-Gotha-Altenburg. Berta
had been living in Sophie's household in Mainz for the last three
years since leaving boarding school in Frankfurt. The couple married
quietly, on 30 March 1835, in the Catholic military garrison church
of St Adalbert in Prague, the Mensdorff-Pouillys having moved back
there when Emmanuel was promoted to a senior military position
in Bohemia in 1834.[17] The close intermarriage of the Saxe-Coburgs
with their own German relatives did not end there: in December
1832 Duke Ernst had no qualms when he chose as his second wife
his own niece – Duchess Marie of Württemberg, daughter of his late
sister Antoinette.

Neither of Julie's children left any personal account revealing
whether they ever found out the truth of their illegitimacy but
Julie clearly did not and could not disguise her deep affection for
them both. Hilda and Eduard met at Elfenau and were friends with
Schiferli's sons and later corresponded with each other. Hilda kept a
diary, alluded to by Julie's biographer Alville in 1962 (from private
information that she did not reveal), in which it would appear she
confided her doubts about her parentage and wondered whether the

kind 'protectress' who was always so solicitous of her welfare was, in fact, her mother. It would seem that she did eventually discover the truth, for among Hilda's papers was a sketch of her sitting with Julie on the terrace at Elfenau.[18] Eduard too would later admit to his own son to 'having suffered a lot from the uncertainty of his descent'; a family member later asserted that he certainly loved and honoured Julie as though she were his mother.[19]

By 1837, and by her own admission, Julie's life had become increasingly circumscribed by ill health, exacerbated by what seemed at times an intolerable burden of grief that she was carrying. Leopold again complained, this time to his widowed brother-in-law Emmanuel, that he had hardly any news of her for she rarely responded to his letters.[20] The reason is probably because she was increasingly preoccupied that her beloved Schiferli – her 'second father' as she referred to him, underlining their long-since platonic relationship – was himself in seriously declining health. He had never got over the death of his elder son, Fritz, in 1834, from tuberculosis and repeated trips to take the cure were having little or no effect. The strain of dealing with Julie's fragile personality must also have taken its toll, for even into her forties she expressed worrying levels of neediness that he must have found overwhelming at times. Julie had always been prone to emotional outbursts and had admitted to Schiferli that she was 'embarrassed by my great sensitivity' and her occasional 'explosions' of tears and inability to cope when he was absent.[21] And then, on 3 June 1837, came the blow from which Julie never fully recovered: after suffering a stroke, Schiferli died at the age of sixty-one, at Elfenau.[22]

In what seems an extraordinary juxtaposition of tragedy with triumph, only seventeen days later news came from England that the old king, William IV, was dead, and that Julie's niece Victoria was now queen. A second scion of the house of Saxe-Coburg was now sitting on a European throne. It is a mark of the young queen's affection for her aunt that soon after her accession she was eager to finally meet her. Word got back to Uncle Leopold in Belgium about her plans to invite Julie to visit her in England, probably passed on by his vigilant friend and personal physician, Baron Christian Stockmar, who was currently based at Kensington Palace.* Leopold and Stockmar had been united in keeping the truth about Julie's unconventional life from the impressionable young queen, and Leopold was swift to intervene. His niece was of course innocent of her aunt's private life and misfortunes and knew nothing of the recent death of Schiferli or Julie's very close bond with him and so Leopold hastened to write to her:

> You seem to have had some intention I understand to ask your [aunt] the Grandduchess to England: it is most amiable of you to have thought of her, and it will please her very much but I think it will be better for the present to *put it off.* She is of very delicate health[,] her life has not been very happy, and her chief aim of late was peace and quiet, this being the case, I think it would place her into difficulties if you were to ask her which it would be better for *her* sake to avoid.[23]

Only one thing had cheered Julie during this terrible year of paralysing grief, and that was to reconnect once more with her former lady in waiting, Renette, whom she had not seen since she had returned to Russia with her mother in 1802. In 1831 she married Count Irénée Khreptovich-Butenev from an eminent family with an estate at Beshankovichy in Vitebsk province (today's Belarus) and she contacted Julie at the end of July 1837 when passing through Switzerland

---

* During the Napoleonic Wars Stockmar had been a physician attached to Saxe-Coburg forces, where he became acquainted with Leopold on campaign. When Leopold married Princess Charlotte he asked Stockmar to join him in England as his physician, from where he rapidly became far more than that: secretary, treasurer, personal advisor and all-round *éminence grise*, in which latter capacity he remained in England until Leopold became king of the Belgians in 1831. Stockmar returned to England in 1837 as an advisor to the young Queen Victoria and became a close friend of Prince Albert, remaining as an unofficial advisor to Victoria and Albert until 1856.

with her daughter Hélène. Renette's letter came only a few weeks after the death of 'my paternal friend of twenty-seven years', as Julie explained to her. Nevertheless, even though she was now 'a poor old invalid, condemned by her health to an almost complete seclusion', she welcomed the opportunity of seeing Renette after so very many years, but warned that 'my house has become a house of mourning' and that in seeing Julie once more 'you will only find a ruin that the storms of life and time have demolished'. Because her household were all in mourning, Julie arranged accommodation for her visitors at a first-class hotel in Bern but looked forward to being 'torn away' from her solitude, as at present she was neither seeing nor receiving any visitors: 'I stretch out my arms to embrace you with the most sincere joy, dear Countess Renette.'[24]

During the course of several days in August when the two friends renewed their friendship and talked of happier times, Julie was left with an overwhelming sense of *Heimweh* – of nostalgia for their shared past. She counted herself lucky to have reconnected with such a treasured friendship and felt that 'it has since doubled and quadrupled and that these precious interests will multiply until eternity.'[25] Their correspondence would be a great comfort to Julie until Renette's death in 1846 and reveal Julie's great warmth and compassion and her deep loyalty to their friendship.[26] They also, disturbingly, chart her declining health, with Julie complaining that she suffered repeated severe headaches that left her unable to write to many friends. But oh, what a thirst she had for Renette's company now that she had once more held her 'good and amiable friend' in her arms. Right now she had a visit from her brother Ernst and his two young sons to look forward to. This had thrown her into a state of anxiety combined with excitement – how she missed her 'irreplaceable friend Schiferli' at such times.[27]

While an impatient Queen Victoria was still unable to meet her intriguing aunt Julie, her cousin Albert was delighted to do so when on a tour of Switzerland and the north of Italy with his older brother Ernst in the autumn of 1837. On 6 September they arrived at Elfenau and stayed for three days, returning briefly on the 22nd and 23rd on their way back from Interlaken, and again on the 30th after visiting Switzerland's most romantic locations before continuing on to the Simplon Pass.[28] By now it had been made clear to Albert that his destiny lay with the young English queen; the previous May, Duke Ernst had taken him and Ernst junior to England for what, for Albert, had been an excruciating inspection by Victoria at Kensington Palace. She had not been impressed by the shy and gawky young prince and had found Ernst far more attractive. Leopold and Baron Stockmar, who together were the unchallenged power brokers of this marriage (and this despite King William's hatred of the Coburgs), had agreed that Albert needed polishing up for his intended role; his virtues must be honed so he could be presented as the perfect bridegroom, and – unlike his father and uncle – as a man without a sexual history. He was therefore dispatched to Brussels for eight months of political and cultural education under Leopold's guidance before moving on to the University of Bonn for two terms and thence to Switzerland.

Julie had found it very hard to say goodbye to Renette and Hélène when they left her at the end of September and wrote wishing them bon voyage in the most loving terms. Less than a month later, on 24 October, she was knocked back by yet another terrible premature death – of Hilda, not long after apparently giving birth to a second child.[29] It was several months before Julie was able to write to Renette again, making no mention of her secret daughter's death; what agony it must have been to not be able to share her grief with her dearest friend.

She also spoke yet again of her terrible eyesight problems. Whenever she tried to fix on a particular point her vision became blurred. The condition was so bad that, at present, she could neither read nor write; indeed, the doctors had completely forbidden her from writing. But she could not bear to be out of touch with her dear, rediscovered friend and took the risk now, in late January 1838, to write a few words. She had been greatly upset to hear of the recent terrible fire at the Winter Palace on 29 December. It had stirred up a lot of mixed and painful feelings. Julie had wept at the destruction of 'this cradle of my happiest Russian memories: of Elise, and Alex'. All her 'green youth partly spent within those walls' was nothing more now than ashes, consumed by the flames like the palace itself.[30] The news had made her shed many tears of regret also for Alexander – for the 'great and paternal sovereign'. More than a year after Schiferli's death Julie confided to Renette that 'my solitude and my misery are always the same' and she had such 'a pain and a weakness in the shoulder and the right hand that I handle a pen with the greatest difficulty'. So weak was her eyesight now that she preferred to sit in the shadows rather than in the light.[31] By degrees her life was being inexorably eaten up by the darkness.

After Schiferli's death Julie found herself bereft of help in the management of her affairs and she wrote to Eduard in Coburg asking him to fill the breach. Although he had rushed to Elfenau in time to attend Schiferli's funeral and stayed for a while to comfort the family, he was loath to abandon his position in Coburg in order to take Schiferli's place, which seems to have been Julie's tacit expectation.[32] Eduard wrote an anxious letter to Duke Ernst on 13 June explaining that although he was concerned that she should find a suitable replacement – an 'older, competent and authoritative man' was needed – a life of seclusion at Elfenau was not what Eduard wanted, nor did he feel, anyway, that his age and experience were suited to the role. His home was Coburg and his family were based there, though had Duke Ernst insisted, he would have had little option but to submit.[33] In the event, Julie must have realised that Eduard's burgeoning career at the Coburg court should not be jeopardised; on his return, Ernst promoted him to the rank of chamberlain, and later to head of the court administration.

With or without Eduard to help her, within a year Julie resolved to leave Elfenau; the memories of Schiferli there were too many and too painful. Elfenau was 'too dark green for me', she said, the trees too tall.[34] She wanted to lose herself somewhere new away from the memory of so many dead friends. She chose a house recommended

to her by a friend that was located a two-day coach ride away to
the southwest, deep in parkland at La Grande Boissière outside
Geneva on the coach road to Chamonix. The house – known as Le
Châtelet – was the smaller of two properties at La Grande Boissière.
In Geneva, as in Bern, foreigners were not allowed to buy property
without government authorisation and Julie wished to preserve her
anonymity, so a Genevese acquaintance – a dental surgeon named
Pierre-Paul Vaucher – bought the property on her behalf for 98,700
French francs.[35] The agreement documents dated 9 June 1838 refer
to her under the name 'Countess Ronau' (perhaps a misspelling of
'Rosenau', her preferred pseudonym).[36]

Le Châtelet was much smaller than Elfenau, with a low roof and
a modest courtyard at the front, a terrace shaded by chestnut trees
and an orangery. It looked out on a large lawn 'framed by beautiful
trees and adorned in summer with a superb flower bed' beautifully
arranged by Julie, and beyond lay a boating pond that was full of
waterlilies. So sweet smelling were the daturas (angel's trumpets)
planted around the house that their aroma 'made you dizzy', according to Countess Ewelina Rzewuska, a visitor at that time; the smell
reminded one of 'the passions that the grand duchess had inspired
and their fatal influence'.[37] Rzewuska enjoyed many conversations
with Julie on warm summer evenings sitting on the terrace, but compared to Julie's residence at Elfenau with its magnificent backdrop
of the River Aare and the mountains beyond, the park here was 'like
Gulliver's Lilliput'; when Leopold first saw it in 1844 he described
the house as being 'reminiscent of Osborne in a daintier way'.[38]

During the twenty-two years she would live in Le Châtelet, Julie
would still return to Elfenau in the summer.[39] But her primary concern right now was to appoint a new major-domo of her household.
She desired, she said, 'someone amiable, spiritual and original, with
taste, talent and fine sentiments, even-tempered, neither pretentious,
nor susceptible, nor wilful'.[40] It was a tall order; the household for
now was managed by a Baron Heldritt, a relative of Julie's lady
in waiting Marianne de Heldritt. He proved to be an ingratiating
Uriah Heep, who irritated Julie with his fawning deference and his

constant kissing of her hand. He was quickly sidelined to gentleman of the chamber by the appointment of the 44-year-old Vaucher as Julie's new major-domo, who was promptly elevated to baron by Duke Ernst at Julie's request.

Monsieur Vaucher, according to Countess Rzewuska, was a poor substitute for the late lamented Schiferli. 'He had neither the figure nor the manners of a romantic hero,' she wrote later. 'Always fearful of displeasing, shy, respectful, his mind, like that of the Genevese in general, was directed only towards practical things. His cows and his garden occupied him a great deal, without the intrusion of any poetic ideas or love.' The gossips in Geneva derided his lowly status as a dentist and talked of Julie surrounding herself with 'vulgar people'. Vaucher was not liked and it reflected badly on the grand duchess, as too did the continuing whispers about her 'frivolous' nature, her dubious past as a separated wife, and her previous close friendship with a married man, and with two – maybe more – illegitimate children. There was no doubt in Rzewuska's mind, however, that for all the calumnies directed against her by Geneva's high-minded *grandes dames*, Julie still possessed 'all the grandeur and all the nobility of the rank to which she had been called ... There was an exquisite grace in the smallest of her actions,' and she showed the greatest care and concern for all those who depended on her.[41]

What people thought of her mattered little to Julie; as she aged, she absorbed herself in her deepening religious faith and her trust in 'justice and divine love'; without it she would despair of life here on earth. With every day, she told Renette, her 'submission to the will of God grows more and more.'[42] 'My principle is to live and let live: I respect the independence of another person, but I will not allow anyone to deprive me of my own. I will ask a friend for advice, but I will not allow myself to be governed or directed, even by my brother [Ernst]. The deceased, the incomparable friend S[chiferli] was the only being in the world who was able to and dared to guide me.'[43]

She was determined to be forgotten, to withdraw from the world, in the belief, much as Balzac had said, that '*aux coeurs blessés, l'ombre et le silence**[44] In her new sitting room Julie placed a bust of Tsar Alexander on the chimney piece and elsewhere one of her friend Queen Luise of Prussia and retreated into her memories. A promised visit from Ernst with his 'beautiful son Albert' would be a 'shaft of silver light in her misty existence'.[45] The Coburg party arrived in mid-May 1839, on their way back from a tour of Italy, and found Aunt Julia, for all her apparent ill health, charming and still handsome. Four months later they travelled on to England, for a revisit to the newly crowned Queen Victoria, who this time cast a most approving eye over an Albert now transformed into the perfect, handsome suitor. Prince Leopold and Baron Stockmar had prepared the ground well. By the end of the year news came that Julie's nephew was to marry the queen of Great Britain.

It is finally with the marriage of Victoria and Albert in 1840 that we get some sense of how Julie was perceived by her British niece. Victoria had in fact first raised the subject of 'Aunt Julia' with her prime minister, Lord Melbourne, in December 1838 when discussing whom she might marry, for after she had become queen considerable pressure was placed on her to choose a husband. Melbourne was not at all keen on the Germans as candidates. 'He said these German princes behaved very ill to us, and were very hostile, and only came to us when they were in difficulties,' Victoria noted in her journal on 9 October. Indeed, according to Melbourne the late King William had not wished intermarriage with 'these small German princes' because 'they always have needy relations'; he had wanted Victoria to marry Alexander, Prince of Orange.[46]

---

*   Popularly translated as 'Wounded hearts are but shadow and silence', the quotation is the title of one of the stories in Honoré de Balzac's *Le Médecin de campagne* (1833). Julie probably fixed on this as a result of a shared interest in the writer with Countess Rzewuska. Rzewuska, a Polish noblewoman, who was also known as Madame Hanska by her first marriage in 1819, was a devoted fan of Balzac's work. She became a regular correspondent and pursued him somewhat obsessively. After her husband's death in 1841 she and Balzac conducted a long and intermittent relationship until they eventually married in 1850. But he died five months later.

Their discussion turned to how women marrying into the Russian imperial family were obliged to change their religion, as had Aunt Julia. Victoria had commented on 'her having only been fifteen when she married [she was actually fourteen]; her disliking it; her temper; the Grand Duke Constantine having been a terrible man'. She was clearly aware of the 'unhappy situation' her aunt was now in, an allusion presumably to her social position as a divorced woman. It was clear too that Konstantin's bad reputation was common knowledge abroad, for Lord Melbourne confirmed that the grand duchess's husband had been 'a very loose youth'. Despite this, Julie's sister Victoire and Uncle Leopold had been 'fond of him', though this would appear to have been the exception in their overall view of the Russians.[47] As far as Victoria was concerned they 'were all rather savage'.[48]

When, in October 1839, Albert and Victoria became engaged, Melbourne crowed that the Russians would be in a 'rage' at the queen's choice, for they hated the Coburgs. The conversation once more turned to the subject of Aunt Julia: Konstantin's abuse of her, and his 'love of insult'. They discussed the fact 'of her *having no children*' (my emphasis) as Victoria noted in her journal; for, 'if she had had, what a difference that would have made.' It would seem from this that the existence of Julie's illegitimate children Eduard and Hilda, which was unlikely to have been common knowledge anyway, had been carefully withheld from the naive young queen.[49]

In the meantime, the British press was sneering in its dismissal of the upstart Coburgers having inveigled their way into the British royal family again: 'Is there no *Man* in Europe worthy of the honour of Queen Victoria's hand? Why should a boy be selected? A branch of the Coburg stock, one of the great swarm of illustrious German beggars.' The British public had not forgotten how, twenty-three years earlier, Julie's brother Leopold had 'emigrated from his German hovel to this country ... to win the heiress apparent'.[50] In discussing the duchy's past history veiled reference was occasionally made to Albert's Aunt Julia and her 'irregular' life.[51] In *Prince Albert, His Country and Kindred*, published in 1840, the anonymous author referred to the prince's aunt and her 1820 divorce from Konstantin having been granted 'through gross cruelty on his part and other circumstances of her own, not necessary to advert to.'[52] Prior to this, *Private Anecdotes of Foreign Courts*, published in London in 1827, had been more explicit. In alluding to the 'rough treatment by Constantine of his first wife' it had pointed out in the most euphemistic terms that 'those who were in the habit of seeing this imperial couple in their domestic hours, can bear witness that the misunderstanding which existed between them, and embittered their comfort previous to her Highness's return to her native country, was at least as much owing to the imprudent levity of the lady as to the abrupt manners of the gentleman.'[53] Another retrospective allusion to Julie's arranged marriage to Konstantin was kinder: it had rightly referred to it as being 'somewhat akin to choosing a horse' and had conceded that from such a connection 'it would be unnatural to expect happiness, except by the merest chance.'[54]

From childhood Victoria seems to have had a particular interest in and affection for Julie and had noted her birthdays in her journal. From Switzerland Julie had sent warm good wishes to 'my sweet niece' via Renette's husband Count Chreptovich when he visited the English court in 1837. But she did not travel to London for Victoria and Albert's wedding in February 1840, instead sending Victoria a 'very kind letter wishing me joy'.[55] The ceremony was a small affair as royal marriages go, with few foreign relatives present beyond Albert's father and brother. Yet Julie had been there in spirit: Victoria could not have known that the 'Baron de Loewenfels' – a member of the Saxe-Coburg entourage who took his place in the bridegroom's procession in the Chapel Royal of St James's Palace – was in fact Julie's illegitimate son.[56] The Saxe-Coburg party remained for some time after the wedding and between February and May Baron de Loewenfels was reported as attending several royal dinner parties at Buckingham Palace, as well as other social events, which confirm his considerable status at the Saxe-Coburg court.[57]

CHAPTER 14

'AUX COEURS BLESSÉS, L'OMBRE ET LE SILENCE'

In July of 1844 Julie, who was now approaching sixty-three, made up for the long separation from her sister Victoire by travelling, albeit reluctantly, to Coburg for a reunion with her and their brother Ferdinand and with Feodore, who came up from Leiningen to see her mother. It had been twenty-five years since the two sisters had seen each other, although they had written and exchanged gifts – often items of jewellery – on birthdays and at Christmas. Victoire was alarmed to see how the years and her chronic ill health had taken their toll on Julie; she wrote home to Victoria to say that she had found her 'grown very old, though she still keeps her good figure'. Feodore was shocked as well to find her aunt 'very much changed, she looks now an old woman, such a pity, for she was so lovely once'.[1]

Perhaps these words prompted Queen Victoria to write soon after, in time for Julie's birthday, to thank her for a 'very pretty brooch' that Julie had sent her. Her mother, she said, had been 'so happy to see you' and it had been 'so sad to see this happy family gathering break up'. She closed her letter with effusive affection: 'Renewing all my prayers for your happiness and prosperity, please believe me for life your devoted niece.'[2] Privately, however, Julie had confided a growing spiritual weariness: she was feeling increasingly negative about life and had been suffering bad attacks of 'gout' in her arm (probably rheumatism or arthritis).[3]

The family in England would not have been aware of the gossip currently being circulated about Julie in Geneva, her request for anonymity having been betrayed in her entry in the census of 1843: under 'Countess Ronau', occupant of Le Châtelet de la Boissière, described as a widow of sixty-two, someone had added: 'This is the Grand Duchess Constantin.'[4] Genevese society seemed to disapprove of Julie, particularly her fondness for the theatre. But, as Julie admitted to Renette, the theatre was one of her few joys and she went four or five times a week. She had particularly enjoyed performances by Madame Albert on tour with the Théâtre des Nouveautés of Paris, which since its opening in 1827 had become popular for its light comedies and vaudevilles. Julie also attended public recitations by the French poet and playwright Eugène de Pradel, of Paris's Royal Athenaeum, and invited him to Le Châtelet to give a performance: 'I have no need of grand receptions, nor of concerts and masked balls,' she wrote, for the theatre 'helped the winter pass more quickly'.[5]

Negative talk about Julie reached such a point that year that a complaint was made to the state council on her behalf by the Russian minister plenipotentiary at Bern, Baron Paul de Krudener. He requested that the council offer Julie the protection due to a woman of her rank and royal connections and defend her personal character. But Julie had moved to Geneva at a time when there was a growing atmosphere of republicanism in the government and society at large, led by state councillor James Fazy, who was violently opposed to the old aristocracy.[6] Krudener's request therefore received an unsympathetic response from the council, which took a cavalier attitude, noting that 'the grand duchess's morals have not always been irreproachable' and that here in Geneva 'a grand duchess was no better than them.'[7] Unfortunately, Julie no longer had Schiferli to defend her: the timid Vaucher, who did not command any respect in Geneva, was not up to the challenge. Although she was sanguine about Vaucher being 'completely incapable of putting himself in the spotlight and asserting himself', in the absence of someone better

Julie made the mistake of investing all her trust in him, much as she had the domineering Seigneux. Always kind and generous, she took a benevolent interest in his family as if they were her own – just as she had done Schiferli's – and Vaucher's name as official owner of Le Châtelet remained on the deeds.[8]

All Julie wanted, she told Renette, was a quiet 'bourgeois life' but that could only be granted to her 'on a desert island'.[9] Instead she retreated into her religious faith and turned to more serious-minded social contacts such as the political economist Jean-Charles Sismondi, until his death in 1842, and Jean Huber-Saladin, a deputy of the Geneva Council, and his wife Ariane. Julie also often visited the Duval family at their estate at Cartigny in the suburbs of Geneva. Jacob-David Duval had been a court jeweller in St Petersburg during the reigns of Catherine the Great and Paul I and had returned to Switzerland in 1803, and their friendship began when Julie was still in Russia. At Cartigny the Duvals maintained an opulent lifestyle complete with Russian cuisine, where they entertained on the grand scale, on Sundays inviting all the local aristocracy in their finest turnouts, with as many as twenty carriages lined up on the courtyard outside. Julie was a frequent guest there, perhaps because her own household was now considerably reduced, as too her income (Tsar Nicholas was no longer as financially accommodating as had been his brother).[10] Such a small social circle suited her evolving life as local interest in Julie faded. She no longer entertained on the scale she had at Elfenau, with only the occasional dinner party for her few close friends. Perhaps the most important friend of all in her final years was Pastor David François Munier, a Protestant theologian whom she turned to as a spiritual advisor and invited to Le Châtelet. To Munier Julie apparently confided all the pain and sorrow of her past, as well as her failings, but as with so many friendships from these later years there is no account to be found of them.[11]

In September 1843 Julie was persuaded at short notice by King Leopold to visit him at his palace at Laeken in Brussels, for their niece Queen Victoria was coming to Belgium on a six-day tour with Prince Albert and it would be a chance for them to finally meet. Julie

had been at Elfenau at the time 'without any toilette' and was thus
'in a great flutter' about having the right clothes for the occasion.[12]
Victoria recorded with great delight their first meeting on the 18th:
'At 2, we reached the Palace ... Aunt Julia, whom we had been
expecting for some days, was at the door, and received us, with her
lady Mme de Hildritt [*sic*]. Aunt is very like Mama, only taller and
slighter. She is quite wonderful for her age, sixty-two.'[13]

Victoria's lady in waiting, Charlotte Canning (Sir Stratford's
second wife), wrote that the grand duchess was very like her
brother Leopold and her sister Victoire and 'has remains of very
great beauty; her manners are very agreeable and she is considered
extremely clever'; though Lady Canning could not refrain from
noting also that her life 'has not always been respectable'.[14] During
her visit to Laeken Julie spent two days with Victoria and Albert and
attended a concert in the park with the royal party. On the day the
couple departed, she accompanied them to Antwerp to see them off
and Prince Albert showed her around the royal yacht, with which
she was 'enchanted'. But parting from her Aunt Julia so soon after
finally meeting her left Victoria in floods of tears and with an over-
riding sense of melancholy: 'She is so cut off from her relatives, her
position is so painful and unfortunate, that I feel most deeply for
her.'[15] Leopold shared that same sense of regret even though Julie
had 'seemed much at home with us' and had recovered some of her
old spirit and been 'very cheerful and friendly'. He never was able to
shake off a tacit sense of guilt at what his gifted and beautiful sister
had lost by being married off to Russia, an act from which he had
greatly profited: 'It is truly a pity that such a handsome personality,
with so many qualities for holding an eminent position, was wasted
so unnecessarily and, it must be admitted, in a way that gave her so
little pleasure.'[16]

At Laeken he was glad that Julie had finally had the chance to
meet his wife Louise, Princess of Orléans, the daughter of King
Louis-Philippe of France, whom he had married in 1832. By all
accounts Louise was a paragon of sweetness and virtue, a loyal and
trusting wife who deserved better than the libidinous Leopold, who

had a mistress installed in a grand house on Brussels's Rue Royale.[17] Victoria had been very taken with Louise; she wrote to Leopold to say how sad she had been to part from her and also from 'poor Aunt Julie, so immediately after making her acquaintance'.[18] Leopold shared his niece's pity: he was certain that knowing his wife would be 'a happy recollection for [Julie] in her solitude', for she had told him how lucky he was to have the blessings of an angelic wife and children (three sons and a daughter had been born by 1840).

Julie sadly did not have that cushion of comfort when deaths came, and her grief reached new heights with that of her eldest brother Duke Ernst at the end of January 1844.[19] She was simply overwhelmed by the loss; of all her brothers, she was closest to Ernst. 'With him I completely lost my family, so to speak, my homeland, my fatherland, yes, even the fatherland; now I don't even know where I belong any more,' she told Renette.[20] His sister's life became ever more 'forlorn' in the eyes of Leopold: her outpouring of grief for Ernst had been 'singularly eloquent in its pain ... I sincerely pity her, she feels more isolated than ever,' he told his wife.[21] 'Forlorn' was a word repeated too by Feodore in a letter to Queen Victoria in March in which she spoke of the sorrow Julie must feel 'if she looks back upon her life full of trials of all kind [sic], her youth thrown away at that court, and now alone amongst strangers here.' It was indeed 'a bitter cup to the last ... poor aunt, life must be a burthen to her; and her feelings are so young still.'[22]

Ernst's death had also brought other, most unwelcome problems: in May Victoire, travelling incognito as the 'Countess of Dublin', made the journey to Switzerland supposedly to commiserate with Julie at Elfenau. Back in England the press revealed that their brother Ernst had died 'considerably involved in debt' and that the real reason for the visit was for the two sisters to 'make certain "pecuniary sacrifices" to satisfy the demands of his creditors'.[23]

The following year Julie once again had to steel herself and leave her hideaway in Switzerland for another big family gathering, this time in Coburg, the event having been organised by Prince Albert, who felt it was time his wife visited his place of birth. Leopold,

Louise and the new Duke Ernst II had welcomed them when they first arrived on 19 August at Duchess Auguste's summer home at Ketschendorf, where Julie stayed for the duration of their visit. From there they processed into Coburg under a triumphal arch garlanded with flowers to be greeted by the rest of the family, including Julie, before they all drove on to the Rosenau, where Victoria and Albert were to be accommodated during their stay. Victoria was entranced by the Gothic beauty of the Rosenau and its forested location. It was Albert's father who had turned it into a fairy-tale residence, 'a long-ago knight's stronghold' with steep gables at either end and a turreted round tower, perched on a knoll surrounded by dense oak forest 4 miles out of Coburg.[24] Julie had always loved spending time there with her mother, and Queen Victoria was equally happy to wake up on their first morning in the room in which Albert had been born: 'If I were not who I am – this would have been my real home, but I shall always consider it my 2nd one.'[25]

As *Hofsmarschall* of Ernst II's court, Julie's son Eduard was closely involved in the arrangements for this gathering of sixty-one relatives – virtually the entire German branch of the Almanach de Gotha. During their stay Victoria and Albert visited all the Coburg family palaces and enjoyed a busy programme of concerts and entertainments, populated by quaintly dressed Coburgers in national costume, as well as a grand banquet to celebrate Albert's twenty-sixth birthday. Victoria took great delight in being in the bosom of her German family, but although she mentions Julie's presence in her journal, Theodore Martin's blow-by-blow account of the visit in the official *Life of the Prince Consort* makes no mention of her. It is only in the list of members of the 'Royal party' that press reports give us a fleeting glimpse of Julie, as though she were more than content to disappear into the background.[26]

Back at Osborne on the Isle of Wight Victoria proudly hung portraits of Julie and her siblings as children together with their parents, which had been copied for her from those at the Ehrenburg Palace. In her bedroom at Windsor she hung a copy by William Corden the Younger of the 1797 Vigée Le Brun portrait of Julie – that bright, vibrant spirit as she, Victoria, had never known her – but she wanted a more recent reminder of the aunt who had a special place in her heart. She therefore commissioned her favourite court painter, Franz Xaver Winterhalter, to go to Le Châtelet specially to paint Julie as a birthday present for her mother Victoire, which she surprised her with on 17 August 1848. It was, she wrote, 'an indescribably like and beautiful picture of Aunt Julia' and shows Julie still beautiful with peachy soft skin and the kindest of brown eyes, painted not long before her sixty-ninth birthday.[27] Dressed in a gown of gossamer-soft lilac muslin and a large bonnet tied with a cream satin ribbon and garlanded with leaves, she wears a bracelet containing an oval miniature of Queen Victoria and stands in her garden at Le Châtelet de Boissière. So taken with Julie had Winterhalter been that he sent his 'heartfelt thanks' to the queen for having commissioned him, for the grand duchess had been 'the kindest and best princess you could meet'.*[28]

At Le Châtelet, and with occasional forays back to Elfenau, Julie continued to receive visits from Leopold and various nephews and nieces. Eduard, his wife Berta and other family members – 'six people deep', she complained – had appeared and stayed for 'six weeks' in the autumn of 1847. She found it a great strain for it had 'robbed me of every free moment'.[29] She perhaps gained greater comfort and a sympathetic ear at this time in the friendship of a woman who like her had suffered at the hands of an abusive husband and who was currently living in Geneva.

Her name was Rosina Bulwer-Lytton. In 1827 she had married the politician and writer Edward Bulwer-Lytton and was herself a talented novelist. But the marriage had been troubled and plagued by financial difficulties. The couple were legally separated in 1836 at a time when women had no rights of custody and Rosina's two children were taken from her. In 1839 she went abroad, living in

---

* The portrait hung at the Duchess of Kent's home, Frogmore House in Windsor Great Park, for many years before and after her death in 1861. It is reported to be a particular favourite of King Charles and is now located at his country home, Highgrove House.

Paris and Florence before settling in Geneva in 1842, all the time struggling to support herself by her writing. It is not known how she and Julie became acquainted but as women who had been separated from their children and had suffered the stigma of social ostracism, they clearly had much in common. 'I think her liking for me began in heartfelt sympathy,' Rosina later wrote, 'as a greater and meaner brute, with one exception, than that Grand Duke Constantine, her husband, could not be.' Rosina was deeply grateful, she said, for Julie's 'great and constant kindness to me during the five years I was in Switzerland'; but sadly, many of her generous gifts of jewellery had had to be 'melted down to pay swindling attorneys and supply my daily bread', though a diamond bracelet from 'the dear Grand Duchess Anne' was handed down to her daughter, Emily, after Rosina's death.[30]

As another decade turned, there came news of more family deaths: in October 1850 Leopold's sickly and neglected wife Louise died of tuberculosis. Julie had managed to travel to Belgium for a few days to see her not long before.* The following August she had to leave Le Châtelet on yet another mournful journey, this time to the deathbed of her brother Ferdinand. Julie took Vaucher and his two daughters for company. But they had only got as far as Augsburg when a telegram arrived to say that Ferdinand had died. At Ratisbon (now Regensburg) Julie continued her journey to Vienna by boat along the River Danube but did not arrive until 31 August – 'too late even to see poor Uncle's remains. How very sad and dreadful for her!' noted Queen Victoria. Julie despaired at being 'ever more and more impoverished of [my] beloved ones in this despoiled life'.[31] But at least Ferdinand had died in the knowledge that his son had, on behalf of the Coburgs, secured another European throne: through

* In her will Louise left Julie a portrait of the Duchess of Kent and two rather curious items: a bracelet of 'stones collected by King Leopold at Claremont' (though quite what kind of stones is puzzling) and 'a brooch imitating an oak branch made with the teeth of a deer killed by the King while hunting at Reinhardsbrunn in 1845'. Prince Albert too had a penchant for presenting Victoria with items of jewellery made from animal teeth (Vachaudez, *Bijoux*).

his marriage – brokered by King Leopold – and the birth of a male heir he had become King Ferdinand II of Portugal in 1837.

As the family sorrows mounted, there remained for Julie one enduring comfort and that was music. In the summer of 1850, she greatly enjoyed the visit to Geneva of a rising star of the concert platform – the 22-year-old American composer and pianist Louis Moreau Gottschalk, who was being lauded in Europe as a *Wunderkind* and the successor to Liszt and Chopin. On the evening of 7 August he was invited to give a concert at the Municipal Casino of Geneva. Playing on a fine concert piano sent specially from Paris, Gottschalk performed Weber's *Konzertstück* and a selection of his own compositions. As he stood in the wings prior to his performance he had noticed that the still unoccupied front row seats were 'equipped with special cushions of a rich red velvet'. He was told the row was permanently reserved for 'Grand Duchess Anna of Russia and her entourage' and that she 'rarely missed a concert when anything from Weber was being played'. After the performance Baron de Vaucher appeared at Gottschalk's dressing room and warmly congratulated him on his performance of the Weber, explaining that the grand duchess had been greatly affected by it, as had he, but that she was very fatigued and had had to leave before the final number on the programme. She had, however, instructed Vaucher to ensure that Gottschalk was accorded the greatest comforts while in the city; thus he left for his hotel in 'the most splendid equipage' provided by Vaucher.[32]

The two men thereafter struck up a friendship and spent much time together during Gottschalk's stay, and he learned much of Julie's story: of her marriage to 'the eccentric son of a mad father' and of how she had fled Russia in 1801. Grand Duke Konstantin, Vaucher told Gottschalk, had claimed that Julie 'was aided in her flight by the man who ha[d] become her lover' and the Geneva gossips, ignorant of Julie's love affair with the long-departed Linev, had assumed that that man had been Vaucher and that he remained her 'consort', indicating the degree of scurrilous gossip still in circulation about Julie.

A week later Gottschalk was invited to meet the grand duchess at Le Châtelet when she held a garden fete in honour of the visit to her of Queen Adelaide of Sardinia and the 'Duchess of Saxe-Weimar'.* He found Julie 'a charming old lady with a great curiosity about America' and in particular about P. T. Barnum's recent promotion of the tour there by the Swedish soprano Jenny Lind, though she appeared to have misconstrued that Barnum was an American states- man. Inevitably, Gottschalk was prevailed upon to play something for Julie and her guests and with a piano moved outside to 'a little platform under the trees' he gave an impromptu rendition of pieces by Bach, Weber, Mendelssohn and Chopin, as well as a composition of his own, the *Polka de salon*, a rather showy piece that he had adapted from an earlier work, *Jerusalem*. The following day at his hotel Gottschalk received a token of Julie's appreciation – a gold jewel case encrusted with silver featuring a cameo surrounded by diamonds on its lid.[33] It is also said she presented him with a brooch of 'diamonds clustered around an enormous pearl' – these being among the first pieces in an extensive collection of valuable honorific gifts made to Gottschalk during his career.[34]

Soon he was asked back to Le Châtelet for luncheon. Once more he played for Julie and her happy and laughing royal guests, at the end of which she presented him with a crown of oak leaves and roses that she had made while he was playing. There is a strong sense in the account of this party of Julie's vivacity, kindness and bright intelligence still shining through. By now the Geneva papers were writing of her patronage of the young American; many of the foreign press, however, confused Julie with her more socially prom- inent sister-in-law, the grand duchess of Saxe-Weimar, referring to *her* as Gottschalk's Geneva patron rather than Julie.[35] When he gave another concert at the Casino on 21 August, Julie and her glamorous

---

*   Adelaide, Archduchess of Austria (1822–55) had married Victor Emmanuel II of Sardinia in 1842. The 'Duchess of Saxe-Weimar' must be Julie's sister-in-law Maria Pavlovna of Russia, who was in fact the grand duchess. She was a great fan of Liszt and had appointed him *Kapellmeister extraordinaire* at the Saxe- Weimar court in 1842.

entourage in the front row were once more the object of everyone's curiosity, as much as Gottschalk's superlative performance.

For his remaining time in Geneva, and in order to escape his increasingly fanatical admirers, Gottschalk retreated to the peace of Le Châtelet whenever he could. There is no doubt that Julie's very visible support directly contributed to his success in Switzerland, which brought him a considerable slice of the box office. The queen of Sardinia and grand duchess of Saxe-Weimar apparently became such devoted groupies that they followed him to concerts in Aix and Lausanne, where they 'overwhelmed him with flowers and bouquets'.[36] But curiously, the enormous acclaim for Gottschalk in Switzerland did not lead to invitations to perform in either London or St Petersburg. It has been suggested that 'given the politics of the situation' Julie's patronage had had a negative effect in the growing atmosphere of Russo-British antipathy in the run-up to the outbreak of the Crimean War in 1854.[37]

Before leaving Geneva for Lausanne in November Gottschalk dedicated his piece *Polka de salon* to Julie – changing the lightweight title to *Danse ossianique*, Opus 12 – in gratitude for her patronage and in the certain knowledge that without it he would never have achieved such dizzy success in Switzerland. He also dedicated another work, the *Grande fantaisie triomphale*, Opus 84, based on themes from Verdi's opera *I Lombardi*, to her and wrote a fantasy on 'God Save the Queen' as a nod to her niece Victoria.[38]

It would seem incongruous that straitlaced Geneva should be the scene of the launch of a musical career such as Gottschalk's, given that a Calvinist revival was in full swing at that time. We know that Julie frequently attended the sermons of her friend Pastor David Munier and sought his opinion on religious matters, as too those of the theologian Pastor Jacques Martin, but her private spiritual life was still dedicated to Russian Orthodoxy. Indeed, her move to Le Châtelet would appear to have had a direct influence on the Holy Synod in Russia allowing the transfer of the Russian Orthodox place of worship from Bern to Geneva, where in fact most of the Russian émigré community lived. In the mid-1850s discussions on the erection of a cathedral in Geneva were initiated by the resident priest of the Russian legation, Father Afanasy Petrov, who set up a committee to raise funds. Julie promised to contribute to it but her involvement appears to have been overstated and she certainly did not fund the building work as has been claimed. In fact, it would not be until 1862, after her death, that a suitable plot was offered by the city of Geneva on which to build the new Cathedral of the Exaltation of the Holy Cross, which was consecrated three years later.[39]

When the eminent Russian poet Pyotr Vyazemsky was travelling in Switzerland in 1855, he attended the Russian Orthodox chapel in Geneva several times and was grateful to be offered hospitality by Julie. He presented her with a portrait of Tsar Nicholas I, who had died suddenly in March; though the question of whether Julie had any sentimental attachment to her austere brother-in-law is moot, for he had only been five years old when she left Russia. But she did receive a visit from Nicholas's widow, Alexandra Feodorovna, in the summer of 1857. The dowager empress arrived in ostentatious style, accompanied by a Russian entourage resplendent in their 'gold embroidered uniforms, orders and ribbons', having taken the steamboat down Lake Geneva from the Hôtel des Trois Couronnes at Vevey. But, as Alexandra's biographer observed, 'these two ladies had been strangers all their lives, and this was their first brief acquaintance, it might therefore rather be called an eternal farewell than a first welcome.' It was a somewhat mournful occasion, no doubt haunted by the ghosts of Julie's Russian past, but Alexandra was glad to have the chance to worship in the Orthodox chapel which Julie conducted her to.[40] Two years later when Alexandra was again at Vevey she made the effort to go and see Julie again.[41] More Russian relatives – Alexandra and Nicholas's son Grand Duke Konstantin Nikolaevich and his wife Maria – also dropped in when passing through Geneva, but for them, as for all her surviving Romanov relatives, Julie was now a relic, a curiosity, one of the last survivors of the Russia of the Napoleonic Age.

During the winter of 1856–7, Queen Victoria's second son

Alfred, no doubt on his mother's instructions, also visited Julie at Le Châtelet when he was in Geneva to improve his French and she invited him and his two equerries to dine with her. By all accounts the old lady was 'wonderfully Russian still', according to Feodore's son, Karl of Hohenlohe-Langenburg, when he visited, but although she was still active enough for her age, Julie's failing eyesight was greatly troubling her.[42] And now, she had sought even further retreat from the world. In around 1857 she rented a small villa named Le Pavillon des Glycines, at Mornex, a remote Alpine village a couple of miles southeast of Geneva on the slopes of Mont Salève. The house, built in 1832 by a former member of King Louis-Phillipe's court, looked out on a magnificent panorama of the Arve valley and the mountains beyond and perhaps fulfilled Julie's romantic idea of the noble, natural world hidden away from civilisation so familiar to her from Rousseau's *Julie ou la Nouvelle Héloïse*, set on the lakeshore at Vevey, as well as the pastoral verse of a favourite poet, Friedrich von Matthisson. The occupancy of Le Pavillon by two celebrated male figures is well known: the composer Richard Wagner had preceded Julie there in 1856, and there is a plaque on the house recording that during 1862–3 the writer John Ruskin rented it.[43] The fleeting shadow of Julie's presence, however, like so much of her life, has to be searched for, though Ruskin was told that the locals, in a nod to her, referred to the house as 'the Empress's Cottage'.[44]

There was another very good reason why Julie chose to go to Mornex: her friend and physician Dr Louis-André Gosse lived there and was a great advocate of the beneficial effects of mountain air.*[45] Gosse was now in regular contact with King Leopold and Prince

---

*   Gosse had studied medicine in Paris and, having spent time in Greece, was a supporter of Kapodistrias and Greek independence. He served as a member of the Geneva State Council between 1822 and 1834 where he had campaigned against the public use of the stocks and branding of criminals as well as pleading for greater tolerance and an end to discrimination against the Jews. A leading philanthropist in Geneva, he served the community during epidemics of cholera in the 1830s and was an advocate of public health reform. King Leopold was another royal patron and in 1856 made him a *chevalier d'honneur* (see *Lettres de Léopold*, 412 note 3).

Albert about the alarming decline in Julie's health, about which she
was clearly becoming depressed. Commiserating with Albert over yet
another family death – in childbirth of her niece Victoria, Duchess
of Nemours (Ferdinand's daughter) – Julie spoke of how 'I always
see the sword of Damocles hanging over my head.' She had recently
suffered another severe attack of pain in her head and chest that
had left her barely able to write a letter of condolence to Victoria's
widower, she told him; the Duchess of Nemours's death had come,
tragically, on the anniversary of Auguste's and left her with such a
'dull confusing feeling', but she offered 'my dear Albert' 'the most
feeling thanks for all the details which you have given me; they cap-
ture my whole being and hold it firmly, as if with an iron hand.'[46]

In September 1859, concerned about Julie's descriptions in her
letters to him of pain in the blood vessels of her head and strong
persistent headaches, Leopold made a long visit to Le Châtelet.[47] She
was worried that she was going blind and Leopold wrote to his son
Leo that it 'threatens what is a horrible misfortune'.[48] By the end
of July 1860, all her natural vivacity had alarmingly ebbed away.
Now, exuding an air of profound exhaustion, Julie began putting
her papers in order; she was doing so, she told her chambermaid,
because 'she felt she could not live long'.[49]

Earlier, in March, she had been greatly preoccupied by news from
Prince Albert that her sister Victoire was very ill; she had suffered
from severe erysipelas for some time and a cancerous tumour had
developed on her arm, although he had kept the truth from his
wife. In probably the last surviving letter we have written by Julie,
on 6 February 1860, she urged Albert to seek out a homeopathic
doctor in Geneva whom she had been consulting, 'who possesses
a *well-proven* and quite harmless, innocent means of healing this
grim malady' – so long as it had not yet 'reached its *most extreme*
state'. The said lady – Madame Benoit – had according to Julie
achieved considerable success with her herbal treatments, and she
knew several people who had recovered from cancer thanks to her.
'The doctors (the most jealous and also the most conscientious) *send
the sick to her*,' she asserted; she knew the doctor would be willing

to travel to England to treat the duchess, who did not need to 'know the pronouncement of *"cancereux"'*.[50]

At the beginning of July Julie suddenly, and inexplicably, announced her desire to return to Elfenau. She was in considerable pain when she left Le Châtelet with Marianne de Heldritt and her maid Jenny Welsch on the 15th, not by carriage but taking the train from Geneva to Bern via Landeron and Bienne. But a long delay in the journey of three hours at Nidau had caused her great distress – leading to temporary paralysis that left her struggling to speak and with loss of strength in her left side and leg. Schiferli's son Maurice, who was in practice as a doctor in Bern, came to see her and thought she had had a stroke (a family letter confirms that she probably had the first of several strokes on 25 July).[51] The following day, despite being weak Julie insisted on being carried into the park at Elfenau in an armchair and for several days after, whatever the weather, she was taken into her favourite grove of trees not far from her little Orthodox chapel, where she would sit lost in thought, taking in the tranquil view of the soft green meadows sloping down to the River Aare, as she made her own private, mental peace with the world.

Dr Schiferli had meanwhile tried and failed to persuade her to consult an allopathic doctor. Julie had insisted on homeopathic treatment only, but the two practitioners in Bern were both out of town and in desperation Schiferli had sent a telegram to Gosse at Mornex. But he was not able to get to Elfenau until the evening of 4 August, by which time Julie had now refused all medical treatment for ten days and was paralysed down most of her left side and particularly in her leg.[52] The following day, and against the better judgement of Schiferli and Gosse, a homeopath, Dr Guder, was found in Bern and between them the three doctors decided on a course of treatment which included a modest amount of 'opium in homeopathic doses'. Vaucher, who had been away on leave at the spa at Evian, arrived back bringing with him another homeopath, Dr Landsmann.* The

---

* It has proved impossible to trace any details, either biographical or professional, for any of these Swiss homeopaths who attended Julie.

medication administered by the homeopaths – rhus tox (for arthritic pain), nux vomica (for a range of symptoms) and teaspoons of marsala wine as a stimulant (soon replaced by an infusion of arnica and acetate of ammonia) – seemed to improve Julie's condition but its effect was merely palliative. Her facial paralysis eased for a while, as too the loss of mobility in her left arm. Gosse was touched to see Julie's old warm disposition return, and hear her speak fondly of those she loved, particularly her parents.

In the meantime, at his palace in Belgium King Leopold had been receiving regular updates and had become greatly alarmed; he sent word to Queen Victoria and Prince Albert, who were on holiday in Scotland, that Aunt Julia had had a 'paralytic stroke'.[53] Victoire (from whom Victoria and Albert kept the full details of Julie's life being in danger) was greatly distressed that she could not go to her sister, for another sixteen years had passed since they had last seen each other. For the next few days the telegrams between Brussels and Balmoral flew thick and fast. Leopold, who felt Julie had not paid sufficient attention to her illness by refusing for too long to see a conventional doctor, was at least relieved to know that she was in the capable hands of 'clever old' Dr Gosse, 'a great friend of ours'.[54]

Feeling better, Julie invited Gosse to have lunch with her and Vaucher, at which, seated looking out at the Bernese Alps, she managed to serve them from the dishes herself. They thought she had turned the corner. But then her strength suddenly gave way and she suffered another stroke. This time her gaze remained fixed, her pulse raced, her ability to speak was strained and she could no longer swallow. Gosse and Schiferli had initially opposed the idea, but now felt that Father Petrov should be sent for from the Russian chapel on Rue Jargonnant in Geneva. They had not wished his presence to alarm Julie and initially only allowed him to pray silently at the foot of her bed; but as her condition worsened and she slipped into unconsciousness during the night of 14 August, he administered the last rites of the Orthodox faith. Just before five on the morning of 15 August 1860, Julie's breathing slowed; she opened her eyes wide and then calmly slipped away. Her end, Gosse told Prince Albert, was 'a death such as I wish for myself and would wish for those I love'.[55]

It took two days for Eduard von Loewenfels to travel the 519 miles from Dresden, where he had moved in 1856 to take up an additional post at the court of Saxony (though he retained his Coburg position). In order to preserve Julie's body in the summer heat until his arrival, Schiferli had covered it with ice and chloride of lime. She was then laid in an oak coffin with an inner one of lead, surmounted with a large gold cross and surrounded by numerous tall candles; downstairs all the shutters were closed and the rooms draped in black.[56] At Balmoral on the 16th Prince Albert received a long letter in French from Gosse describing Julie's final days and his attempts to treat her in the face of her insistence on homeopathic treatments.

Julie's funeral was held at the Rosengarten cemetery in Bern on 18 August. Father Petrov and a small choir intoned the Russian *panikhida* for the dead, according to the rites of the Russian Orthodox Church, before her coffin was lowered into a simple grave. No relatives attended from abroad, the only British presence being Edward Harris, minister plenipotentiary to the Swiss Federation. But other members of the diplomatic corps in Bern were there, as too were many local dignitaries who had known Julie. A small marble slab was placed on the grave, without titles, royal arms or coronet, or even the usual Russian Orthodox crucifix. It poignantly captured the duality of Julie's Russian and German personas:

Julie–Anne

Christ est ma vie

et la mort m'est un gain[*]

I Phil. V. 21

1781–1860

---

[*]   St Paul's Letter to the Philippians 1: 21: 'For me, to live is Christ and to die is gain'.

In death, as so often in her life, Julie clung to anonymity, to obscurity. But the official protocols had to be observed: across Europe, the royal courts went into mourning. The British royals donned black for two weeks: 'Her Majesty the Queen and His Royal Highness the Prince Consort have been observing the strictest retirement since the melancholy intelligence,' it was announced.[57] The news of Julie's death was syndicated across the British press, albeit generally as a one-liner. In its obituary, the *Morning Chronicle* made very belated acknowledgement of how Julie's union with Grand Duke Konstantin 'with all its early brilliant prospects, turned out an unhappy one', due to the temperament of the 'morose and despotic, but whimsical prince' who had 'treated his wife with indifference' when she failed to produce any children. It made no criticism of Julie's unorthodox life, emphasising instead that she had been 'a most virtuous and pious lady' who after her divorce had 'retired into privacy, and rarely sought society even among the members of her own family'.[58] The *Gentleman's Magazine* did not observe such niceties about Konstantin in its obituary, defining him as 'little better than a lunatic' who treated his wife not just with initial indifference but 'positive cruelty and outrage'. It also made mention of Julie's 'piety and charity' and the 'many poor persons who depended on her bounty for subsistence'.[59]

At Balmoral, Victoire's birthday on 16 August was celebrated 'without any of the usual festivities'. Prince Albert was greatly distressed by Julie's death and his letters reflect his deep affection for the 'special charm' of his beloved aunt's 'romantic character'. 'Until the end she remained lively in mind and soul, in her love of life and her kindliness,' he told his stepmother Marie.[60] No one who ever met her would forget Julie's warm and gentle personality. On hearing of her death, Rosina Bulwer-Lytton in England remembered her thus: 'She had, besides her great beauty, that greatest of all charms, – the sweetest of sweet voices; a truer heart, brighter soul, or nobler mind never went to heaven . . . oh! How additionally dark and cold the world looks and feels when these pure unworldly spirits quit it to return home! Poor soul, she was but a few days ill, and her death was as gentle and lovely as her life had been. Peace be with her.'[61]

In her will, Julie bequeathed Elfenau to Eduard von Loewenfels and all her personal effects, jewels and the contents of Le Châtelet to Vaucher. In a codicil to her will she left 2,000 francs to the poor of Bern and 1,000 to those at the nearby village of Muri.* But, as Leopold discovered from Eduard, her will 'had not been very regularly made'; he could not afford to maintain Elfenau and asked Leopold to buy it from him.[62] 'People have such extravagant notions of one's richesse,' Leopold tut-tutted to Victoria. Elfenau was 'uncommonly pretty', certainly, but there was no way he could indulge in 'such a distant possession de luxe'.[63] Eduard turned to Prince Albert but he too declined the offer to buy the house.[64] In April 1861 Eduard sold it – along with most of its art and furnishings – to Bernard de Watteville, whose family had been close friends with Julie and whose granddaughter Alix published two biographies of her, in 1942 and 1965.[65] In 1918 the Wattevilles sold Elfenau to the Municipality of Bern for 2.3 million francs. Some of the original contents owned by Julie are today in the Bern Historical Museum.[66]

Maurice Schiferli later discovered from Vaucher that the Russian emperor, Alexander II, had designated 15,000 francs to be sent to pay for Julie's funeral costs, as well as an annual grant of 179 francs to cover the upkeep of her grave by the Russian legation at Bern. Another 500 francs were set aside for prayers to be said there by the

---

* The obituary in the *Journal de Genève* spoke of Julie's involvement in 'our city's charities' and how 'no man suffering who asked for aid was ever turned away,' which could be attested to by 'Geneva's clergy'. Alville similarly makes passing mention of Julie's patronage of charities but offers no details, perhaps because Julie insisted on anonymity in this regard. It has therefore proved impossible to trace anything beyond the fact that, for example, she was a patron of the Great St Bernard Hospice in Valais close to the Italian border, which was founded as a refuge for travellers as well as a place of worship and which is where the first St Bernard mountain-rescue dogs were bred and trained. The charity apparently holds records which mention Julie's support for it.

resident Orthodox priest three times a year – on Julie's birthday, her name day (15 February) and the anniversary of her death.[67]

In October of 1860 Prince Albert, in a sentimental gesture, sent word to the British legation in Bern to commission a noted local professional, Carl Durheim, to take photographs of Julie's grave.[68] Two years later, the queen's eldest daughter, Vicky, visited it and picked some flowers to send her as a memento, but she found the grave 'extremely simple, too much so I think' and the little black slab of marble with its cryptic inscription seemed far too stark.[69] Leopold felt the same when he saw his sister's tomb in 1864; he deeply regretted the 'lonely miserable place of rest which that distinguished sister of mine had chosen for herself'.[70]

In a strange twist of fate Julie's grave has not survived; nor have the photographs taken of it; nor indeed is there any known photograph of Julie herself, although she lived well into the age of the daguerreotype.* In 1913 the Rosengarten, having closed as a cemetery in 1877, was turned into a public park. Julie's coffin was exhumed and moved to the Schosshalden cemetery a mile away. The Russian embassy in Bern continued to pay for the grave's maintenance until, with the Revolution of 1917, the payments suddenly ceased. Many years later the grave was lost, swallowed up in a landslip at the cemetery. Its precise location today is unknown, but a small commemorative plaque bearing the words of the original marble slab has been placed in the vicinity. In death the ever-elusive Julie still holds onto the anonymity she so longed for, but the lovely, green and peaceful oasis of Elfenau, with the glorious Swiss landscape surrounding it, is her enduring memorial.[71]

---

*   Queen Victoria was an avid collector of photographs of her European relatives, both alive and even on their deathbeds. Did she ever solicit a photograph of Julie and was she politely refused? No image of Julie is to be found anywhere in Victoria and Albert's vast collection of family photographs in the Royal Collection at Windsor, nor in King Leopold's archive in Brussels.

'HER FATE MIGHT HAVE BEEN VERY BRILLIANT'

King Leopold was deeply distressed by the loss of the good, warm-hearted sister whom he had loved so tenderly. He had thought it a merciful release that Julie had not recovered from her stroke, he told Victoire, for it would have only been partial at her 'advanced age': 'Infirm and crippled, with mental faculties enfeebled, and her sensibility of feeling over-strong, quite alone among strangers, *without children of her own* who would regard it as a privilege and a pleasure to nurse her, life would have been certain to become insupportable to her!'[1] He expressed his appreciation of his sister in more gentle terms to Queen Victoria: 'she had many many qualities of the heart and there was something noble and high minded in her character, with much loveliness in her manners.' Julie was 'much beloved by all who knew her well' – and that included Tsar Alexander, who had 'loved and admired her'. Had she received more support from the dowager empress, he was certain that 'she would have been an ornament to her position'.[2]

Leopold had always believed that his sister's life in Russia 'might have been very brilliant' and he greatly regretted his failure to effect a reconciliation between her and Konstantin during that week at Elfenau in 1814.[3] He had always done his best to defend his brother-in-law against his critics and believed that – in his own idiosyncratic way – Konstantin had 'admired [Julie] of all things', and that for those brief few days there had been 'the possibility of regaining a great position'.[4] Indeed, as Julie's obituary in the *Allgemeine Zeitung* in Munich reiterated, Princess Juliane of Saxe-Coburg had seemed 'destined for greatness' when she married into the Russian imperial family.[5] Perhaps Konstantin was not entirely to blame for Julie's misery; Leopold had always been aware of the negative role that the dowager empress Maria Feodorovna had played in her Russian life, as he explained to Queen Victoria: 'If the late Empress mother ... had not had but one object in view viz: to ruin the marriages of the two elder brothers, to get *Nicholas to succeed*, [Julie] might have comparatively had a better existence. She was a very lovely and distinguished creature. The grand duke Constantine *told me himself of all the <u>intrigues</u> of the mother to destroy his marriage*.'[6]

Duchess Auguste also sensed that her daughter had been emotionally damaged by her maltreatment in Russia. Writing in November 1805, she talked of how Julie had acquired 'a habit of psychological and moral suffering' that had given her 'a gentle, quiet resignation early on'. Despite her imperial status, she had shown 'no striving for power' during her self-imposed exile in Switzerland but had sought 'merely to recover from her difficult years in Russia'. We shall never know the true extent of those difficulties for Julie never spoke of them. But an obscurely published article in Russian that appeared in 1870 questioned why the 'august persona' of the grand duchess had not been better presented in Russia, 'as would befit a woman of undoubted historical importance'. Pointing out that he could 'recall only a single mention' of Julie – in the *Moscow Gazette* of 1857 when Grand Duke Konstantin had visited her in Geneva – the anonymous author went on to state that 'in her brief sojourn at our court, Grand Duchess Anna Fyodorovna had suffered much unpleasantness, alongside the Empress Elisaveta Alexeevna, from her mother-in-law.'[7]

The suggestions are certainly there of Maria Feodorovna's malevolent role, but we can pursue it no further. Much of Julie's life remains hidden from us. Quite aside from her natural secrecy, such of her correspondence that survives is scattered across the royal houses of Europe and is largely uncatalogued and untranslated. But a great deal has been deliberately lost. Julie and Elise had an agreement to destroy each other's letters, though thankfully we do at least have Elise's valuable testimony on Julie from her letters to her mother in Baden. The letters that Julie's other key correspondent, Renette, received from her were carefully preserved and published in 1910 by her family, although Renette's side of their intimate correspondence was no doubt destroyed by Julie herself, along with all her other letters and private papers. This was confirmed by King Leopold not long after Julie's death when he told Queen Victoria that his sister 'was very prudent about papers and will have destroyed what might be dangerous'.[8]

The implication here is that Julie worried that anything she wrote or received might be found to be politically compromising at a time when Russian relations with western Europe were very unstable and spies were everywhere. It also perhaps explains why many of her letters do not survive elsewhere; along with those from her correspondents they appear to have been burned – on Julie's explicit instructions.* Those that do survive are largely unrevealing, full of stream-of-consciousness chatter that switches constantly from French to German and back again, about family weddings, birthdays and deaths; Julie's problems with her entourage; melancholy preoccupations with death and religion; and her chronic ill health. Worse – certainly for the biographer – is the revelation by King Leopold in a letter to Victoria in 1864, that he had recently been going through and destroying his letters to Ernst, Victoire and Stockmar, where he adds: 'I have now also the journal kept by poor Aunt Julia when she was in Russia, but I have not yet opened it.'[9] That journal has never come to light; it is likely that having read its contents Leopold was so horrified at Julie's unhappiness that he destroyed it.

---

* See for example a letter written to Julie by Prince Albert from Osborne on 18 December 1846 which was marked and underlined by her on the front of the envelope 'Verbrennen' ('Burn') but which is a very fortunate survival, now in the Ian Shapiro collection.

We do at least have a valuable record of Julie kept by Duchess Auguste in her journals that take us from that first fateful journey to Russia in 1795 until 1821.[10] But even this crucial source has not come through to us unscathed. In 1941 Queen Victoria's youngest daughter Princess Beatrice produced a privately printed translation of the journals, but only for 1806–21, covering mainly the Napoleonic Wars. A check of the clean transcription of the German original in the Royal Archives reveals that some references to Julie in the original have been tampered with and attempts have been made to obliterate her name, perhaps by Julie herself when she had the journals in her possession after her mother's death. In Princess Beatrice's highly selective published translation many allusions to Julie have been omitted altogether, probably because of the complications of her personal life, but also because Beatrice had thought them peripheral to the more important comparison she wished to make, at the height of the Second World War, between wartime/occupied Europe under Napoleon and under Hitler.[11]

If you search today, you will still find little or nothing in mainstream sources on Princess Juliane of Saxe-Coburg-Saalfeld aka Grand Duchess Anna Feodorovna of Russia, beyond the fact of her unhappy marriage to Grand Duke Konstantin. She remains an unjustifiably neglected footnote in history. But perhaps, in many ways, this is what she wanted: she was, in the end, the architect of her own deliberate effacement from the record.

Notes

Abbreviations

AP	Chreptowitch-Bouténeff, *Lettres d'augustes personnages*
Bachmann	'Die Reise der Coburger Erbprinzessin'
Benson and Esher	Benson and Esher, *Letters of Queen Victoria*
Cours	Alville, *Des cours princières*
Czartoryski	Czartoryski, *Memoirs of Prince Adam Czartoryski*
Danilova	Danilova, *Sud'by zakon pechal'nyi*
Golovina	Golovina, *Memoirs of Countess Golovine*
Jahrbuch	Bachmann, 'Die Reisetagebücher der Herzogin Auguste'
Kucherskaya	Kucherskaya, *Konstantin Pavlovich*

LATh – HStA   Landesarchiv Thüringen, Hauptstaatsarchiv Weimar

Lettres de Léopold Puraye and Lang, *Lettres de Léopold*

LIE   Nicolas Mikhailovitch, *L'Impératrice Elisabeth*

Masson   Masson, *Secret Memoirs*

Mitteleuropa   Lohausen, *Mitteleuropa 1658–2008*

ND   Beatrice, *In Napoleonic Days*

QVJ   Queen Victoria's Journals online

RA   Royal Archives

'Reminiscences'   Leopold, 'Reminiscences', in Victoria, *Early Years*

StA CO   Staatsarchiv Coburg

Tagebuch   Arnswaldt, *Petersburger Tagebuch der Frau Erbprinzessin*

Vie   Alville, *Vie en Suisse*

Vigée   Vigée Le Brun, *Memoirs*

NOTES

Prologue: The Coburg Marriage

1 Dressel, 'Ein „Pumpernickel-Staat"?', 49–50. See Thackeray, *Vanity Fair*, vol. II, 312–13; Nisbet, *Caroline Bauer and the Coburgs*, 328.

2 Leighton, *The Correspondence of Charlotte Grenville, Lady Williams Wynn, and Her Three Sons*, 193; *Spectator*, 2 January 1864, 6.

3 See Shoberl, 'Memoirs of the House of Saxe-Coburg-Saalfeld', 161; D'Auvergne, *The Coburgs*, 14–17.

4 Render, *A Tour Through Germany*, vol. II, 319. In 1801 the annual revenue was calculated at £36,364; see *Annual Register* 1810, 428.

5 'House of Saxe-Coburg', *Kentish Weekly Post*, 31 May 1816.

6 Ibid.; Croly, *Lines on the Death of HRH Princess Charlotte*, 45, Notes.

7 Croly, *Lines on the Death of HRH Princess Charlotte*, 45, Notes. See Beéche, *The Coburgs of Europe*, 30–5.

8 Many sources talk of Leopold staying above Mr Hole's grocer's shop just before his wedding in 1816 but this is not so; he stayed there in 1814 on his first visit. See Hone, *Hone's Authentic Account of the Royal Marriage*, 17.

9 'My Cousins the Coburgs', *Dublin Weekly Nation*, 24 June 1854.

10 Belien, *A Throne in Brussels*, 11.

11 Cases, *Private Life and Conversations of the Emperor Napoleon*, vol. IV, 98.

12 See e.g. her letters in Aspinall, *Letters of Princess Charlotte*, 210 etc.

13 Aspinall, *Letters of Princess Charlotte*, 187, 225.

14 *Kentish Weekly Post*, 31 May 1816; Scheele and Scheele, *Prince Consort*, 14.

15 Nisbet, *Caroline Bauer and the Coburgs*, 21.

16 Cases, *Private Life and Conversations of the Emperor Napoleon*, vol. IV, 99; Aronson, *Coburgs of Belgium*, xvi; Greville, *Greville Memoirs*, vol. 2, 157.

17 *Northampton Mercury*, 10 February 1816.

18 Bury, *Diary of a Lady-in-Waiting*, vol. II, 17; *London Courier and Evening Gazette*, 8 February 1816.

19 'The Sun Review', *Sun*, 13 June 1816 quoted extensive extracts. For Leopold see Shoberl, 'Memoirs of the House of Saxe-Coburg-Saalfeld', 161–96.

20 *London Chronicle*, 23 February 1816; *The Picture of London for 1820*, 412.

21 'The Royal Wedding', *London Chronicle*, 3 May 1816.

22 Urbach, *Royal Kinship*, 97.

23 Sergeant, *Courtships of Catherine the Great*, 272; Potemkin, *Memoirs of Prince Potemkin*, 2nd ed., 93.

24 Schnitzler, *Secret History of the Court and Government of Russia*, 95.

Chapter 1: A Pumpernickel State

1 Aspinall, *Letters of Princess Charlotte*, 226.

2 Crawford, *Victoria*, 233, 238.

3 Stanford, *Rambles and Researches in Thuringian Saxony*, 123.

4 Ibid.

5 Crawford, *Victoria*, 232; Weintraub, *Uncrowned King*, 59.

6 Marie, *Story of My Life*, 143–4.

7 Panam, *A German Prince and His Victim*, 60–1. See also Crawford, *Victoria*, 231–2 for a forgotten and fascinating account of the German *Residenzstaat*.

8 Belien, *Throne in Brussels*, 1; Shoberl, 'Memoirs of the House of Saxe-Coburg-Saalfeld', 161.

9 Cottineau de Kloguen, *Geographical Compilation*, vol. I, 494; Gill, *We Two*, 100.

10 Diesbach, *Secrets of the Gotha*, 151.

11 D'Auvergne, *The Coburgs*, 30.

12 'Reminiscences', 372.

13 D'Auvergne, *The Coburgs*, 30–1; *Tagebuch*, 33.

14 Fiedler, *Auguste Caroline Sophie*, 7.

15 Ibid., 6–7.

16 Flantzer, 'Augusta Reuss of Ebersdorf'.

17 Fiedler, *Auguste Caroline Sophie*, 9–10.

18 Victoria, *Early Years*, 17; Ponsonby, *Lost Duchess*, 22–3.

19 Richardson, *My Dearest Uncle*, 17.

20 Stanford, *Rambles and Researches*, 129.

21 Mönning and Riedel, 'Zur Gründung des Herzoglichen Kunst- und Naturcabinets', 185.'

22 Her Royal Highness the Duchess of Kent', *La Belle Assemblée*, vol XVIII New Series, September 1818, 99.

23 Gill, *We Two*, 127; Stanford, *Rambles and Researches*, 129.

24 Shoberl, 'Memoirs of the House of Saxe-Coburg-Saalfeld', 168–9.

25 Victoria, 'Reminiscences of Early Childhood', 32.

26 Ponsonby, *Lost Duchess*, 33; Nisbet, *Caroline Bauer and the Coburgs*, 21; Diesbach, *Secrets of the Gotha*, 151.

27 St Aubyn, *Queen Victoria*, 287; Benson and Esher, vol. I, 18. See also Timms, 'My Dear Grandmama'.

28 Nisbet, *Caroline Bauer and the Coburgs*, 21.

29 *Cours*, 5–6; Benson and Esher, 13.

30 Auguste spoke of this governess briefly in a later letter: see Kruse, 'Franz Friedrich Anton', 194; Auguste's journal for 9 November 1805, in *Mitteleuropa*, 63.

31 See e.g. Fiedler, *Auguste Caroline Sophie*.

32 'Karoline Bauer, Leopold I, and Baron Stockmar', 467. See also Stockmar, *Memoirs of Baron Stockmar*, vol. I, xxxvi.

33 Nisbet, *Caroline Bauer and the Coburgs*, 21.

34 Crawford, *Victoria*, 234.

35 *Penny Cyclopaedia*, 304.

36 D'Auvergne, *Coburgs*, 35.

37 Journal for 9 November 1805, in *Mitteleuropa*, 63.

Chapter 2: Journey to St Petersburg

1 Czartoryski, vol. I, 97.

2 Wortman, *Scenarios of Power*, 122.

3 Golovina, 53, 52.

4 'Draft Dispatch concerning a Project of Marriage between the Grand Duke Constantine and a Princess of Naples (1793)', in Maroger, *Memoirs of Catherine the Great*, 392–3.

5 Masson, 29.

6 Ibid., 30; 'Royal Sweethearting', *Era*, 29 December 1839.

7 For the Stockmars of Coburg, see 'Karoline Bauer, Leopold I, and Baron Stockmar', 467–8. Ernst Friedrich's son by his first marriage was Johann Ernst Stockmar, father of the Baron Stockmar who later became Prince Leopold's personal physician. Christine who played with Julie and her siblings as a child was Ernst Friedrich's daughter by his second marriage. Her daughter, Caroline, born 1807, was an actress and the mistress of Prince Leopold 1828–9. Her memoirs of that relationship and the Saxe-Coburg family were published posthumously in 1884.

8 *Cours*, 1. Catherine's letters are to be found in the Coburg Staatsarchiv.

9 Ibid., 2.

10 Ibid., 3.

11 Ibid., 7.

12 Ibid., 9.

13 Ibid.

14 Scherer, *Melchior Grimm*, 328.

15 Grot, *Pis'ma Grimma*, 632.

16 Ibid, 628–9.

17 *Bayreuther Zeitung*, 7 September 1795.

18 Klöffler, 'Last und Lust des Reisens', 6.

19 Fiedler, *Auguste Caroline Sophie*, 13.

20 For an account of a similar journey to St Petersburg in 1781, see the
    journal of Baroness Elizabeth Dimsdale, in Cross, *An English Lady*.

21 O'Brien, *Mrs Adams in Winter*, 53–4.

22 Catherine the Great's mother Johanna to her husband, quoted in Cronin,
    Catherine, 44.

23 Dixon, *Catherine the Great*, 38; Maroger, *Memoirs of Catherine the
    Great*, 54.

24 After Auguste's death in 1831 the journals were sent to her youngest
    daughter, Victoire, Duchess of Kent, in England. According to Louise
    Segschneider (see 'Die Tagebücher der Herzogin Auguste', 185–9), who
    had sight of them at the Royal Archives, Auguste's original diary entries
    were made somewhat randomly on small pieces of paper which were
    all later neatly glued onto larger sheets and bound into six volumes.
    These are held in the Royal Archives at RA VIC/MAIN/M/26–31. At
    the request of various Saxe-Coburg family members, including Julie, a
    copy of the journal was made some time later and sent to them. This was
    apparently privately printed in Darmstadt but no trace can be found of
    that edition according to Segschneider. Auguste's St Petersburg letters to
    Duke Franz were, however, published separately there at around the same
    time.

25 Bachmann, 17.

26 Ibid., 16.

27 Ibid., 21.

28 Ibid., 23.

29 Ibid., 13; Fiedler, *Auguste Caroline Sophie*, 16.

30 Bachmann, 21–3.

31 Karamsin, *Travels from Moscow*, vol. I, 35.

32 Bachmann, 24.

33 Vigée, 158.

34 Karamsin, *Travels from Moscow*, vol. I, 27.

35 Ritchie, *Journey to St Petersburg and Moscow*, 2, 3.

36 O'Brien, *Mrs Adams in Winter*, 113.

37 Karamsin, *Travels from Moscow*, vol. I, 14.

38 Bachmann, 25–6.

39 Vigée, 158.

40 Kohl, *Russia*, 340.
41 Ibid., 255–6.
42 Vigée, 158.
43 *Tagebuch*, 10.
44 Madariaga, *Russia in the Age of Catherine the Great*, 5; Cronin, *Catherine*, 44.
45 Carr, *A Northern Summer*, 264.
46 *Tagebuch*, 10.

Chapter 3: 'The Largest and Most Brilliant Court in Europe'

1 *Tagebuch*, 10; Granville, *St Petersburgh*, vol. I, 412.
2 *Tagebuch*, 11; Staël-Holstein, *Ten Years' Exile*, 389.
3 Masson, 90.
4 'A New Description of St Petersburg', 195; Storch, *Picture of Petersburg*, 10.
5 'A New Description of St Petersburg', 195.
6 Cross, *St Petersburg and the British*, 58.
7 Storch, *Picture of Petersburg*, 30, 29.
8 Staël-Holstein, *Ten Years' Exile*, 361, 364.
9 *Tagebuch*, 11.
10 Ibid.
11 Ibid.
12 Coxe, *Travels into Poland*, vol. II, 287.
13 Ibid., 267.
14 Vogüé, *Czarevitch*, 248–9.
15 Cronin, *Catherine*, 289.
16 See Madariaga, *Russia in the Age of Catherine the Great*, 573.
17 Cronin, *Catherine*, 292.
18 Grot, *Pis'ma Imperatritsy Ekateriny*, 658.
19 Golovina, 95; Czartoryski, 105 specifies the Diamond Room as being used during the season spent at the Winter Palace.
20 *Tagebuch*, 11; Golovina, 95.
21 *Tagebuch*, 11–12.
22 Czartoryski, 98, 97.
23 Masson, 38.
24 Golovina, 95.
25 Masson, 32; *Tagebuch*, 14; Golovina, 32.
26 *Tagebuch*, 14–15.
27 Ibid., 15.
28 Ibid., 16.
29 Golovina, 95.
30 9/20 October 1795, *LIE*, vol. I, 219.

31 *Tagebuch*, 17.

32 *LIE*, vol. I, 219.

33 *Tagebuch*, 18–19.

34 Ibid., 19–20.

35 Ibid.

36 Masson, 39; Ramenskii, *Tsesarevich Konstantin Pavlovich*, 18; Nisbet, *Caroline Bauer and the Coburgs*, 21–2; Joyneville, *Life and Times of Alexander I*, vol. I, 71.

37 Golovina, 97.

38 Letter 03716 to Friedrich Melchior Grimm, between 23 September and 14 October 1795, Correspondence of Catherine the Great online, https:// catcor.seh.ox.ac.uk/texts/ Also in Grimm, Pis'ma Imperatritsy, 658.

39 Nesbit, *Caroline Bauer and the Coburgs*, 22. Precisely the same story was quoted in 'Domestic Life of Alexander', 120 – but in relation to Louise of Baden and not the Coburg sisters. However, she had arrived with only one sister, not two, so it seems likely the stories have been muddled.

40 Golovina, 33.

41 *LIE*, vol. I, 221.

42 *Tagebuch*, 32, 34, 35.

43 Ibid., 23.

44 Ibid., 24.

45 Ibid., 26–7.

46 Ibid., 29–30.

47 Ibid., 31, 33.

48 'Reminiscences', 295.

Chapter 4: 'Jülchen's Star Has Prevailed'

1 Grot, *Pis'ma Imperatritsy Ekateriny*, 658.

2 Ibid., 660.

3 Cronin, *Catherine*, 260.

4 See 'Instructions to Prince Nikolay Ivanovich Saltykov with regard to the upbringing of the grand dukes', in *Sochineniya Imperatritsy Ekateriny II*, 201–10, quoted in Kucherskaya, 32.

5 Kucherskaya, 32–3.

6 Rey, *Alexander I*, 26.

7 Kucherskaya, 35; Rey, *Alexander I*, 34.

8 *Russkaya Starina*, 1, 42, 121–4, quoted in Kucherskaya, 38.

9 Potemkin, *Memoirs of the Life of Prince Potemkin*, 76.

10 Kucherskaya, 38–9.

11 Ibid., 39.

12 Ibid., 41.

13 'Private History of Constantine of Russia', 162.

14 Ibid.
15 Kucherskaya, 37.
16 Golovina, 42; Vogüé, *Czarevitch*, 282.
17 Quoted in Chavchavadze, *Grand Dukes*, 20.
18 *Tagebuch*, 41.
19 Letter to La Harpe, 28 October 1795, in Biaudet and Nicod, *Correspondance de Frédéric-César de La Harpe et Alexandre Ier*, vol. III, 633.
20 *Cours*, 36–7.
21 *LIE*, vol. I, 220.
22 Ibid.
23 *Tagebuch*, 36.
24 Slabáková, 'Le Destin d'une famille noble', 74.
25 *Tagebuch*, 36–7.
26 Ibid., 38.
27 Ibid., 39.
28 *Tagebuch*, 40.
29 *LIE*, vol. I, 221, 223; *Tagebuch*, 40.
30 Golovina, 97.
31 *Tagebuch*, 43.
32 Grot, *Pis'ma Grimma*, 661; *LIE*, vol. I, 224.

Chapter 5: 'Alexander Is an Angel, but Constantine Is a Fury'

1 Letter to Auguste, from St Petersburg, 1 November 1795, StA CO LA A 5518/5.
2 Letter 71, 11/22 March 1796, in *Sbornik imperatorskago russkago istoricheskago obshchestva*, vol. V, 60, St Petersburg, 1870.
3 Golovina, 98; Kucherskaya, 49.
4 *LIE*, vol. I, 223.
5 Ibid., 225.
6 Czartoryski describes the function of the Diamond Room at this time in his *Memoirs*, 104–6.
7 *Vie*, 24.
8 Madariaga, *Russia in the Age of Catherine the Great*, 573.
9 Czartoryski, 106; *Cours*, 51.
10 Czartoryski, 101–2.
11 Ibid., 103.
12 Krylov-Tolstikovich, 'Nemetskie printsessy v Rossii'.
13 Letter from Catherine to Grimm, 18 February 1796, in *Sbornik imperatorskago russkago istoricheskago obshchestva*, vol. XXIII, 1878, 668–9; Krylov-Tolstykovich, Potselui Psikhei, 65.
14 *Vie*, 26–7; Bolotov, 'O brakosochetanii'.

15　Bolotov, 'O brakosochetanii'.
16　Ibid.
17　Ibid.
18　*Vie*, 27.
19　See, for example, Potts and Potts, *Queen Victoria's Gene*, 11–12.
20　Rey, *Alexander I*, 33.
21　*Vie*, 28.
22　Czartoryski, 103–4; 'Private History of Constantine of Russia', 162.
23　Masson, 188–9.
24　'Pridvornoe torzhestvo 1796 goda', http://history-gatchina.ru/article/ celebrations.htm
25　Grot, *Pis'ma Grimma*, 669; Dixon, *Catherine the Great*, 313.
26　Bolotov, 'O brakosochetanii'.
27　Melissino, 'Opisanie feierverka'/'Déscription du Feu d'Artifice'.
28　Grot, *Pis'ma Grimma*, 669, 671.
29　Czartoryski, 104.
30　Ibid.; letter, 11/22 March 1796, La Harpe, vol. I, 158.
31　Golovina, 98, 102.
32　Letter, 21 February 1796, La Harpe, vol. I, 158.
33　'Sketch of the Grand Duke Constantine of Russia', 197. The anonymous author of this very telling study of Konstantin declared that he was 'most anxious that no individual should be compromised' by the shocking revelations in his article about Konstantin's cruelty, not just to animals but to Julie, and he assured his readers of their veracity (see 194); Golovina, 98, 97.
34　Letter, 21 February/3 March 1796, StA CO LA A 5498 ff1–2.
35　Danilova, 152–3; Kucherskaya, 51–2.
36　'Sketch of the Grand Duke Constantine of Russia', 199, quoting Tooke, *Life Catharine II*, vol. III, 375.
37　Ibid., 197, original emphasis.
38　Potts and Potts, *Queen Victoria's Gene*, 11.
39　*Vie*, 29; Danilova, 156.
40　*Cours*, 57.
41　Masson, 29.
42　Golovina, 102–3.
43　Ibid.
44　Golovina, 98, 102–3; Schönle and Zorin, *On the Periphery*, 66.
45　Rousseau, *Julie*, 569.

Chapter 6: 'A Life of Brilliant Misery'

1　Masson, 14; Vogüé, *Czarevitch*, 260.
2　Masson, 14.

3 Ibid., 15. Catherine's letter to Saltykov is reproduced in *Istoricheskii sbornik*, vol. 1, 1–2; Danilova, 154–5.
4 Danilova, 154–5.
5 Ibid., 155; Masson, 190.
6 Masson, 16, 18, 19.
7 Brown, *Memoirs of the Courts*, vol. II, 247–9; Masson, 20.
8 Brown, *Memoirs of the Courts*, vol. II, 253.
9 Ibid., 256; Masson, 22–3.
10 Madariaga, *Russia in the Age of Catherine the Great*, 576; Vogüé, *Czarevitch*, 260.
11 Madariaga, *Russia in the Age of Catherine the Great*, 572.
12 Ibid., 577; Vogüé, *Czarevitch*, 265.
13 Madariaga, *Russia in the Age of Catherine the Great*, 577.
14 Masson, 122.
15 Ibid., 48.
16 Vigée, 198; Golovina, 133.
17 Masson, 137.
18 Vigée, 198.
19 Vigée, 198–9; Cronin, *Catherine*, 301.
20 Danilova, 157.
21 *LIE*, vol. I, 241.
22 Ibid., 242.
23 Letter, 29 January/10 February 1797, ibid., 239–40.
24 Czartoryski, 140.
25 Golovina, 156–7; Czartoryski, 140–2.
26 Vogüé, *Czarevitch*, 282.
27 Kaznakov, 'Pavlovskaya Gatchina', 136–7.
28 Ibid., 139–40; Czartoryski, 142.
29 Kucherskaya, 54. See also 'Further Characteristics of the Emperor', *Fraser's Magazine*, vol. 72, 1865, 237.
30 Kucherskaya, 54–5.
31 Golovina, 132; Kucherskaya, 8.
32 Golovina, 96.
33 Vigée, 169.
34 Golovina, 124; Vigée, 159, 170–1. Vigée painted five portraits of Elizaveta Alexeevna as grand duchess and then as empress during her six years in Russia.
35 Vigée, 171.
36 Ibid.
37 Golovina, 146.
38 Golovkine, *La Cour et le règne de Paul Ier*, 144.
39 Ibid., 148.
40 Ibid., 147.

41 Golovina, 146–7.
42 Ibid., 149.
43 24 January 1797, StA CO LA A 5498 f 3.
44 18 February 1797, StA CO LA A, 5498 f 5.
45 14 October 1797, StA CO LA A 5498, f 6.
46 8/19 April 1797, *LIE*, vol. I, 232.
47 27 June 1797, *LIE*, vol. I, 293.
48 Czartoryski, 184.
49 See Kucherskaya, 53–4, 57–8.
50 Kaznakov, 'Pavlovskaya Gatchina', 140–1.
51 *Vie*, 41; Vigée, 171; Danilova, 162.

Chapter 7: 'She Has Come Back to Us After All'

 1 Golovina, 141.
 2 *Vie*, 40; A. M. Turgenev, quoted in Balyazin, *Tainy doma Romanovykh*, 192.
 3 See e.g. Golovina, 167–8.
 4 'Reminiscences', 374.
 5 *LIE*, vol. I, 253.
 6 *Cours*, 63, 250 note 28; Danilova, 163.
 7 'Reminiscences', 375.
 8 Vigée, 171.
 9 Jackman, *Romanov Relations*, 9.
10 Golovina, 185.
11 'Private History of Constantine of Russia', 162.
12 Danilova 163–4; *LIE*, vol. I, 336–7.
13 Undated letter, *AP*, 83.
14 Golovina, 185.
15 *Vie*, 45; *Cours*, 66–7; Danilova, 165.
16 *LIE*, vol. I, 337.
17 Golovina, 187; *Vie*, 45–6.
18 Pienkos, *Imperfect Autocrat*, 9.
19 Danilova, 165.
20 See *Kamer-fur'erskie zhurnaly*, 397–9, 407–8; Golovina, 186.
21 *LIE*, vol. I, 341; *Cours*, 67.
22 Dressel, 'Ein „Pumpernickel-Staat"?', 41–2.
23 *LIE*, vol. I, 345; *Cours*, 67.
24 'Badechronik 1: Bericht aus Carlsbad' Journal des Luxus und der Moden, 24 July 1799, 462. I have identified this Tischbein portrait of Julie as being the uncredited plate opposite p. 152 in *AP*. See also 'Johann-Friedrich-August Tischbein, *Portrait of a Lady*', MutualArt, https://www.mutualart.com/Artwork/Portrait-of-a-lady/62DDBB1BD4CC651C

25 'Route 260 – Eger to Franzensbrunn and Carlsbad', in *Hand-Book for Travellers in Southern Germany*, 372, 369–75.
26 Ibid., 375.
27 10/21 June, *AP*, 3.
28 'Jeu de l'Arquebuse à Carlsbad', in Carro, *Almanach de Carlsbad*, 221, 226. The Swiss-born physician Jean de Carro (1770–1857) was a pioneer of vaccination against smallpox.
29 Adams, *Traveled First Lady*, 68, 69.
30 *Vie*, 46; Danilova, 166.
31 *Cours*, 67–8.
32 Golovina, 203.
33 Ibid., 205.
34 Ibid., 204–5.
35 *LIE*, vol. I, 361.
36 See *Cours*, 68–9, 251.
37 *LIE*, vol. I, 363–4; Kucherskaya, 72.
38 Kucherskaya, 72; Golovina, 208.
39 Golovina, 209.
40 Nisbet, *Caroline Bauer and the Coburgs*, 22.
41 Kucherskaya, 80.
42 Komarovskii, *Zapiski*, 94.
43 See letters of 3 December 1799 and 11 April 1800, in LA A 5498 StA CO; *Cours*, 70.
44 Golovina, 222–3; Kucherskaya, 73.
45 *Cours*, 71.
46 Kotzebue, *Merkwürdigste Jahr*, vol. II, 228.
47 *Cours*, 71.
48 McGrigor, *Tsar's Doctor*, 21.
49 Ibid., 29; Troubetzkoy, *Imperial Legend*, 37.
50 Golovina, 226.
51 Troubetzkoy, *Imperial Legend*, 38–9; Kucherskaya, 74.
52 Golovina, 228.
53 Troubetzkoy, *Imperial Legend*, 51.
54 Ibid., 51, 234–5, 238; *Cours*, 75. See also Sebag-Montefiore, *The Romanovs*, 253–78.
55 *Cours*, 74; Golovina, 235.
56 Pienkos, *Imperfect Autocrat*, 12.
57 This fanciful story was related in Gagarin, 'Anecdotes recueillies', 85.
58 Shavrov, 'Pridvornaya i velikosvetskaya zhizn'', 62–3.
59 Kucherskaya, 81–2.
60 Golovina, 184–5.
61 Smirnova-Rosset, *Dnevnik*, 567, 569.
62 Accounts of the supposed affair vary and are at best contradictory, but see

Kucherskaya 80–1; Shavrov 'Pridvornaya i velikosvetskaya zhizn'', 62–3. Shavrov suggests Julie was sent abroad in 1801 because of this pregnancy, which would be her second inside a year, as Kucherskaya says she had miscarried in March.

63 *Corriere Milanese*, 10 September 1801, no. 73, report from Berlin of 22 August.

64 *Sbornik biografii kavalergardov*, vol. II, 401–2.

65 'Royal Sweethearting', *Era*, 29 December 1839; Hyde, *Private Anecdotes*, *vol. I*, 354.

66 Undated letter *c.* May/June 1801, *AP* 264; 31 July 1801, *AP*, 269.

67 8/20 November 1801, *AP* 276.

68 Constantin Chreptowitch Bouténeff, 'Avant propos', *AP*, xii.

69 Turgenev, 'Zapiski', 163.

70 22 April 1802, *AP*, 254–5.

71 *Vie*, 50.

72 Kucherskaya, 84, citing Onuchkov, 'Zapreshchennye pesni'.

Chapter 8: 'The Catastrophe from the North'

1 Letter to Auguste, 25 July 1801, LA A 5518, StA CO.

2 Letter to Franz, 25 July 1801, LA A 5450 StA CO.

3 Diary of Friedrich Josias, 22 October 1801, StA CO LA A 5518. See also entries for 19 August and 5, 12 September. For the apartment see *Cours*, 84.

4 *Mvon Thümmels Sammtliche Werke*, vol. I, 84–6.

5 Belien, *Throne in Brussels*, 6; letter to Kretschmann, July 1800, StA CO LAA 5517.

6 Letter, 30 August/11 September 1801, LA A 5549, StA CO; *Bamburger Zeitung*, 20 March 1802.

7 Letter to Auguste, 15 April 1802, LA A 5549, StA CO.

8 These letters, to be found in GARF 641-1-43, were, at the time the research for this book was carried out in 2019, only made available in very poor quality microfilm and are very hard to read. They have been wrongly identified as being written to Empress Maria Alexandrovna, who was the wife of Nicholas I, and although they are numbered 1–13, they have not been catalogued in the correct chronological order. This confusion is not helped by Julie's inconsistent and incomplete dating of them, but they appear to start on 14 September 1801, shortly after her arrival in Saalfeld, and tail off by May the following year.

9 *Mitteleuropa*, 62.

10 According to Ernst's lover Caroline Bauer; see Nisbet, *Caroline Bauer and the Coburgs*, 24.

11 Kruse, 'Franz Friedrich Anton', 170; *Lettres de Léopold*, 80.

12 Rothkirch, *Königin Luise*, 188.
13 See Laszlo Vajda, 'Erläuterungen zur Geschichte von Grossfürstin
    Anna Feodorowna .. und Ihr erster Sohn Alexander', https://ia801902.
    us.archive.org/14/items/ErlauterungenAlexanderDE2015Aug/
    Erl%C3%A4uterungen%20Alexander%20DE%202015%20aug.pdf.
    The author is descended from the Sandor Vajda, born *c.* March 1802,
    whose birth was registered in 1803 in Mártonfalva in Upper Hungary,
    now Slovakia, his parents being Joseph Vajda and Katalin Csontos. Vajda
    family legend claims he was Alexander I's illegitimate son by Julie.
14 Victoire letter, 19 December 1802, *AP*, 211–12.
15 See *AP*, 271; *Augsburgische Ordinari Postzeitung*, 22 March 1802;
    Journal de Francfort, 21 March 1802; Kostgelder accounts, Min E 205,
    StA CO.
16 This was stated by Alexander in his 1820 manifesto when he granted the
    divorce. See Tondini, *Pape de Rome*, 99.
17 Letter to Renne, August 1802, *AP*, 131. See also Julie's long disjointed
    letter to Renne of 24 February 1803, *AP*, 133, also summarised in *Vie*,
    53–5.
18 *Vie*, 55–6; *Cours*, 84; résumé in French of original German letter to
    Renne, 24 February, 1803, *AP*, 133–41.
19 *Vie*, 53; Renne, 24 February 1803, *AP*, 133; letter, 10 August 1802, *LIE*,
    vol. II, 98.
20 Letter to Renne, 21 April/3 May 1802, *AP*, 11, 10; *Cours*, 86. Grenier,
    Mémoires de la Comtesse Rosalie Rzewuska, 285, refers to him as
    'Linoff'.
21 Heins, 'Das Herzogspaar', 169; 'Reminiscences', 375.
22 Slabáková, 'Sophie von Sachsen-Coburg-Saalfeld', 2–3.
23 Letter to Christian Otto, 3 November 1802, Jean Paul – Sämtliche Briefe,
    https://www.jeanpaul-edition.de/brief.html?num=IV_329
24 See the review of *Hesperus* in Ferrier, 'Jean Paul', 284–9.
25 Victoire, letters to Renette, 19 December, 26 November 1802, *AP*, 209,
    211.
26 See *AP*, 135–8.
27 Victoire, letter to Renette, 26 November 1802, *AP*, 210.
28 Victoire to Renette, 28 February 1803, *AP*, 214; *Cours*, 81, 82.
29 Julie, letter to Renne, 24 February 1802, *AP*, 140.
30 Letter to Renne, 26 August/7 September 1803, *LIE*, vol. II, 101–2.
31 Wortman, *Scenarios of Power*, 123.
32 'Pis'mo Imp. Marii Fedorovny vel. kn. Konstantinu Pavlovichu, 1803',
    Istoricheskii sbornik, vol. 1, 7–8.
33 Jean Paul to Johann Georg von Ahlefeldt, Coburg, 22 October 1803,
    Jean Paul – Sämtliche Briefe, https://www.jeanpaul-edition.de/brief.
    html?num=IV_415

34 Albert, *Queen Victoria's Sister*, 17.
35 Ponsonby, *Lost Duchess*, 28; Stuart, *Mother of Victoria*, 8.
36 Victoria, *Early Years*, 19; Redman, *House of Hanover*, 186; Stuart, *Queen Victoria's Sister*, 18; Antoinette to Renne, 8 July 1805, *AP*, 94; *Cours*, 83–4.
37 Queen Luise to Julie from Charlottenburg, 28 May 1804, Rothkirch, *Königin Luise*, 232.
38 Reported in *Le Publiciste*, 6 July 1804. Queen Luise to Julie from Charlottenburg, 21 June 1804, Rothkirch, *Königin Luise*, 235–6; 'Greek pagan', Rothkirch, *Königin Luise*, 231.
39 *Manchester Mercury*, 6 February 1810.
40 *LIE*, vol. II, 142.

Chapter 9: 'She Lives in the Most Perfect Oblivion'

1 *Cours*, 23; *Vie*, 87; Julie, letter to Duke Franz, 9 September 1804, StA CO LA A 5450.
2 *Lettres de Léopold*, 33.
3 See *LIE*, vol. II, 50 re. the sale of the diamonds. *Cours*, 87; Julie, letter to Duke Franz, 9 September 1804, StA CO LA A 5450. Antoinette's disapproval in letter of 18 July 1805, *AP*, 93.
4 *Cours*, 86; *LIE*, vol. II, 131.
5 *AP*, 93–4.
6 Julie at Schloss Fantaisie, reported in *L'Abeille du Nord*, Altona, 7 May 1805, 213. See Jean Paul, letter from Bayreuth, 25 April 1805, Jean Paul – Sämtliche Briefe, https://www.jeanpaul-edition.de/brief.html?num=V_98
7 Auguste's diary for 7 and 9 November 1805, quoted in *Mitteleuropa*, 62–3.
8 Julie, letter to Alexander I, 26 November 1805, RGADA; the original letter in the Russian archives is without introduction or salutation, indicating that the first page is missing.
9 Maria Pavlovna, letter to Maria Feodorovna, 19 March 1806, LATh – HStA, Grossherzogliches Hausarchiv A XXV Korrespondenzen R 153, Bl. 83.
10 Maria Pavlovna, letters to Maria Fedorovna, 7 May 1806 and 11 June 1806, LATh – HStA, Grossherzogliches Hausarchiv A XXV Korrespondenzen R 153, Bl. 75–6, 99.
11 Ibid.; letter, 14 June 1806, LATh – HStA, Grossherzogliches Hausarchiv A XXV Korrespondenzen R 153, Bl. 102.
12 *ND*, 1.
13 *ND*, 1, 2.
14 *ND*, 4; 'Reminiscences', 376.
15 'Battle of Saalfeld', 140; Wright, *Beautiful Enemy*, 119–21.

16 *ND*, 6.
17 'Battle of Saalfeld', 140–2; *ND*, 7.
18 'Battle of Saalfeld', 143; *ND*, 9.
19 *ND*, 10.
20 Letter to Emmanuel Mensdorff-Pouilly, 10 November 1806, *Lettres de Léopold*, 37; *ND*, 21.
21 *ND*, 12; D'Auvergne, *The Coburgs*, 41.
22 *ND*, 22.
23 *ND*, 23.
24 *ND*, 23, 24.
25 Julie to King Friedrich Wilhelm, 14 August 1807, GARF 663-1-74.
26 Ibid.
27 Ibid.
28 *ND*, 31.
29 *Cours*, 96.
30 'Reminiscences', 378; Auguste's diary, 4 August 1808, RA VIC/MAIN/M/26/267.

Chapter 10: 'Some Things of Which I Do Not Wish to Speak'

1 *Cours*, 101.
2 Letter to Renne and Renette, 8 July 1805, *AP*, 94.
3 Reported in *Journal des curés, ou Mémorial de l'Eglise gallicane*, 15 February 1809, 4. See *Le Publiciste*, 13 February 1809, where Seigneux's name is given as Signen.
4 See Kostgelder in StA CO LReg 5502 with regard to the purchase of the Wangenheim garden 1803; documents in StA CO Min E 1660, 1103 also refer to it. Julie left the house and garden to her nephew Alphonse von Mensdorff-Pouilly in her will; he sold it back to the Coburg state and the house was demolished around December 1860. See StA CO Min E 1103.
5 Tagebuch for 28 June 1808, VIC/MAIN/M/26, 263–4.
6 *Cours*, 102–3.
7 Wolfe, *Literary Pilgrimage*, 228.
8 See Marlowe, *Single Summer*, 41, which although a work of fiction contains a useful description of the house.
9 *Cours*, 103, 104.
10 *ND*, 49.
11 'Reminiscences', 379.
12 See Tafel 343b, 'Die von Schauenstein und die von Löwenfels', in Freytag von Loringhoven and Schwennicke, *Europäische Stammtafeln*. Ferrand's book was self-published in Paris 1995; see page 79. Neither book provides any contextual detail or explanation backed up by documentary evidence that Alexander was Eduard's father. In his article 'The Grand Duchess

Anna Feodorovna: "Poor Dear Aunt Julie"', William Mead Lalor dismissed the claim, confirming, as does this narrative, that Alexander was nowhere near Coburg at the time of Eduard's conception and that even if he were, he could hardly have dropped in to visit Julie without it being noticed. In fact, he was in Russia, and did not return to Germany until September 1808, when he stopped off at Königsberg to visit the Prussian royals and then Weimar to see Maria Pavlovna, en route to the Erfurt congress that began on 27 September – not long before Eduard was born. The only conclusion Lalor could come to was that 'the pedigree was embroidered by a Loewenfels descendant' at some later date, perhaps in an attempt to provide Eduard with a more illustrious royal pedigree than the notorious Jules-Gabriel Seigneux, and particularly bearing in mind that Eduard had been ennobled by Duke Ernst to Baron Schmidt von Loewenfels in 1815. See Lalor, 'Grand Duchess Anna Feodorovna', 12–13. Alexander Jordis Lohausen in his detailed account of Eduard also argues that the paternity of Alexander I 'seems very unlikely': *Mitteleuropa*, 79.

13 See Pestalozzi, *Sämtliche Werke*, vol. 15, 53.
14 *ND*, 51; the mention of Julie's teeth problems does not appear in *ND* but in the full unexpurgated original for 11 January 1809, RA VIC/ MAIN/Y/116.
15 Julie mentions her eye problem in her letter to Friedrich Wilhelm of 27 May 1808 and says she has been plagued by it since February. See GARF 663-1-74.
16 North, *'Material Delight'*, 37.
17 Karamsin, *Travels from Moscow*, 230, 242. Auguste's copious journal entries for this trip can be found in *Jahrbuch*, 38–90, but have not been translated. Regretfully the entire sequence of her Swiss travels was redacted from *ND*, probably because they were too extensive and not relevant to the Napoleonic Wars.
18 *Handbook for Travellers in Switzerland*, xxxvi.
19 *Jahrbuch*, 59, 69; *Cours*, 109.
20 *Cours*, 109–10.
21 10 June, *Jahrbuch*, 59.
22 'Private History of Constantine of Russia', 162.
23 *Jahrbuch*, 69; *Cours*, 110, 111.
24 *Cours*, 111.
25 *Le Publiciste*, 16 July 1810.
26 *Cours*, 111, 112.
27 The *Saint James's Chronicle* reported on 13 October that Hortense and Josephine had visited the Mer de Glace at Chamonix in the second week of September and were supposedly meeting up with Julie at Neuchâtel.
28 Josephine to Hortense, before 1 November 1810, Abbott, *Confidential Correspondence*, 297.

29 Avrillon, *Mémoires*, vol. I, 262.

30 See Ebel, *Traveller's Guide Through Switzerland*, 80–2; *Handbook for Travellers in Switzerland*, 221.

31 'Memorie inedite di Giuseppe Bossi', *Archivio Storico Lombardo*, V, Milan, 1878, 275–313, at 290–2.

32 *ND*, 83.

33 *Cours*, 115; *Mitteleuropa*, 65.

34 For biographical details on Schiferli see *Cours*, 258, note 29; Buess, 'Rudolf Abraham Schiferli'. It is worth noting, given Julie's recurring eye trouble, that Schiferli also had a specialism in ophthalmics (he had written a dissertation on the treatment of cataracts in 1797). See *Cours*, 115, 258, note 29.

35 *Lettres de Léopold*, 75.

36 Sophie's letter is quoted with no date given, or the name of the recipient, in *Cours*, 118, but dates from around March 1812. Frustratingly Alville cites the source merely as a 'private archive'.

37 Auguste, journal entries for 2 April, 18 April and 4 June 1812, RA VIC/MAIN/Y/117, RA VIC/MAIN/M/28.

38 *Cours*, 119.

39 Journal, 21 July 1812, RA VIC/MAIN/M/28.

40 Journal, 23 and 25 September 1812, RA VIC/MAIN/M/28.

41 See StA CO LReg 6221.

42 Journal, 3 February 1813, RA VIC/MAIN/M/28.

43 *ND*, 89, 93.

44 *ND*, 95, 100.

45 *ND*, 102.

46 Letter to Renne and Renette, 8 July 1805, *AP*, 94.

47 *Cours*, 120.

48 *Cours*, 105; 'Reminiscences', 382; letter of 13 September 1813, *AP*, 100.

49 The European press appears well apprised of Julie's movements that summer of 1813, all sightings referring to her as 'Madame la grande-duchesse Constantin'. See *Le Moniteur westphalien*, 26 August 1813; *Journal de Lyon*, 28 August 1813; *Courrier de Turin*, 28 September 1813; *Le Moniteur universel*, 12 September 1813.

Chapter 11: 'That Haven of Peace She So Longed For'

1 Friedrich Wilhelm of Prussia in 1814; Rey, *Alexander I*, 35.

2 *Vie*, 67.

3 For Kapodistria's role in Switzerland see Koukkou, *Ioannis A. Kapodistrias; Vie*, 113–14. Andreev, 'Ioann Kapodistriya'. Kapodistria also later lobbied Alexander and Julie for support for the cause of Greek independence during the revolt against Turkey in 1821.

4 For details of the sales, see *Vie*, 203–4, note 73.

5 *Vie*, 70.

6 Some fine examples from Hopfengärtner's workshop can be seen at Schloss Jegenstorf on the outskirts of Bern. For a while some of Julie's furniture, including pieces by Hopfengärtner, was on view in the Empire Room at Schloss Oberhofen on Lake Thun, but it is now in storage at the Bern Historical Museum. See https://www.museum.de/event/anna-feodorowna

7 Some of Julie's books, donated to the Bern Historical Museum by her biographer Alville, are held in the museum's archives.

8 See *Vie*, 68–71. An exhibition of Julie's furniture, '200 Jahre Elfenaugut Bern 1814–2014', was held at Schloss Oberhofen, Lake Thun in October 2019, but unfortunately there is no catalogue. The Bern Historical Museum holds some of Julie's furniture as well as various decorative table pieces – some donated by Alville, whose family owned Elfenau until 1918, but these items are all in storage and there is no accessible photographic record of them.

9 *Cours*, 172–3.

10 *Vie*, 75; the house name was officially changed on 19 September 1816.

11 *AP*, 134–5; *Vie*, 56. The Wieland poem was later the basis for an opera by Julie's favourite composer, Carl Maria von Weber.

12 For descriptions of Elfenau see *Vie*, 70–2, 103; *Cours*, chapter 8; Hermann and Eichenberger, 'Bern, Elfenau'; Ritter-Lutz, *Die Elfenau in Bern*. For a history of the estate see Alville, *Elfenau*.

13 *Vie*, 93–4. A watercolour of the *hermitage* by Luternau on page 92 of *Vie* depicts the chapel romantically snuggled in between the trees in the park, but sadly it has not survived.

14 Leopold, letter to Schiferli, 15 July 1817 from Claremont, quoted in *Vie*, 81–2.

15 Schiferli to Ernst, 17 March 1812, *Cours*, 115.

16 *Cours*, 123.

17 Leopold, letter, 15 June 1817, *Vie*, 82–3; Leopold, letter to Sophie, 28 August 1817, *Lettres de Léopold*, 160; Lavater-Sloman, 'Die Schweizerjahre', 695.

18 *Vie*, 61; *Cours*, 117, which gives details of the jewellery pieces sold, including a parure from Catherine the Great which appears to have been split up.

19 Grenier, *Mémoires de la Comtesse*, 287–8; Kucherskaya, 159; *Cours*, 146.

20 *Cours*, 147.

21 *ND*, 123; *Cours*, 147; Leopold to Queen Victoria 22 August 1860, RA VIC/Y 82/72.

22 *ND*, 142.

23 *ND*, 149.

24 ND, 163; Beéche, *Coburgs of Europe*, 25.

25 ND, 164.

26 Letter to Renne and Renette, 29 June 1816, *AP*, 108; Leopold to Sophie,
15 February 1817, *Lettres de Léopold*, 138.

27 Princess Caroline in Bern, see *Liverpool Mercury*, 28 October 1814;
Carlisle Journal, 29 October 1814. Robert Huish, *Memoirs of Her Late
Majesty*, vol. I, 587.

28 Christin, *Ferdinand Christin*, 332, 337.

29 *Jahrbuch*, 98.

30 Ibid., 110.

31 Ibid., 110, 112, 117.

32 See *Vie*, 68–9. Although Julie's biographer clearly asserts her subject's
friendship with these leading Bernese politicians and dignitaries it has
proved impossible to find any published sources that shed light on their
relationship with her. Sources in French and German beyond Alville are
very thin indeed, as too are details of the Bernese social scene at this time.
Simond, *Switzerland*, vol. I, 404.

33 *Jahrbuch*, 114, 116, 117.

34 Lane-Poole, *Life of The Right Honourable Stratford Canning*, vol. I. For
the Cannings' take on Switzerland at this time, see chapter VII.

35 *Jahrbuch*, 112; *Cours*, 184.

36 The story of Metilde Dembowski's encounter with Julie can be found in
a very rare article by Adolfo Fermi, 'Metilde Dembowski Viscontini in
Svizzera', *Archivio Storico Lombardo*, vol. 7, 1957, which quotes from
letters she wrote to Caroline Wasmer, her lady in waiting, and Schiferli,
of which there is a résumé in *Cours*, 182–4. See also Marta Boneschi,
La Donna Segreta: Storia de Metilde Viscontini Dembowski, Venice:
Marsilio, 2010, 85–9.

37 *Jahrbuch*, 117.

38 Ibid., 121–2.

39 Ibid., 123–4.

40 Ibid., 125.

41 Ibid., 125.

42 ND, 185; Auguste, letter from Coburg to Schiferli, 23 November 1817,
Vie, 101–2; *Vie*, 103.

43 Pigott, *Records of Real Life*, vol. II, 13.

44 'My Cousins the Coburgs', *Dublin Weekly Nation*, 24 June 1854.

45 Ibid.

46 ND, 20; Rostislava, 'Nesostoyavshayasya imperatritsa'.

47 Ponsonby, *Lost Duchess*, 100; ND, 203.

48 ND, 202, 203.

49 Baillie, *First Impressions*, 303.

50 Pigott, *Records of Real Life*, 151.

51 Stockmar, *Memoirs of Baron Stockmar*, vol. I, 78.
52 Hibbert, *Queen Victoria*, 12.
53 Crawford, *Victoria*, 48.
54 Ponsonby, *Lost Duchess*, 106.

Chapter 12: 'Die Elfenkönigin'

1 A detailed explanation of the circumstances leading up to the divorce can be found in a letter written by Empress Elizaveta Alexeevna to her mother on 16 March 1820; see *LIE*, vol. III, 126–9.
2 Kucherskaya, 160–1, quoting letters in GARF 728,1.X1104 but no dates given.
3 Alexander I to Julie, 6 January 1820, original in French, *Russkii Arkhiv*, vol. 5, 1902. 81–4. Quoted in Krylov-Tolstykovich, *Potselui Psikhei*, 247–8.
4 Kucherskaya, 161; *Annual Register*, 1820, part 1, 140–1; Tondini de Quarenghi, 'Divorce of Grand-Duke Constantine', 61.
5 Schiferli explained the settlement in a letter to Auguste, 27 December 1825, pointing out that Julie's appanage was paid in paper money, not in gold as it was to other members of the imperial family, and that she lost out considerably as a result – to the tune of a million rubles. See *Cours*, 201; *Public Ledger*, 4 July 1820; *Daily Advertiser*, 4 July 1820.
6 Jackman, *Chère Annette*.
7 *LIE*, vol. III, 128.
8 *LIE*, vol. III, 128; letter of 31 January 1821, 118–19.
9 The comments here on Julie's excessively long, erratically written and at times indecipherable letter of 14 February 1820 in *Kurrenschrift* (old German cursive script) are a brief paraphrase of the content of a more legible transcription in German in RA M/3/34, ff 1–3, which at some point was made, perhaps for the use of Princess Beatrice. I am most grateful to Oliver Walton for tackling this difficult text on my behalf.
10 Heinrich Zschokke, *Stunden der Andacht zur Beförderung wahren Christentums und häuslicher Gottesverehrung* ['Hours of Devotion for the Promotion of True Christianity and the Domestic Worship of God'], vol. II, Aarau: Sauerländer, 1815. Zschokke published one of these volumes annually for a number of years.
11 See note 7 above.
12 See *Vie*, 134, 136, 138.
13 Julie to Ernst, 17 April 1815, *Mitteleuropa*, 70; Ernst to Julie, 10 January 1818, *Mitteleuropa*, 70; Schiferli's genealogy quoted in *Mitteleuropa*, 71.
14 *Mitteleuropa*, 68.
15 *Jahrbuch*, 175.
16 Zach to Schiferli, 22 October 1827; Zach to Schiferli, 24 July 1826.

In 1827 Zach spent several months there recuperating after treatment in Paris for bladder stones and visited again the following year. Cunningham, *Collected Correspondence of Baron Franz Xaver von Zach*. The electronic edition is not paginated.

17 *Vie*, 138–9.

18 *Cours*, 285–91 contains a detailed list of all the eminent visitors 'presented to Her Imperial Highness' at Elfenau between 1814 and 1837, compiled from Schiferli's visitors' book.

19 Villèle, *Mémoires et correspondance*, vol. V, 179; *Cours*, 120–1.

20 *Vie*, 109 note 137; *Cours*, 198–9.

21 Leopold, letter to Ernst, 19 October 1817, StA CO.

22 Bonstetten, *Briefe von Bonstetten an Matthisson*, 111.

23 Matthisson, *Schriften*, 220; Bonstetten, *Briefe an Friederike Brun*, 250.

24 Sources on Antoinette are very hard to find in any language but see her Russian Wikipedia entry under Antuanetta Saksen-Koburg-Zaalfeldskaya. A little more can be found in Russian web sources on her husband Alexander. He left Russia after resigning from military service in 1832 and settled in Gotha. On his death in 1833 he was buried in the crypt at Gotha alongside Antoinette.

25 'Alberinchen', in Martin, *Life of HRH the Prince Consort*, vol. I, 3; Victoria, *Early Years*, 24.

26 Letter, 29 June 1825, *Briefe der Herzogin Auguste von Sachsen-Coburg*, 22.

27 'Queen Victoria's Grandmama Visits England', in Cathcart, *Royal Bedside Book*, 15–16.

28 Ibid., 16.

29 Ibid., 23, 24.

30 Victoria, 'Reminiscences of Early Childhood', 32.

31 Rey, *Alexander*, 363.

32 *Cours*, 202.

33 *Vie*, 150.

34 See Benckendorff letter to Schiferli quoted in *Cours*, 205–6; *Vie*, 153–4.

35 A detailed description of the mourning worn by Julie's household can be found in *Vie*, 217.

36 *Cours*, 204.

37 *Mitteleuropa*, 72–3.

38 Richardson, *My Dearest Uncle*, 101.

39 Ibid., 98; Rappaport, *Queen Victoria*, 243–4.

40 *Vie*, 157.

41 Tosato-Rigo and Wick-Werder, 'Marguerite Wildermeth', 69.

42 Ibid., 115; Taillandier, 'Les Souvenirs du médecin de la Reine Victoria', 109.

Chapter 13: 'My House Has Become a House of Mourning'

1 Baring-Gould, 'The Coburg Mausoleum', 120.

2 Letter, 26 November 1831, RA VIC/MAIN/Z/479/14 (original emphasis).

3 'Baring-Gould, 'The Coburg Mausoleum', 123–8.

4 *Cours*, 209–10; *Vie*, 68 note 201.

5 Leopold to Sophie, 24 May 1833, in *Lettres de Léopold*, 242; Sophie to Ferdinand, 9 March 1831, StA Co Kohary-Archive 220.

6 Sophie's life is not well documented but see the work of Radmila Slabáková, who has written a thesis on the Mensdorff-Pouilly family and an article, 'Sophie, Gräfin Mensdorff-Pouilly' (see Bibliography for full details).

7 *Vie*, 150.

8 *Vie*, 65–6.

9 See Petrov and Shchapova, 'K izucheniyu istoriko-dokumental'nogo naslediya Velikoy knyagini Anny Fedorovny', 53–4.

10 Lehmann, *Hôtel de Musique*, 143; *Mitteleuropa*, 105.

11 Petrov and Shchapova, 'K izucheniyu istoriko-dokumental'nogo naslediya Velikoy knyagini Anny Fedorovny', 54; *Vie*, 66.

12 Petrov and Shchapova, 'K izucheniyu istoriko-dokumental'nogo naslediya Velikoy knyagini Anny Fedorovny', 55.

13 Ibid., 55.

14 Ibid., 55–6. Julie's musical archive that is now in the Burgerbibliothek originally passed into the hands of the well-known Watteville family of Bern, who bought Elfenau after Julie's death and restored it.

15 An image is online at Münchener Digitale Bibliothek. The piece was composed and dedicated to 'Madame la Grande Duchesse de Russie', but on the original title page the 'Feodorovna' part of 'Anna Feodorovna' has, interestingly, been crossed out with red chalk, though it is not known by whom. It is possible that this Späth may have been related to Baroness Späth, the Duchess of Kent's lady in waiting from Coburg.

16 Entry in the marriage register at Bursinel, 15 December 1834, *Cours*, 119. See *Cours*, 260–1 note 62. The birth of Hilda and Jean's son Ernest was noted in a letter written by Edward von Loewenfels to Duke Ernst on 9 January 1836: see *Mitteleuropa*, 81. Jean Dapples later became active in Swiss politics, rising to president of the Council of Lausanne. Ernest died in 1895 without issue but with five half-siblings by his father's second marriage in 1840 to Marie Suzanne Elisabeth Curchod.

17 See *Mitteleuropa*, 78–9. Eduard and Berta had a long 57-year marriage that produced five children and many descendants, including members of the von Wangenheim family, who may have misconstrued the link to Alexander I. See Thornton, 'Prince Albert's Sister'.

18 This image of Hilda and Julie and the letters from her half-brother Eduard

were kept in a box among Hilda's effects but according to Alville it was 'lost during the war'; *Cours*, 119.

19 Eduard von Loewenfels to his son Ernst, 13 December 1864, *Mitteleuropa*, 104.

20 Leopold to Emmanuel Mensdorff-Pouilly, 26 November 1836, *Lettres de Léopold*, 295.

21 *Vie*, 84–5.

22 *Vie*, 157; Buess, 'Rudolf Abraham Schiferli', 94.

23 Leopold to Victoria, 1 July 1837, RA VIC/MAIN/Y/63/5070 (original emphasis).

24 Julie to Renette, 18 July 1837, *AP*, 144–5.

25 Julie to Renette, 14 August 1837, *AP*, 147–8.

26 See Julie's letters between 1837 and 1845 in *AP*, 144–202.

27 *AP*, 150, 151.

28 See Victoria, *Early Years*, 110–13.

29 *Vie*, 158.

30 *AP*, 155–6, 156–7.

31 *AP*, 158.

32 *Mitteleuropa*, 81.

33 See letter to Ernst, 13 June 1837, *Mitteleuropa*, 82–3.

34 *Vie*, 159.

35 *Cours*, 278.

36 For details of the former ownership of Le Châtelet and Julie's purchase of it see *Vie*, 160–1 and the notes on 219–20. Alville is the only source for the purchase of the property but does not explain how Julie was able to afford it, given that she held onto Elfenau as well. Very little is known of Vaucher or his career but see *Vie*, 220.

37 Grenier, *Mémoires de la Comtesse*, 287–8.

38 To Louise, 16 February 1844, Fonds Goffinet, 769.

39 *Cours*, 214.

40 *Vie*, 163.

41 *Vie*, 165; Grenier, *Mémoires de la Comtesse*, 288.

42 *Vie*, 86.

43 *Vie*, 163.

44 *AP*, 15.

45 *AP*, 159, 167.

46 QVJ, 9 October 1838, 1 March 1839.

47 QVJ, 31 December 1838, 22 September 1839.

48 QVJ, 31 December 1838.

49 QVJ, 16 October 1839.

50 'A Boy Husband for the Queen', *Bell's Weekly Messenger*, 25 August 1839 (original emphasis).

51 This term was applied as late as 1968 by Roger Fulford in his collection

of the queen's letters, *Dearest Mama*, 113, where he wrote of Julie's life being 'reputedly irregular' in an unnecessarily censorious turn of phrase.

52 *Prince Albert, His Country and Kindred*, 80.
53 *Private Anecdotes of Foreign Courts*, vol. I, 354.
54 'Sketch of the Life of the Grand Duke Constantine', 199.
55 QVJ, 16 December 1839.
56 *Dublin Morning Register*, 10 February 1840.
57 See for example *Morning Post* between 24 February and 9 May 1840 and many other UK papers; also e.g. 'Guests at the Royal Table' for 2, 9 and 16 March 1840, *Court Magazine and Monthly Critic*, January–June 1840, 264, 384, 481, 593.

Chapter 14: 'Aux coeurs blessés, l'ombre et le silence'

1 *Letters of Feodora*, 14 July 1841 – these appear to have been redacted.
2 MS letter from Victoria to Julie, Windsor Castle, 17 September 1841. Courtesy Ian Shapiro Collection.
3 Letter to Renette, 23 October 1840, *AP*, 172–3.
4 *Vie*, 222.
5 *Vie*, 175.
6 *Vie*, 170, 260.
7 *Cours*, 217; *Vie*, 168–9.
8 *Vie*, 173.
9 Letter to Renette, 20 October 1841, *AP*, 187.
10 *Cours*, 228; Beglova, 'Shveitsarskie yuveliry', note 31.
11 Munier's wife, Amélie Munier Romilly, was an artist who painted Julie's portrait, now lost. She was a student of Firmin Massot and an acquaintance of the painter Henriette Rath, both of whom also painted Julie: *Vie*, 227, 182–3. Alville relates what little she was able to glean of Julie's Genevese friends in *Vie*, 179–82, but published sources on them are almost non-existent.
12 Leopold to Victoria, from Laeken, 8 September 1843, RA VIC/MAIN/Y/70/10.
13 QVJ, 18 September 1843.
14 QVJ, 19 September 1843; Surtees, *Charlotte Canning*, 117.
15 QVJ, 20 September 1843.
16 *Lettres de Léopold*, 329.
17 Belien, *Throne in Brussels*, 66.
18 21 September 1843, Benson and Esher, vol. II, 492.
19 Her aunt Victoria's outpouring of grief for the undeserving Ernst matched Julie's. See letter to Leopold, 6 February 1944, ibid., vol. II, 7.
20 26 February 1844, *AP*, 198.
21 To Louise, 14 February 1844, Fonds Goffinet 767.

22 Feodore writing to Victoria from Langenburg, 2 March 1844, RA VIC/MAIN/Y/37/19.

23 *Morning Chronicle*, 20 May 1844; *Oxford University and City Herald*, 1 June 1844, citing *Britannia*.

24 Ponsonby, *Lost Duchess*, 57.

25 QVJ, 20 August 1845.

26 See e.g. *Morning Post*, 22 August 1845.

27 QVJ, 17 August 1848.

28 22 July 1848, RA VIC/ADD/C/4/85.

29 Julie to Leopold, 7 October 1847, Fonds Goffinet, 740.

30 Devey, *Life of Rosina*, 362. Julie makes no mention of this friendship in her surviving correspondence, nor does the extensive literature on Rosina Bulwer Lytton beyond a brief mention in Devey's biography, which is a great shame.

31 *Vie*, 173; *Cours*, 229; QVJ, 8 September 1851; Julie to nephew Charles of Leiningen, 20 September 1851, RA /VIC/MAIN/Z/194/44.

32 Loggins, *Where the World Ends*, 90–1.

33 Ibid., 92–3.

34 Offergeld, 'The Gottschalk Legend'.

35 See e.g. *La France musicale*, 18 August 1850.

36 *Mémorial des Pyrénées*, Pau, 6 August 1851.

37 Starr, *Louis Moreau Gottschalk*, 87.

38 Loggins, *Where the World Ends*, 94–5. Dedicated '*A son Altesse impérial Mme la Grande Duchesse de Russie*', the original score of the *Danse ossianique* is in the Gottschalk Collection, Washington University libraries, http://omeka.wustl.edu/omeka/exhibits/show/gottschalk/item/2642

39 Grezin, 'Iz istorii stroitel'stva Russkikh khramov', 138–41.

40 Grimm, *Alexandra Feodorowna*, vol. II, 405.

41 According to Leopold in a letter to Queen Victoria, 15 October 1859, RA VIC/MAIN/Y/82/12.

42 QV to Leopold, 8 September 1857, RA VIC/MAIN/7/102/30; QV to Leopold, 17 February 1857, RA VIC/MAIN/Y/102/6.

43 For Wagner at Le Pavillon see Guy 'Richard Wagner à Mornex'; for John Ruskin see Häusermann, *Genevese Background*, chapter 5.

44 Weber, 'Grande Duchesse', 10–12.

45 The Duchess of Kent explained Julie's need for a change of air, as advised by her physician, in a letter to Queen Victoria of 30 September 1857; see RA VIC/MAIN/Z/131/48. Häusermann, *Genevese Background*, 159–64, devotes a chapter to Dr Gosse, 'Ruskin's Friend and Physician in Geneva' – but it fails to say anything about Gosse's close relationship with Julie. In 1862 when Ruskin rented the house at Mornex, Gosse treated him for a mental breakdown.

46 Julie to Prince Albert, 23 November 1857, RA VIC/MAIN/M/54/72.

47 In a long, rambling letter to Leopold of 1857 Julie gave an almost incoherent, scribbled description of her aches and pains. She also complained in other letters of recurring pain in her right arm and hand that made it difficult to write. See 7 September 1857, Fonds Goffinet, 740.

48 Leopold to Prince Leo, 7 September 1859, Fonds Goffinet, 1078; Leopold to QV, 26 August 1859, RA VIC/MAIN/Y/82/12.

49 Gosse provided Prince Albert with a detailed account of Julie's final days and his attempts at treatment in a very long letter written from Elfenau, 16 August 1860, RA VIC/MAIN/M/54/138. It can be read online in Prince Albert's Personal Papers, Royal Collection Trust, https://albert.rct.uk/collections/royal-archives/prince-alberts-personal-papers/letter-from-dr-louis. Alville's résumé of the Gosse letter can be seen in *Cours*, 235–7.

50 Julie to Prince Albert, 6 February 1860, RA VIC/MAIN/M/54/130 (original emphasis).

51 Prince Albert to his stepmother, Duchess Marie of Saxe-Coburg-Gotha, 29 August 1860, in Bachmann, *Herzogin Marie*, 319.

52 See Dr Gosse letter, note 49 above.

53 QVJ, 10 and 11 August 1860.

54 Leopold to Victoria, 7 August 1860, RA VIC/MAIN/Y/82/65918.

55 See Dr Gosse letter, note 49 above.

56 *Globe*, 18 August 1860.

57 See e.g. *Taunton Courier*, 29 August 1860.

58 'Death of Her Imperial Highness the Grand Duchess Anne of Russia', *Morning Chronicle*, 16 August 1860.

59 *Gentleman's Magazine*, vol. 9, 1860, 319.

60 *Herts Guardian*, 23 August 1860; Prince Albert to Stockmar, 21 August 1860, in Martin, *Life of HRH the Prince Consort*, vol. V, 173; Prince Albert to Duchess Marie, 29 August 1860, in Bachmann, *Herzogin Marie*, 318.

61 Devey, *Life of Rosina*, 363.

62 Leopold to QV, 14 December 1860, RA VIC/MAIN/Y/82/65.

63 21 December 1860, RA VIC/MAIN/Y/82/93.

64 Eduard's daughter Sophie (1836–1920) married into the influential von Wangenheim family in Coburg, who had connections at the Saxe-Coburg court. See *Mitteleuropa*, 65.

65 Published in French in 1942, the first biography, *La Vie en Suisse*, is a valuable starting point, written by a Swiss national who had lived at Elfenau as a child and who drew on extensive local knowledge. Watteville spoke with many people whose families had known Julie and who shared documentary material with her that was in private hands. Unfortunately, the location of that material remains unknown. Due to the onset of the Second World War in Europe, Watteville was unable to access any of the

important material in the Staatsarchiv Coburg. She therefore wrote an additional volume, *Des cours princières*, published in 1962, which adds much of this missing material, but unfortunately lacks any source material from Russia and the Royal Archives at Windsor. Alix de Watteville might well have added more detail to the Swiss side of Julie's story but she died in 1964 at the age of only sixty-five. Such papers of Julie's that survive are in the Von Wattenwyl Family and Bonstetten Family archives in the Burgerbibliothek Bern.

66 The contents are few and not particularly ostentatious, given Julie's high status. Nothing survives of her once fabulous collection of Russian jewellery. Julie made many gifts of jewellery, including to Queen Victoria. She also presented some magnificent diamonds to Luise of Saxe-Gotha-Altenburg when she married her brother Duke Ernst in 1817: see https://royal-magazin.de/german/sachsen-coburg/sachsen-coburg-luise-saalfeld-hochzeit-loop-tiara-necklace-diamonds.htm

67 *Cours*, 283–4.

68 A Captain Harris at the British legation was asked to commission Durheim to take the photographs, but although the Royal Archives hold the invoice for the work, the actual photographs cannot be found anywhere in the Royal Collection. See RA PPTO/PP/QV/PP2/49/1590/17/; Prince Albert's Personal Papers, https://albert.rct.uk/collections/royal-archives/prince-alberts-personal-papers/bill-letters-and An email to author from Royal Collection, 28 September 2021 confirms their loss. An enquiry to the Fonds Goffinet confirms they are not in King Leopold's archive either.

69 Fulford, *Dearest Mama*, 113.

70 Leopold to QV, 23 and 27 October 1864, RA VIC/MAIN/Y/86/69 and 70.

71 For a summary of the house's history after Julie's death see Petrov and Shchapova, 'K izucheniyu istoriko-dokumental'nogo naslediya Velikoy knyagini Anny Fedorovny', 56–7.

Epilogue

1 Letter of 15 August 1860, Martin, *Life of HRH the Prince Consort*, vol. V, 172 (my emphasis).

2 Letter to Victoria, 22 August 1860, RA VIC/MAIN/Y/82/72; *Mitteleuropa*, 66.

3 26 September 1856, RA VIC/MAIN/Y/80/81.

4 See Leopold's comments on Konstantin in his 'Reminiscences', Appendix A to Victoria, *Early Years*, especially 384.

5 *Allgemeine Zeitung*, 22 August 1860.

6 Leopold to QV, 18 August 1860, RA VIC/MAIN/Y/82/71 (original emphasis).

7 'Sobstvennoruchnyya zapiski neizvestnago avtora', 43–4.

8 28 August 1860, RA VIC/MAIN/Y/82/73.

9 16 February 1864, RA VIC/MAIN/Y/86/10.

10 The German text of Auguste's letters to Duke Franz from St Petersburg was published in Darmstadt in 1907 but has not been translated into English, neither have her valuable travel diaries from 1810 to 1825, which were published in the *Jahrbuch der Coburger Landesstiftung*, vol. 51, 2006. Auguste's original *Tagebuch* is held at the Royal Archives at RA VIC/MAIN/Y/115–21; there is also a transcript at RA VIC/MAIN/M/26–31 which may have been used by Princess Beatrice for her expurgated edition, *In Napoleonic Days*.

11 A close comparison of key periods in Auguste's journal made by my research assistant Oliver Walton shows that there were considerable differences between the clean, and reliable transcription (RA VIC/MAIN/M/26–31) which may have been made by Prince Albert or his German secretaries, and the text of *In Napoleonic Days*. In the original journal, (RA VIC/MAIN/Y/115–21), in the first volume in particular, there are numerous crossings-out and attempts at obliteration or alteration of names, made – presumably – in the years after Auguste's death by members of her family who had the journals at one time in their possession. There is a concerted attempt in entries for 1818 in particular to erase Julie's name. But who was the culprit? This explanation from Leopold to Queen Victoria of 14 April 1854, is highly ambiguous: 'You will read with interest the Journal of my dear mother. My sister has t[ruly] with a sort of insanity scratched out most of the names in things that are without the *slightest* danger, I confess that it put me out of all patience.' (RA VIC/MAIN/Y/79/45, original emphasis) But the question is: does Leopold mean Julie, or Victoire? It seems logical that it was Julie, for she wrote to Victoire on 25 December 1831 begging her to agree that Ernst, who had taken possession of his mother's papers, send this 'most wonderful inheritance' to her first. 'I also have some right to it,' she wrote, 'because she read to me often and a great deal from her diary and initially wanted to leave it to us undivided. . . *please, dear, allow me to have it to read first before it is transferred to you!*' (RA VIC/MAIN/Z/479/28, original emphasis) At some point after that, Julie had sent the original to Victoire in England.

BIBLIOGRAPHY

ARCHIVES

Bibliothèque de Genève
Burgerbibliothek, Bern
Fonds Goffinet, Brussels
GARF, Moscow
Landesarchiv Thüringen, Hauptstaatsarchiv Weimar
Prince Albert's Personal Papers, Royal Collection Trust,
    https://www.rct.uk/collection/themes/Trails/
    prince-albert-his-life-and-legacy
Queen Victoria's Journals, http://www.queenvictoriasjournals.org/
    home.do
RGADA, Moscow
Royal Archives, Windsor
Royal Collection, Windsor
Russian National Library, https://primo.nlr.ru/primo-explore/
    search?vid=07NLR_VU1
Staatsarchiv Coburg

Electronic Sources

Newspapers and Journals

Bayerische StaatsBibliothek DigiPress, https://digipress.digitale-sammlungen.de/search/simple

British Newspaper Archive, https://www.britishnewspaperarchive.co.uk/

e-newspaperarchives.ch, https://www.e-newspaperarchives.ch/?l=en

Gallica, French archives, https://gallica.bnf.fr/services/engine/search/advancedSearch/

German newspaper archive, https://www.deutsche-digitale-bibliothek.de/newspaper?lang=en

Imperial Russian Newspapers, https://www.eastview.com/resources/gpa/crl-irn/

Journal des Luxus und der Moden 1787–1812, https://zs.thulb.uni-jena.de/receive/jportal_jpjournal_00000029

Kamer-fur'erskie zhurnaly 1799 goda, https://vivaldi.nlr.ru/bv000020329

Kamer-fur'erskie zhurnaly 1801 goda, https://vivaldi.nlr.ru/bv000020331

Revue historique vaudoise, https://www.e-periodica.ch/digbib/volumes?UID=rhv-001

Le Temps archives, https://www.letempsarchives.ch/

Articles and Letters

Andreev, Andrei, 'Ioann Kapodistriya – pervyi russkii posol v Shveitsarii!', 1 June 2014, https://shorturl.at/iWWk1

Beglova, Natal'ya Spartakovna, 'Shveitsarskie yuveliry v Rossii', https://beglova.com/shveicarskie-juveliry-v-rossii/

Beglova, Natal'ya Spartakovna, 'Velikaya Knyagina Anna Fedorovna: "Izranennym serdtsam – sumrak i tishina!"', http://beglova.com/anna-fjodorovna

Catherine the Great letters online, CatCor, https://catcor.seh.ox.ac.uk/texts/

Cunningham, Cliff, *Collected Correspondence of Baron Franz Xaver von Zach*

Duchhardt, Heinz, 'The Dynastic Marriage', EGO European History Online, 4 August 2011, http://ieg-ego.eu/ en/threads/european-networks/dynastic-networks/ heinz-duchhardt-the-dynastic-marriage

'L'Eglise Orthodoxe en Suisse', Switzerland.isyours.com, https:// switzerlandisyours.com/F/guide/religion/christianisme/ orthodoxe.html

Flantzer, Susan, 'Augusta Reuss of Ebersdorf, Duchess of Saxe-Coburg-Saasfeld', Unofficial Royalty, 2015, http://www.unofficialroyalty.com/ augusta-reuss-of-erbersdorf-duchess-of-saxe-coburg-saalfeld/

Grezin, Ivan, 'Grand Duchess Anna Feodorovna: In Search of Simple Happiness in the Midst of Big Politics', *Nasha gazeta*, 15 June 2011, https://nashagazeta-ch.translate.goog/fr/ node/11890?_x_tr_sl=ru&_x_tr_tl=en&_x_tr_hl=es

Guy, Lucien, 'Richard Wagner à Mornex en 1856', Munich and Company, 19 March 2017, http://munichandco.blogspot. com/2017/03/richard-wagner-mornex-en-1856-par.html

'Juliane von Sachsen-Coburg-Saalfeld', German Wikipedia, https:// de.wikipedia.org/wiki/Juliane_von_Sachsen-Coburg-Saalfeld

Klöffler, Martin, 'Last und Lust des Reisens oder von der Unbequemlichkeit der Fortbewegung zu Lande 1750–1815 Teil 2: von dem Reisen selbst, der Fortbewegung und den Hindernisssen', Düsseldorf, 8 April 2023, https://www. academia.edu/99882413/Last_und_Lust_des_Reisens_ Oder_von_der_Unbequemlichkeit_der_Fortbewegung_zu_ Lande_1750_1815_Teil_2_Von_dem_Reisen_selbst_der_ Fortbewegung_und_den_Hindernissen

Krylov-Tolstykovich, Aleksandr, 'Nemetskie printsessy v Rossii', https://www.proza.ru/2012/11/18/404

Offergeld, Robert, 'The Gottschalk Legend', http://thompsonian. info/gottschalk-legend-offergeld.htm

Rostislava, 'Nesostoyavshayasya imperatritsa', part 1, 25 July

2009, https://rostislava.livejournal.com/23613.html ; part 2, 28 July 2009, https://rostislava.livejournal.com/39742.html

Sbornik Imperatorskago Russkago istorichestkago obschchestva, H-Russia, https://networks.h-net.org/node/10000/ pages/138851/sbornik-imperatorskago-russkago-istoricheskago-obshchestva-sirio

Slabáková, Radmila Švařičková, 'Sophie, Gräfin Mensdorff-Pouilly, geborene Prinzessin von Sachsen-Coburg-Saalfeld', https://www.academia.edu/8613608/ Sophie_Gr%C3%A4fin_Mensdorff_Pouilly_geborene_ Prinzessin_von_Sachsen_Coburg_Saalfeld

Timms, Elizabeth Jane, '"My Dear Grandmama": Queen Victoria's memories of her grandmother', Royal Central, 26 July 2020, https://royalcentral.co.uk/features/my-dear-grandmama-queen-victorias-memories-of-her-grandmother-146117/

PUBLISHED SOURCES

English

Abbott, John S. C., ed., *Confidential Correspondence of the Emperor Napoleon and the Empress Josephine*, New York: Mason Brothers, 1856

Adams, Louisa Catherine, *A Traveled First Lady: Writings of Louisa Catherine Adams*, Harvard: Belknap Press, 2014

Albert, Harold A., *Queen Victoria's Sister: The Life and Letters of Princess Feodora*, London: Robert Hale, 1967

Aronson, Theo, *The Coburgs of Belgium*, London: Cassell, 1969

Ashdown, Dulcie M., *Victoria and the Coburgs*, London: Robert Hale, 1981

Aspinall, A., ed., *The Letters of Princess Charlotte 1811–1817*, London: Home & Van Thal, 1949

Baillie, Marianne, *First Impressions on a Tour upon the Continent in the Summer of 1818*, London: John Murray, 1819

Baring-Gould, Sabine, 'The Coburg Mausoleum', in *Historic*

Oddities and Strange Events, Second Series, London: Methuen, 1891, 120–8

'The Battle of Saalfeld (1806) Reported by an Eyewitness', in George Sherburn, *Roehenstart, A Late Stuart Pretender*, Chicago: Chicago University Press, 1960, Appendix III

Beatrice, HRH Princess, ed., *In Napoleonic Days: Extracts from the Private Diary of Augusta, Duchess of Saxe-Coburg-Saalfeld, Queen Victoria's Maternal Grandmother, 1806–1821*, London: John Murray, 1941

Beéche, Arturo, *The Coburgs of Europe: The Rise and Fall of Queen Victoria's European Family*, Eurohistory.com, 2013

Belien, Paul, *A Throne in Brussels: Britain, the Saxe-Coburgs and the Belgianisation of Europe*, Exeter: Imprint Academic, 2005

Benson, Arthur Christopher and Viscount Esher, *Letters of Queen Victoria*, 3 vols, London: John Murray, 1911

Bischoff, Ilse, 'Madame Vigée Le Brun at the Court of Catherine the Great', *Russian Review*, vol. 24, no. 1, 1965, 30–45

Bosbach, Franz, John R. Davis and Karina Urbach, eds, *Documents and Sources Relating to German–British Relations in the Archives and Collections of Windsor and Coburg, vol. 1: The Archives*, Berlin: Duncker & Humblot, 2015.

Brown, John, *Memoirs of the Courts of Sweden and Denmark During the Reigns of Christian VII. of Denmark and Gustavus III. and IV. of Sweden*, 2 vols, London: Grolier Society, 1904

Bury, Lady Charlotte Campbell, *The Diary of a Lady-in-Waiting*, 2 vols, London: J. Lane, 1908

Carr, John, *A Northern Summer; or Travels Round the Baltic . . . in the Year 1804*, Hartford: Lincoln & Gleason, 1806

Cases, Count de las, *Journal of the Private Life and Conversations of the Emperor Napoleon at Saint Helena*, 4 vols, New York: Worthington, 1890

Cathcart, Helen, *The Royal Bedside Book*, London: W. H. Allen, 1969

Chavchavadze, David, *The Grand Dukes*, New York: Atlantic International, 1990

Cottineau de Kloguen, Denis, *Geographical Compilation for the Use of Schools ...*, Baltimore: John West Butler, 1806

Coxe, William, *Travels into Poland, Russia, Sweden and Denmark*, 3 vols, Dublin: S. Price, 1784

Crabitès, Pierre, *Victoria's Guardian Angel: A Study of Baron Stockmar*, London: G. Routledge & Sons, 1937

Crawford, Emily, *Victoria, Queen and Ruler*, London: Simpkin, Marshall, 1903

Croly, Rev. George, *Lines on the Death of HRH Princess Charlotte*, London: John Murray, 1818

Cronin, Vincent, *Catherine, Empress of All the Russias*, London: Harvill Press, 1989

Cross, A. G., ed., *An English Lady at the Court of Catherine the Great: The Journal of Baroness Elizabeth Dimsdale 1781*, Cambridge: Crest, 1989

Cross, Anthony, *St Petersburg and the British: The City Through the Eyes of British Visitors and Residents*, London: Frances Lincoln, 2008

Czartoryski, Adam, *Memoirs of Prince Adam Czartoryski and his Correspondence with Alexander I*, ed. Adam Gielgud, 2 vols, London: Remington, 1888

D'Auvergne, Edmund B., *The Coburgs: The Story of the Rise of a Great Royal House*, London: Stanley Paul, 1911

Devey, Louisa, *Life of Rosina, Lady Lytton*, London: Swan, Sonnenschein, Lowry, 1887

Diesbach, Ghislain de, *Secrets of the Gotha*, London: Chapman & Hall, 1967

Dixon, Simon, *Catherine the Great*, Harlow: Longman, 2001

'The Domestic Life of Alexander Paulowitz, Emperor of Russia', *Littell's Living Age*, vol. 28, 1851, 120–4.

Dziewanowski, M. K., *Alexander I: Russia's Mysterious Tsar*, New York: Hippocrene, 1990

Ebel, Johann Gottfried, *The Traveller's Guide Through Switzerland*, London: Samuel Leigh, 1820

Edwards, Andrew and Suzanne Edwards, *His Master's Reflection: Travels with John Polidori, Lord Byron's Doctor and Author of 'The Vampyre'*, Eastbourne: Sussex Academic Press, 2018

Feodora, Princess of Hohenlohe-Langenburg, *Letters of Feodora, Princess of Hohenlohe-Langenburg, from 1828 to 1872*, London: Spottiswoode, 1874

Ferrier, 'Jean Paul', *English Review*, vol. 7, no. 14, 1847, 276–313

Fulford, Roger, ed., *Dearest Mama: Letters between Queen Victoria and the Crown Princess of Prussia 1861–1864*, London: Evans Brothers, 1968

Gill, Gillian, *We Two: Victoria and Albert – Rulers, Partners, Rivals*, New York: Ballantine, 2009

Golovina, Countess Varvara, *Memoirs of Countess Golovine*, London: David Nutt, 1910

'The Grand Duchess Anne of Russia', *Gentleman's Magazine*, vol. 70, 1860, 319.

'The Grand Dukes: Konstantin in the Marble Palace, Part 1: Grand Duke Konstantin Pavlovich', *Imperial Russian Journal*, vol. 5, no. 2, 2001

Granville, Augustus Bozzi, *St Petersburgh: Travels to and from that Capital*, 2 vols, New York: Arno Press, 1971

Green, George, *An Original Journal from London to St Petersburgh*, London: T. Boosey, 1813

Greville, Charles C. F., *The Greville Memoirs: A Journal of the Reigns of King George IV, King William IV and Queen Victoria, vol. 2*, ed. Henry Reeve, Cambridge: Cambridge University Press, 2011

Grimm, A. Th. von, *Alexandra Feodorowna, Empress of Russia*, 2 vols, Edinburgh: Edmonston & Douglas, 1870

A Hand-book for Travellers in Southern Germany, 2nd ed., London: John Murray, 1840

A Hand-Book for Travellers in Switzerland and the Alps of Savoy and Piedmont, London: John Murray, 1839

A Hand-Book for Travellers on the Continent, 4th ed., London: John Murray, 1843

Häusermann, H. W., *The Genevese Background: Studies of Shelley, Francis Danby, Maria Edgeworth, Ruskin, Meredith, and Joseph Conrad in Geneva*, London: Routledge & Kegan Paul, 1952

Hibbert, Christopher, *Queen Victoria: A Personal History*, London: HarperCollins, 2000

Hone, William, *Hone's Authentic Account of the Royal Marriage*, London: W. Hone, 1816

Huish, Robert, *Memoirs of Her Late Majesty Caroline, Queen of Great Britain*, 2 vols, London: T. Kelly, 1821

Hyde, Catherine, *Private Anecdotes of Foreign Courts*, 2 vols, London: H. Colburn, 1827

Jackman, S. W. ed., *Chère Annette: Letters from Russia 1820–1828*, Stroud: Sutton, 1994

Jackman, S. W., ed., *Romanov Relations: The Private Correspondence of Tsars Alexander I, Nicholas I and the Grand Dukes Constantine and Michael with Their Sister Queen Anna Pavlovna 1817–1855*, London: Macmillan, 1969

Jackman, Sydney W. and Hella Haase, eds, *A Stranger in The Hague: The Letters of Queen Sophie of the Netherlands to Lady Malet 1842–1877*, Durham, NC: Duke University Press, 1989

Joyneville, C. *Life and Times of Alexander I: Emperor of all the Russias*, 3 vols, London: Tinsley Brothers, 1875

Karamsin, Nicolai, *Travels from Moscow Through Prussia, Germany, Switzerland, France and England*, 2 vols, London: J. Badcock, 1803

'Karoline Bauer, Leopold I, and Baron Stockmar', *Westminster Review* 123, 1885, 460–87

Kelly, Laurence, *Moscow: A Travellers' Companion*, London: Constable, 1983

Kelly, Laurence, *St Petersburg: A Travellers' Companion*, London: Constable, 1981

Kohl, J. G., *Russia: St Petersburg, Moscow, Kharkoff, Riga, Odessa*, London: Chapman & Hall, 1844

Koukkou, Helen E., *Ioannis A. Kapodistrias, the European Diplomat and Statesman of the 19th Century, Roxana S. Stourdza, a Famous Woman of Her Time*, Athens: Society for the Study of Greek History, 2001

Lalor, William Mead, 'The Grand Duchess Anna Feodorovna: "Poor Dear Aunt Julie"', *Royalty Digest*, no. 61, July 1996, 11–14

Lane-Poole, Stanley, *The Life of The Right Honourable Stratford Canning, Viscount Stratford de Redcliffe*, 2 vols, London: Longmans, Green, 1888

Leighton, Rachel, *The Correspondence of Charlotte Grenville, Lady Williams Wynn, and Her Three Sons 1795–1832*, London: John Murray, 1920

Leopold, King of the Belgians, 'Reminiscences', in Victoria, *Early Years*

Letters of Feodora Princess of Hohenlohe-Langenburg from 1828 to 1872, London: Spottiswoode, 1874

Loggins, Vernon, *Where the World Ends: The Life of Louis Moreau Gottschalk*, Baton Rouge: Louisiana State University Press, 1958

McGrigor, Mary, *The Tsar's Doctor: the Life and Times of Sir James Wylie*, Edinburgh: Birlinn, 2010

Madariaga, Isabel de, *Russia in the Age of Catherine the Great*, New Haven, CT: Yale University Press, 1981

Marie, Queen of Roumania, *The Story of My Life*, New York: Charles Scribner's Sons, 1934

Marlowe, Derek, *A Single Summer with L.B.: The Summer of 1816*, Harmondsworth: Penguin, 1973

Maroger, Dominique, ed., *The Memoirs of Catherine the Great*, London: Hamish Hamilton, 1955

Martin, Theodore, *The Life of His Royal Highness The Prince Consort*, 5 vols, London: Smith, Elder, 1880

Masson, C. F. P., *Secret Memoirs of the Court of Petersburg*, London: T. N. Longman & O. Rees, 1801

Mikaberidze, Alexander, *Kutuzov: A Life in War and Peace*, New York: Oxford University Press, 2022

'My Cousins the Coburgs', *Dublin Weekly Nation*, 24 June 1854

'A New Description of St Petersburg, the Metropolis of the Russian Empire', *Scots Magazine*, vol. 58, March 1796

Nicholas, Grand Duke, ed., *Scenes of Russian Court Life, Being the Correspondence of Alexander I with His Sister Catherine*, London: Jarrolds, 1917

Nikolenko, Lada, 'The Russian Portraits of Madame Vigée Le Brun', *Gazette des Beaux Arts*, July–August 1967, 92–120

Nisbet, Charles, *Caroline Bauer and the Coburgs*, 2nd ed., London: Vizetelly, 1887

North, Michael, *'Material Delight and the Joy of Living': Cultural Consumption in the Age of Enlightenment in Germany*, Aldershot: Ashgate, 2008

O'Brien, Michael, *Mrs Adams in Winter: A Journey in the Last Days of Napoleon*, New York: Farrar, Straus & Giroux, 2010

Ostler, Catherine, *The Duchess Countess: The Woman Who Scandalised a Nation*, London: Simon & Schuster, 2021

Panam, Pauline, *A German Prince and His Victim*, London: John Long, 1915

Penny Cyclopaedia of the Society for the Diffusion of Useful Knowledge, vol. VII: Char–Copy, London: Charles Knight, 1837

The Picture of London for 1820; Being a Correct Guide for the Stranger . . ., London: Longman, Hurst, Rees, Orme, 1820

Pienkos, Angela T., *The Imperfect Autocrat: Grand Duke Constantine Pavlovich and the Polish Congress Kingdom*, Boulder, CO: East European Monographs, 1987

Pigott, Miss Harriott, *Records of Real Life in the Palace and the Cottage*, Rev. John Galt, 3 vols, London: Saunders & Otley, 1839

Ponsonby, D. A., *The Lost Duchess: The Story of the Prince Consort's Mother*, London: Chapman & Hall, 1958

Porter, Robert Ker, *Travelling Sketches in Russia and Sweden During the Years 1805, 1806, 1807, 1808*, Philadelphia: Hopkins & Earle, 1809

Potemkin, Prince Grigory, *Memoirs of the Life of Prince Potemkin*, London: Henry Colburn, 1812

Potemkin, Prince Grigory, *Memoirs of the Life of Prince Potemkin*, 2nd ed., London: Henry Colburn, 1813

Potts, D. M. and W. T. W. Potts, *Queen Victoria's Gene: Haemophilia and the Royal Family*, Stroud: Alan Sutton, 1995

Prince Albert, His Country and Kindred, London: Thomas Ward, 1840

'Private History of Constantine of Russia', *London and Paris Observer: Or Chronicle of Literature*, 1826, vol. II, 161–3

Rappaport, Helen, *Queen Victoria: A Biographical Companion*, Santa Barbara, CA: ABC Clio, 1999

Redman, Alvin, *The House of Hanover*, New York: Funk & Wagnalls, 1968

Render, Rev. Dr William, *A Tour Through Germany*, T. N. Longman & O. Rees, 1801

Rey, Marie-Pierre, *Alexander I: The Tsar Who Defeated Napoleon*, DeKalb: Northern Illinois University Press, 2012

Richardson, Joanna, *My Dearest Uncle: A Life of Leopold, First King of the Belgians*, London: Jonathan Cape, 1961

Rimmer, Alfred, *The Early Homes of Prince Albert*, Edinburgh: William Blackwood & Sons, 1883

Ritchie, Leitch, *A Journey to St Petersburg and Moscow Through Courland and Livonia*, London: Longman, Rees, Orme, Brown, Green & Longman, 1836

Rounding, Virginia, *Catherine the Great: Love, Sex, and Power*, New York: St Martin's Press, 2008

Rousseau, Jean-Jacques, *Collected Writings of Rousseau, vol. 6: Julie, or the New Héloïse*, Hanover, NH: Dartmouth College Press, 1990

St Aubyn, Giles, *Queen Victoria: A Portrait*, New York: Atheneum, 1992

Scheele, Godfrey and Margaret Scheele, *The Prince Consort: Man of Many Facets*, London: Oresko, 1977

Schnitzler, Johann Heinrich, *Secret History of the Court and Government of Russia under the Emperors Alexander and Nicholas*, 2 vols, London: Richard Bentley, 1847

Schönle, Andreas and Andrei Zorin, *On the Periphery of Europe 1762–1825: The Self-Invention of the Russian Elite*, DeKalb: Northern Illinois University Press, 2018

Sebag-Montefiore, Simon, *The Romanovs 1613–1918*, London: Weidenfeld & Nicolson, 2016

Sergeant, Philip, *The Courtships of Catherine the Great*, Philadelphia: Lippincott, 1905

Seume, J. G., *A Tour Through Part of Germany, Poland, Russia, Sweden, Denmark, &c., During the Summer of 1805*, London: Richard Phillips, 1807

Shoberl, Frederic, 'Memoirs of the House of Saxe-Coburg-Saalfeld', in *Historical Account Interspersed with Biographical Anecdotes of the House of Saxony ... and Containing a Memoir of the Life of His Serene Highness Leopold*, London: R. Ackermann, 1816, 159–96.

Simond, Louis, *Switzerland; or, A Journal of a Tour and Residence in That Country, in the Years 1817, 1818, and 1819*, 2 vols, London: John Murray, 1822

'Sketch of the Grand Duke Constantine of Russia', *New Monthly Magazine*, vol. 16, 1826, 194–206

Staël-Holstein, Baroness de, *Ten Years' Exile*, Fontwell: Centaur Press, 1968

Stanford, John Frederick, *Rambles and Researches in Thuringian Saxony*, London: John W. Parker, 1842

Starr, S. Frederick, *Louis Moreau Gottschalk*, Urbana: University of Illinois Press, 2000

Stockmar, Baron E. von, *Memoirs of Baron Stockmar*, 2 vols, London: Longman, Green, 1873

Storch, Heinrich Friedrich von, *The Picture of St Petersburg*, London: T. N. Longman & O. Rees, 1801

Stuart, Dorothy Margaret, *The Mother of Victoria: A Period Piece*, London: Macmillan, 1942

Surtees, Virginia, *Charlotte Canning: Lady-in-Waiting to Queen Victoria and Wife of the First Viceroy of India 1817–1861*, London: John Murray, 1975

Temperley, Harold, ed., *The Unpublished Diary and Political Sketches of Princess Lieven*, London: Jonathan Cape, 1925

Thackeray, William Makepeace, *Vanity Fair*, London: Smith, Elder, 1869

Thornton, Richard, 'Prince Albert's Sister and Other Shady Coburgs', *Royalty Digest Quarterly*, 2008, no. 2, 39–43

Tondini de Quarenghi, Cesare, 'Divorce of Grand-Duke Constantine', in *The Pope of Rome and the Popes of the Oriental Orthodox Church*, London: R. Washbourne, 1875

Tooke, William, *The Life of Catharine II, Empress of Russia*, 3 vols, Dublin: J. Moore, 1800

Troubetzkoy, Alexis S., *Imperial Legend: The Disappearance of Tsar Alexander I*, Staplehurst: Spellmount, 2002

Tyrrell, H., and Henry A. Haukeil, 'The Grand Duke Constantine', in *The History of Russia from the Foundation of the Empire to the War with Turkey in 1877–'78*, London: London Printing & Publishing Co., 1879, vol. II, ch. 8

Urbach, Karina, ed., *Royal Kinship: Anglo-German Family Networks 1815–1918*, Munich: K. G. Saur, 2008

Victoria, Queen, *The Early Years of His Royal Highness the Prince Consort*, London: Smith, Elder, 1867

Victoria, Queen, 'Reminiscences of Early Childhood', in Cathcart, *Royal Bedside Book*, 29–33

Vigée Le Brun, Elisabeth, *The Memoirs of Elisabeth Vigée Le Brun*, London: Camden Press, 1989

Vogüé, Viscomte E. M. de, *A Czarevitch of the Eighteenth Century and Other Studies in Russian History*, London: Arthur L. Humphreys, 1913, 260

Ward, Lucy, *The Empress and the English Doctor: How Catherine the Great Defied a Deadly Virus*, London: Oneworld, 2022

Weintraub, Stanley, *Uncrowned King: The Life of Prince Albert*, New York: Free Press, 1997

Wolfe, Theodore Frelinghuysen, *A Literary Pilgrimage Among the Haunts of Famous British Authors*, 10th ed., Philadelphia: J. B. Lippincott, 1897

Wortman, Richard S., *Scenarios of Power: Myth and Ceremony in Russian Monarchy, from Peter the Great to the Abdication of Nicholas II*, Princeton: Princeton University Press, 2006

Wright, Constance, *Beautiful Enemy: A Biography of Queen Louise of Prussia*, New York: Dodd, Mead, 1969

French

Alville, *Des cours princières aux demeures helvétiques*, Lausanne: La Concorde, 1962

Alville, *La Vie en Suisse de S.A.I. la Grande-Duchesse Anna Feodorovna née Princesse de Saxe-Cobourg-Saalfeld*, Lausanne: F. Rouge, 1942

Avrillon, Marie-Jeanne-Pierrette, *Mémoires de Mademoiselle Avrillon: première femme de chambre de l'impératrice*, 2 vols, Paris: Garnier, 1913

Biaudet, Charles and Francoise Nicod, eds, *Correspondance de Frédéric-César de La Harpe et Alexandre Ier, suivie de la correspondance de Frédéric-César de La Harpe avec les membres de la famille impériale de Russie*, 3 vols, Neuchâtel: La Baconnière, 1980

Bronne, Carlo, *Lettres de Leopold Ier: premier roi des Belges*, Brussels: Office de Publicité, 1943

Carro, Jean de, *Almanach de Carlsbad*, Carlsbad: Franiek, 1846

Chreptowitch-Bouténeff, Constantin, *Lettres d'augustes personnages, adressées à Madame de Roenne et à sa fille la Comtesse Caroline Chreptowitch 1798–1845*, Lausanne: Imprimeries Réunies, 1910

Christin, Ferdinand, *Ferdinand Christin et la princesse*

Tourkestanow: lettres écrites de Pétersbourg et de Moscou 1813–1819, Moscow: Université Imperiale, 1882

Corti, Comte E., and Baron C. Buffin, *Léopold Ier: oracle politique de l'Europe*, Brussels: Albert Dewit, 1927

Defrance, Olivier, *Léopold Ier et le clan Cobourg*, Brussels: Racine, 2004

Dufoux, Georges, *Une dynastie mythique: Les Saxe-Cobourg-Gotha*, 2 vols, privately printed, 2000

Gagarin, P., 'Anecdotes recueillies à Saint-Pétersbourg par le Comte de Maistre', *Etudes Religieuses, Historiques et Littéraires*, July 1869, 84–100

Golovkine, Comte Fédor, *La Cour et le règne de Paul Ier: portraits, souvenirs et anecdotes*, Paris: Plon-Nourrit, 1905

Grenier, Giovanella Caetani, ed., *Mémoires de la Comtesse Rosalie Rzewuska (1788–1865)*, 2 vols, Rome: Cuggiani, 1939

Kotzebue, Auguste, *Souvenirs de Paris en 1804*, 2 vols, Paris: Barba, 1805

Nicolas Mikhaïlovitch, Grand-Duc, *L'Impératrice Elisabeth, épouse d'Alexandre Ier*, 3 vols, St Petersburg: Manufacture des Papiers de l'État, 1908–9

Puraye, Jean and Hans-Otto Lang, eds, *Lettres de Léopold Ier*, Liège: Vaillant-Carmanne, 1973

Scherer, Edmond, *Melchior Grimm: l'homme de lettres, le factotum, le diplomate*, Geneva: Slatkine, 1968

Slabáková, Radmila, 'Le Destin d'une famille noble emigrée d'origine française dans l'empire des Habsbourg et en Tschécoslovaquie de la fin du XVIII aux années trente du XX siècle: le Mensdorff-Pouilly', thesis, University of Grenoble, 1999

Taillandier, Saint-René, 'Les Souvenirs du médecin de la Reine Victoria, III: le Prince Leopold et le Comte Capodistrias', *Revue des deux mondes*, 46th year, 3rd period, vol. 14, 1876, 73–109

Tassigny, Eddie de, *Les Mensdorff-Pouilly: le destin d'une famille émigrée en 1790*, Bihorel: Bois d'Hélène, 1998

Tondini, Césaire, *Le Pape de Rome et les papes de l'Eglise orthodoxe d'Orient*, Paris: Plon, 1876

Tosato-Rigo, Danièle and Margrit Wick-Werder, 'Marguerite Wildermeth: une gouvernante biennoise entre les cours de Berlin et de Saint-Pétersbourg', *Intervalles*, no. 128, 2024.

Vachaudez, Christophe, *Bijoux des reines et princesses de Belgique*, Brussels: Racine, 2003

Villèle, Joseph de, *Mémoires et correspondance du Comte de Villèle*, 5 vols, Paris: Perrin, 1890

Waliszewski, Kazimierz, *La Russie il y a cent ans: le règne d'Alexandre Ier, vol. 1: La Bastille russe et la Révolution en marche 1801–1812*, Paris: Plon-Nourrit, 1923

Weber, Claude, 'Une Grande Duchesse à Mornex', *Salèves*, vol. 25, no. 3, 1996

German

Alville, *Elfenau: Die Geschichte eines bernischen Landsitzes und seiner Bewohner*, Bern: Paul Haupt, 1959

Arnswaldt, Werner Konstantin von, ed., *Petersburger Tagebuch der Frau Erbprinzessin Auguste Karoline Sophie von Sachsen-Coburg-Saalfeld 1795*, Darmstadt: C. F. Wintersche Buchdruckerei, 1907

Bachmann, Gertraude, *Herzogin Marie von Sachsen-Coburg und Gotha*, Coburg: Schriftenreihe der Historischen Gesellschaft Coburg EV, 1999

Bachmann, Gertraude, 'Die Reise der Coburger Erbprinzessin Auguste Caroline Sophie an den Hof der Zrain Katharina II in St Petersburg 1795', Coburg, 1992

Bachmann, Gertraude, 'Die Reisetagebücher der Herzogin Auguste Caroline Sophie von Sachsen-Coburg-Saalfeld (1757–1831) als Europäischer Zeit- und Kulturspiegel', *Jahrbuch der Coburger Landesstiftung*, vol. 51, 2006, 1–414

Berger, Joachim, and Joachim von Puttkamer, eds, *Von Petersburg nach Weimar: Kulturelle Transfers von 1800 bis 1860*, Frankfurt: Peter Lang, 2005

Bestenreiner, Erika, *Die Frauen aus dem Hause Coburg*, Munich: Piper, 2008

Bichsel, Therese, *Grossfürstin Anna: Flucht vom Zarenhof in die Elfenau*, Bern: Zytglogge, 2012

Bonstetten, Karl Viktor von, *Briefe an Friederike Brun*, Frankfurt: Wilhelm Sachaefer, 1829

Bonstetten, Karl Viktor von, *Briefe von Bonstetten an Matthisson*, Zurich: Orell, Füssli, 1827

Briefe der Herzogin Auguste von Sachsen-Coburg-Gotha geb. Prinzessin Reuss-Ebersdorf aus den Jahren 1801, 1825 und 1831, Gera: Isslieb u. Rietzschel, 1890

Buess, Heinrich, 'Rudolf Abraham Schiferli 1775–1836', *Berner Zeitschrift für Geschichte und Heimatkunde*, vol. 8, 1946, 86–99

Dmitrieva, Katja, and Viola Klein, eds, *Maria Pavlovna: die frühen Tagebücher der Erbherzogin von Sachsen-Weimar-Eisenach*, Cologne: Böhlau, 2000

Dressel, Carl-Christian H., 'Ein „Pumpernickel-Staat"? Sachsen-Coburg im frühen 19. Jahrhundert', in John R. Davis, ed., *Prinz Albert – ein Wettiner in Grossbritannien*, Munich: K. G. Saur, 2004, 37–50

Fiedler, Heinz-Dieter, *Auguste Caroline Sophie, Herzogin von Sachsen-Coburg-Saalfeld geborene Reuss-Ebersdorf: Die Stammmutter des europäischen Hochadels*, Norderstedt: Books on Demand, 2015

Freytag von Loringhoven, Frank Baron and Detlev Schwennicke (eds), *Europäische Stammtafeln, neue Folge, Bd. 3:2: Nichtsandesgemässe und illegitime Nachkommen der regierenden Hauser Europas*, Frankfurt: Klostermann, 1983

Griep, Wolfgang, and Hans-Wolf Jäger, eds, *Reisen im 18. Jahrhundert*, Heidelberg: Winter, 1986

Grinsted, Mark, *Coburg Darmstadt Windsor: Deutsch-englische Geschichten und Geschichte aus den Fürstenhäusern des 19. Jahrhunderts*, Norderstedt: Books on Demand, 2020

Heins, Dr Walther, 'Die Erbprinzessin Auguste von Sachsen-Coburg-Saalfeld', *Nordfrankische Monatsblatter*, July 1954

Heins, Dr Walther, 'Das Herzogspaar Franz und Auguste
    von Sachsen-Coburg-Saalfeld', *Jahrbuch der Coburger
    Landesstiftung*, vol. 27, 1982, 161–82

Hermann, Volker and Pierre Eichenberger, 'Bern, Elfenau: Ein
    Beitrag zur Park- und Gartenarchäologie in Kanton Bern',
    Archäologie Bern, 2014, 62–4

Jordis-Lohausen, Alexander, *Mitteleuropa 1658–2008: Die
    Chronik einer Familie*, Munich: Grin, 2008

Kotzebue, August von, *Das merkwürdigste Jahr meines Lebens*, 2
    vols, Berlin: 1801

Kruse, Christian, 'Franz Friedrich Anton von Sachsen-
    Coburg-Saalfeld (1750–1806), *Jahrbuch der Coburger
    Landesstiftung*, vol. 40, 1995, 1–448.

Langbein, Heinrich, 'Lebensbild der Herzogin Auguste von
    Sachsen-Coburg-Saalfeld, geb. Prinzessin von Reuss-
    Ebersdorf', Coburg: Albrecht, 1904

Lavater-Sloman, Mary, 'Die Schweizerjahre der Grossfürstin Anna
    Feodorowna', *Neue Schweizer Rundschau*, vol. 15, 1947–8,
    693–6

Lehmann, Claudia, ed., *Hôtel de Musique und Grande Société in
    Bern 1759–2009*, Bern: Cercle de la Grande Société de Berne,
    2009

Matthisson, Friedrich von, *Schriften*, Zurich: Orell, Fussli, 1833

Mönning, Eckhart and Jana Riedel, 'Zur Gründung des
    Herzoglichen Kunst- und Naturcabinets in Coburg 1844 –
    175 Jahre Naturkunde-Museum Coburg', *Jahrbuch der
    Coburger Landesstiftung* 64, 2020, 172–267

Pestalozzi, Johann Heinrich, *Sämtliche Werke, vol. 15*,
    Brandenburg: Adolph Müller, 1872

Ritter-Lutz, Susanne, *Die Elfenau in Bern*, Bern: Gesellschaft für
    Schweizerische Kunstgeschichte, 1992

Rothkirch, Malve Gräfin, ed., *Königin Luise von Preussen,
    Briefe und Aufzeichnungen 1786–1810*, Berlin: Deutscher
    Kunstverlag, 1995

Segschneider, Louise, 'Die Tagebücher der Herzogin Auguste

von Sachsen-Coburg-Saalfeld', *Jahrbuch der Coburger Landesstiftung*, vol. 8, 1963, 185–9

Slabáková, Radmila, 'Sophie von Sachsen-Coburg-Saalfeld, verheiratate Gräfin Mensdorff-Pouilly, eine unbekannte Prosadichterin', *Coburger Geschichtsblätter*, vol. 6, 1998, 108–13

Thümmel, Moritz von, M. *von Thümmels Sammtliche Werke*, 4 vols, Leipzig: Göschen, 1820

Witzleben, A. von, *Prinz Friedrich Josias von Coburg-Saalfeld, Herzog zu Sachsen*, Berlin: Verlag der Königlichen Geheimen, 1859

Russian

Balyazin, Vol'demar, *Tainy doma Romanovykh: braki s nemetskimi dinastiyami v XVIII – nachale XX vv*, Moscow: Olma, 2010

Bolotov, Andrei, 'O brakosochetanii velikogo knyazya Konstantina Pavlovicha i Peterburgskikh torzhestvakh', in *Zapiski Andreya Timofeevicha Bolotova 1737–1796*, Tula: Priokskoe Knizhnoe Izdatel'stvo, 1988, vol. II, 251–2

Danilova, Al'bina, *Sud'by Zakon Pechal'nyi: Zheny synovei Pavla I*, Moscow: Eksmo, 2007

Danilova, Al'bina, *Russkie imperatory, nemetskie printsessy: dinasticheskie svyazy, chelovecheskie sud'by*, Moscow: Eksmo, 2004

Dmitrieva, Ekaterina, and Franziska Schedewie, *Aleksandr I, Mariya Pavlovna, Elizaveta Alekseevna: perepiska iz trekh uglov 1804–1826*, Moscow: Novoe literaturnoe obozrenie, 2016

Grezin, I. I., 'Iz istorii stroitel'stva russkikh khramov v Shveitsarii', *Vestnik PSTGU, seriya II: istoriya russkoi pravoslavnoi tserkvi*, vol. 1, no. 56, 2014, 137–44

Grot, Jacques, ed., *Pis'ma Imperatritsy Ekateriny II k Grimmu*, in *Sbornik imperatorskago russkago istoricheskago obshchestva*, vol. 23, St Petersburg: Sovet Imperatorskago

Russkago Istorichskago Obshchestva, 1878 (NB many letters are in French)

Grot, Jacques, ed., *Pis'ma Grimma k Imperatritse Ekaterine II*, in *Sbornik imperatorskago russkago istoricheskago obshchestva*, vol. 44, St Petersburg: Sovet Imperatorskago Russkago Istorichskago Obshchestva, 1885 (NB many letters are in French)

Istoricheskii sbornik vol'noi russkoi tipografii v Londone, 2 vols, London: Trübner, 1859

Karnovich, E., 'Tsesarevich Konstantin Pavlovich 1779–1831', *Russkaya starina*, vol. 19, 1877, 217–254, 361–88, 539–57

Karnovich, E., *Tsesarevich Konstantin Pavlovich*, St Petersburg: A. S. Suvorin, 1899

Kaznakov, S., 'Pavlovskaya Gatchina', *Starye gody*, July–September 1914, 101–88

Komarovskii, E. F, *Zapiski grafa E F. Komarovskago*, St Petersburg: Ognim, 1914

Kotlubitskii, N. A., 'Razskazy o starine', *Russkii arkhiv*, no. 7–8, 1868

Krylov-Tolstikovich, Aleksandr, *Potselui Psikhei: Aleksandr I i imperatritsa Elizaveta*, Moscow: Ripol Klassik, 2005.

Krylov-Tolstikovich, Aleksandr, and B. Arutyunov, *Chuzhaya krov': nemetskye printsessy v Rossii*. Moscow: Ripol Klassik, 2003

Kucherskaya, Maiya, *Konstantin Pavlovich*, 2nd ed., Moscow: Molodaya Gvardiya, 2013

Melissino, Petr, 'Opisanie feierverka, pri torzhestve brakosocheshaniya . . .'/'Déscription du feu d'artifice, tiré à St. Pétersbourg sur la Neva . . .', pamphlet, 1796, available at Russian National Library, https://rusneb.ru/catalog/000200_000018_RU_NLR_A1_11422/

Moriol, Graf, 'Velikii Knyaz Konstantin Pavlovich i ego dvor', *Russkaya starina*, vol. 111, no. 8, August 1902.

Onuchkov, N. E., 'Zapreshchennye pesni o Konstantine i Anne', *Izvestiya po russkomu yazyku i slovesnosti*, vol. 2, no. 1, 1929, 275–6

Pchelov, E. V., *Romanovy: istoriya i genealogiya 1613–1917*, Moscow: Akademicheskii proekt, 2017

Petrov, Igor and Elena Shchapova, 'K izucheniyu istoriko-dokumental'nogo naslediya Velikoy knyagini Anny Fedorovny v Berne v svete mezhkul'turnykh svyazei Rossii i Evropy', *Muzykal'naya Akademiya*, no. 2 (762), 2018, 51–7

'Pis'ma Imperatora Aleksandra I i drugikh osob tsarstvuyushago doma k F. Ts. Lagarpu', *Sbornik Russkago Istoricheskago Obshchestva*, St Petersburg: A. Devrient, 1870

Ramenskii, A., *Tsesarevich Konstantin Pavlovich*, Moscow; Delo, 1913

Sbornik biografii kavalergardov 1724–1899, St Petersburg: Ekspeditsiya zagotovleniya gosudarstvennykh bumag, 1904

Shavrov, A. V. and I. M. Smirnov, 'Pridvornaya i velikosvetskaya zhizn' XVIII – nachalo XIX v. v rasskazakh P. P. Lopukhina', *Otechestvennye arkhivy*, no. 4, 1998, 43–72

Smirnova-Rosset, Aleksandra, *Dnevnik, Vospominaniya*, Moscow: Nauka, 1989

'Sobstvennoruchnye zapisii neizvestnago avtora', *Izvestiya tambovskoi uchenoi arkhivnoi komisssii*, no. 56, 1915, 35–44.

Sverbeev, Dmitrii, *Moi zapiski*, Moscow: Nauka, 2014

Turgenev, A. M., 'Zapiski A M Turgeneva', *Byloe*, no. 13, 1918, 149–77

ACKNOWLEDGEMENTS

When I decided to try to uncover the lost story of Juliane of Saxe-Coburg, I must admit to being apprehensive about the amount of foreign language research involved, particularly as most of it was in German and my knowledge of German was pretty basic. But I knew that there would be people who could help and so in I plunged. But I really could not have got going on this book without the crucial help of my German specialist researcher and translator Oliver Walton, who expertly handled the difficult handwritten German material from the Staatsarchiv Coburg and the Royal Archives. I was backed up by the late Melanie Florence in Oxford, who provided excellent translations of Auguste's account of the family's journey to St Petersburg and her 1816 Swiss journal at a time when she was already very ill. My bilingual granddaughter, Cheyenne Rappaport, in Vienna, helped me with some of the briefer published sources in German and Christopher Guyver heroically deciphered Julie's rambling *Kurrentschrift* scrawl in letters to her brother Leopold in Brussels. Susan Ronald assisted with difficult handwritten sources in French.

In Switzerland, Alessandra Reeves-Gehrig was most generous in helping with German sources in the Bern archives and translating them for me, as well as being an invaluable expert advisor on the Swiss cultural background to the Napoleonic period and Julie's life in Switzerland. On a wonderful sunny day in October she showed me Julie's home and the glorious park at Elfenau, providing unique insights into Julie's life there. At Schloss Jegenstorf, where she is curator, Alessandra brought to life for me the style and ambiance of the interiors in which Julie lived, by providing a fascinating guided tour of the furniture of the period in their collection.

During my research I contacted numerous fellow historians who shared their knowledge as well as material gleaned from their own research. I must start by thanking Sarah, Duchess of York, with whom I first shared an enthusiasm for the Saxe-Coburg women. Her special interest in Prince Albert's mother Luise and our discussions about her story sent me in search of the other Saxe-Coburg brides, which led me to Julie. Sarah's researcher Susan Lovejoy was a great help in the early stages in obtaining some rare published sources. Before Covid and the war in Ukraine, Anna Erm in Moscow spent much time trying to track down Julie's scattered letters in the Russian archives, which was made very difficult by the lack of modern, user-friendly cataloguing in many cases and very blurred old microfilm copies. With the shutdown of access to Russian archives, Rudy de Casseres in Finland helped me access material from St Petersburg libraries and Nick Nicholson helped with translation of a particularly difficult Russian source.

Josef Dreesen in Germany kindly took considerable trouble to find the relevant Julie material I needed in the Staatsarchiv in Coburg and ordered scans for me. Christopher Guyver generously passed on references to Julie in the correspondence of Leopold, King of the Belgians, and his family while researching his biography of Leopold in Fonds Goffinet in Brussels and the Royal Archives at Windsor. Franziska Schedewie in Jena shared valuable unpublished letters between Maria Pavlovna and her mother, Maria Feodorovna. Cliff Cunningham sent me the electronic text of his edited volume of the Zach letters that I had been unable to locate in print. Matthias Memmel at the Bayerische Schlösserverwaltung sent me German material that I had had difficulty getting hold of. When I visited Bern in October 2023, Annette Kniep, Early Modern Period curator at the Bern Historical Museum, generously arranged a private view for me of Julie's porcelain vases and china, books and other ephemera held in storage at the museum. Mme Cathérine Ballaire, maître d'hôtel at the Grande Société de Berne, arranged for Alessandra to take me round the private reception rooms at the Hôtel de Musique, which survive as Julie would have known them.

Peter Morrell offered advice on Julie's homeopathic treatments and my good friend Sue Woolmans sent photocopies of useful Saxe-Coburg material from her own extensive library. Josh Provan of Adventures in Historyland was a great help with the background to the Napoleonic Wars, a historical period that was new to me. I must also say a particular thank you to László Vajda in Budapest, who inspired me to search for answers to the many puzzling aspects of Julie's private life and her illegitimate children, and who generously shared material with me from his own research files. Other friends, contacts and fellow historians along the way responded helpfully to emails and encouraged the writing of this book; my thanks to: Daniel Schönpflug, Christophe Guy, Christian Sepp, David M. Bellos, Ulrike Grunewald, Joseph Baillio, Peter Armitage, Mark Andersen, Michael Holman, Michael Rowe, Jessie Childs, Celia Brayfield, Lucy Ward, Clare Mulley, Doug Smith, Lynne Hatwell and Paul Frecker.

I am grateful to the following for providing material from their archives: Baudouin D'hoore on behalf of Fonds Goffinet in Brussels; Johannes Staudenmaier at the Staatsarchiv Coburg; Gerald Raab at the Staatsbibliothek Bamberg; Katja Deinhardt at the Landesarchiv Thüringen (LATh–HSIA Weimar), Ian Shapiro for letters from his private collection and Julie Crocker at the Royal Archives for most kindly organising scans of sources that the Covid pandemic prevented me from seeing. I am most grateful to King Charles III for permission to quote from correspondence in the Royal Archives and also to Lucy Peter, assistant curator of paintings at the Royal Collection, for organising reproduction of their two very fine portraits of Julie.

I began this project when Covid was still making travel difficult, which precluded visits to foreign archives. It was not until I had completed the book that I was able to make a long-wished-for trip to Coburg and Bern. This was made possible thanks to the generosity and chivalry of my friend Nick Short, who volunteered to drive me on a most memorable 2,850-mile magical mystery tour across Germany and down to Switzerland and back in search of many of the places connected with Julie's life and the historical and geographical context of her story. It was a great pleasure to have his enthusiastic company for the trip and share with him my own voyage of discovery.

My final thanks go, as always, to my family for their unstinting support in all my literary endeavours, and my agent Caroline Michel and the dedicated team at PFD who take such good care of me. Thanks are due also to my friend and publisher Charles Spicer at St Martin's Press in New York; to Fran Jessop at Simon & Schuster in London for sharing my enthusiasm for this project; my publicists Kathryn Hough in New York and Sabah Khan in London; and not forgetting Ian Marshall for having had faith in my proposal and signing it.

INDEX